FAITH
SCIENCE
AND
THE
FUTURE

BL
226
.F34
1979

EDITORIAL COMMITTEE

Charles Birch
John Francis
Paulos Gregorios
Shem Olende
Keith Roby
David Rose
Roger Shinn
Paul Abrecht - Editor

FORTRESS PRESS   Philadelphia

First Fortress Press Edition 1979

Second printing 1979
Third printing 1980

Library of Congress Cataloging in Publication Data

Main entry under title:
Faith, science and the future.

   Preparatory readings for the World Conference on Faith, Science and the Future, to be held at Massachusetts Institute of Technology, July 12-24, 1979.
   1. Religion and science—1946-   —Addresses, essays, lectures. 2. Nature (Theology)—Addresses, essays, lectures. 3. Human ecology—Moral and religious aspects—Addresses, essays, lectures.
I. Abrecht, Paul. II. World Conference on Faith, Science and the Future, Massachusetts Institute of Technology, 1979.
BL226.F34   1979   261   79-7035
ISBN 0-8006-1365-1

Cover design: John Taylor
Photo inside front cover: by Lennart Nilsson from Ten Commandments Today Exhibit

8326L79   Printed in the United States of America   1-1365

Contents

Preface

This book, originally published by the World Council of Churches as readings for the participants in its 1979 Conference of Faith, Science and the Future, is a significant contribution to the continuing debate about the role of science and technology in our societies, particularly as churches look for fresh theological and ethical insights applicable to current problems. *Faith, Science and the Future* sets out, in terms the nonspecialist can understand, the issues in the debate today. Its main aim is to highlight a number of problem areas and to reveal the variety of opinion within the churches and within society at large.

This book is the work of an editorial group drawn largely from the membership of the WCC's Working Committee on Church and Society. Each member contributed a chapter or helped in editing the whole. Where chapters are not the work of a member of the editorial group, this is so indicated. The staff of the Church and Society have assembled and edited the final text.

Philadelphia

1979

1 · Science and Technology in the Struggle for a Just, Participatory and Sustainable Society

Until about 1970, the main focus of ecumenical social thought and action was the struggle for a more just and socially responsible society. In the ecumenical movement social justice was broadly defined. It included the more equitable distribution of wealth and income, and the transformation of political and economic institutions which caused injustice. It included also the definition and defense of human rights, equal treatment for all races and concern for movements of national liberation and self-determination. More recently (especially since the 1960's), the latter was dramatically widened to include the struggle of the countries of Africa, Asia, Latin America, the Middle East, and the Pacific to achieve political independence and economic development, and to overcome the consequences of centuries of domination and exploitation by the Western industrialized nations.

In pursuit of these goals, the churches engaged in support of many causes: movements for the rights of workers, especially their right to organize into trade unions for collective bargaining; movements for racial justice and political liberation; the challenge to extreme theories of the free market society, and the promotion of the responsible society as the alternative to both laissez-faire capitalism and totalitarian political systems.

After 1970, a new issue emerged, posing a fresh set of problems for ecumenical consideration — the concern for what is now called the technologically and ecologically sustainable society. This emphasis arose as a result of an awareness of the growing human pressures on finite resources and the ecological and social risks associated with increasingly large technological systems. Whereas before 1970 it was generally assumed that economic and technological growth was nearly always beneficial and could be practically unlimited, there were now doubts about both the desirability and the possibility of continuing unchecked technologically based expansion. This new critical assessment of the consequences of seeking unlimited economic growth included also questions about the human and social consequences of the science and technology which made such growth possible. Thus the idea of the sustainable society came to embody a quite new range of concerns previously outside the scope of Christian action in society.

The emergence of this concern for a sustainable society startled, confused and often antagonized many of those working for social justice as traditionally conceived. They had come to accept without question the promises of a technological society to provide the affluent life for all. They feared that the ecological concern was a ruse of conservatives and reactionaries who were using the defense of nature as a rationale to halt world economic growth in the service of justice. Most traditional Christian social movements were persuaded that the whole world might some day enjoy the affluence which the most technologically developed peoples and countries had achieved. They believed that fears about "limits" — to resources, to growth, to technology — would prove unfounded and that, as in the past, new technological breakthroughs would provide new possibilities for human welfare and freedom from toil.

However, the questioning about the future of technologically based societies has not diminished in the seven years since the debate was launched. On the contrary, the anxiety about the deterioration of the physical environment, about the exhaustion of resources and about the threats to human welfare, has grown and spread gradually even to countries that are still only beginning their industrial development. The latest studies on future economic prospects, including the enquiry undertaken for the United Nations by a group of eminent economists on *The Future of the World Economy*, have not resolved the queries about long-term resource limits.

As a result, there is still much uncertainty about how to evaluate this concern for sustainability and how to relate it to the traditional Christian concern for justice. Is sustainability a high priority issue, equivalent in importance to justice? Or is it a secondary issue which should not be allowed to distract attention from the more fundamental and central issue of economic development with justice? Is the achievement of the sustainable society primarily a question of better social cost accounting so that the full economic and environmental costs of industrialization are understood and equitably distributed? Or does it, as some would claim, pose a much more fundamental question: that of the viability of the total scientific and technological world view on which the whole edifice of modern industrialized, urbanized society has rested? We do not have clear answers to any of these questions. And the public debates about such matters as energy policy and appropriate technology reveal the large measure of disagreement on these basic issues. In this book, we try to trace where the churches are in the debate and the kind of questions and issues which might now be the focus of their attention.

What is a Sustainable Society?

The phrase "the sustainable society" was first used in the report of an ecumenical study conference on Science and Technology for Human Development convened by the World Council of Churches in 1974 in Bucharest, Rumania. This conference followed a series of international consultations between 1970 and 1973 on the problems of technology, environment and the future of society.

The Bucharest conference report called for a "long-term concept of a sustainable and just society" based on four considerations:

"*First*, social stability cannot be obtained without an equitable distribution of what is in scarce supply or without common opportunity to participate in social decisions. *Second*, a robust global society will not be sustainable unless the need for food is at any time well below the global capacity to supply it, and unless the emissions of pollutants are well below the capacity of the ecosystem to absorb them. *Third*, the new social organization will be sustainable only as long as the rate of use of non-renewable resources does not outrun the increase in resources made available through technological innovation. *Finally*, a sustainable society requires a level of human activity which is not adversely influenced by the never ending, large and frequent natural variation in global climate."

It was made clear in this statement that the idea of the sustainable society should not be used by Christians to defend the status quo — the affluent nations and peoples holding on to their power and wealth and the poor ones accepting the limits imposed by newly understood economic and environmental constraints. The report emphasized that sustainability had to be achieved in relation to a new measure of human solidarity and justice.

"Feeling a responsibility at least for our grandchildren, and sensing an incapacity of the physical environment to support for long a load significantly higher than today's, we believe that the rich segments of the world have now reached the critical point where material expansion will reduce the quality of life for some people at some time within the period of concern to us. The remaining poorer members of humanity are at a stage where the current benefits of material expansion, except in terms of population, are far larger than the probable costs in terms of reduced quality of life now or in the relevant future. Thus today the worldwide quality of life will be increased by material growth among the poor and by stabilization and possibly contraction among the rich."

The idea of the sustainable society was developed further by Prof. Charles Birch in his address to the Fifth Assembly in Nairobi, December 1975. On that occasion he said:

"A prior requirement of any global society is that it be so organized that the life of man and other living creatures on which his life depends can be sustained indefinitely within the limits of the earth. A second requirement is that it be sustained at a quality that makes possible fulfilment of human life for all people. A society so organized to achieve both these ends we can call a sustainable global society in contrast to the present unsustainable global society. If the life of the world is to be sustained and renewed, ... it will have to be with a new sort of science and technology governed by a new sort of economics and politics. That is what the sustainable global society is all about. It will not come without radical and revolutionary transformations in science and technology and in economics and politics. The decisions we have to make are not just economic and political ones, they are also scientific and technical."

The Assembly incorporated some of this thinking into its own report on "Social Responsibility in a Technological Age". There it is said:

"The responsibility that now confronts humanity is to make a deliberate transition to a sustainable global society in which science and technology will be mobilized to meet the basic physical and spiritual needs of people, to minimize human suffering and to create an environment which can sustain a decent quality of life for all people. This will involve a radical transformation of civilization, new technologies, new uses for technology and new global economic and political systems. The new situation in which humanity now finds itself has been created in less than a generation. There is even less time to create the transition to a sustainable global society if humanity is to survive."

The Assembly's report added that,

"For the developed countries it means in the first instance a sustainable core of economic activity relating to patterns of indigenous resource consumption, for example, land use, food supply, and energy production, in a far longer time frame than suggested by trends in current commodity markets. It implies a substantial reallocation of power controlling the patterns of world trade in essential resources. It also implies increased participation by workers in the decision-making process in industry.

For the developing countries, it means emphasis on production for essential human needs, including food and energy; the search for technologies which will guarantee this result and which will at the same time avoid a continuing dependence on technology imported from industrialized countries which is in direct conflict with social and cultural identity."

The Assembly report indicated specific areas like energy, food, and other resources where the realization of the sustainable society would in the long-term depend on new and appropriate uses of technology.

Origin of the 1979 World Conference

This vision of a global sustainable society was considered sufficiently important by the Assembly that it authorized a continuing WCC programme to explore "The Contribution of Faith, Science and Technology in the Struggle for a Just and Sustainable Society" [1]. In 1976, at its first meeting, the new Central Committee of the WCC, endorsed this concern, under the heading of "The Struggle for the Just, Participatory and Sustainable Society", as one of the four major programme emphases of the World Council for the period up to the next Assembly.

The deliberations about the new programme by the Working Group on Church and Society, meeting in Switzerland in May 1976, emphasized the essential link between the issues of justice and sustainability.

"The twin issues around which the world's future revolves are justice and ecology. 'Justice' points to the necessity of correcting maldistribution of the products of the earth and of bridging the gap between rich and poor countries. 'Ecology' points to humanity's dependence upon the earth. Society must be so organized as to sustain the earth so that a sufficient quality of material and cultural life for humanity may itself be sustained indefinitely. A sustainable society which is unjust can hardly be worth sustaining. A just society that is unsustainable is self-defeating. Humanity now has the responsibility to make a deliberate transition to a just and sustainable global society."

At this meeting the Working Group outlined a programme of study and action on the scientific and technical problems and the ethical issues involved in the transition to a just, participatory and sustainable society, leading up to a World Conference in 1979 on this theme.

The Working Group envisaged five levels of concern:

1. The theological and ideological critique of the prevailing scientific and technological world views, including an examination of the theological and ethical dilemmas posed by developments in such areas as biological research and nuclear energy.

2. The development of appropriate (i.e. sustainable) technologies in relation to energy, agriculture and industrial development.

---

[1] *Breaking Barriers, Nairobi, 1975*. The official report of the Fifth Assembly of the WCC, London, 1976, p. 303.

3. The re-examination of traditional political and economic principles, policies and systems in light of the demands for a sustainable society.

4. The ethical and social issues involved in the transfer of technology between rich and poor countries.

5. The consequences for Christian social thought and witness of these new concerns.

In a general way the chapters in this book reflect these five concerns.

The Sustainable Society — No Blueprint and No Panacea

It must be emphasized that within the ecumenical movement we are far from reaching any measure of consensus about the role of science and technology in achieving the just, participatory and sustainable society, and for good reason. The churches have themselves only truly begun their enquiries and for some time to come there are bound to be wide differences of opinion on these issues. Christians who are still debating the meaning of social justice will not find it easier to continue that debate when it is enlarged to incorporate the discussion of responsible ecological options and the ethical choices to be faced in framing technological policies today. Furthermore, the strong challenge to reductionist, triumphalist and materialist views of man and the world which have dominated thinking in our time must shake the confidence of all persons of whatever ideological or theological persuasion, because in some measure all their hopes have rested and, in large part, continue to rest on obtaining and using technological power.

The ethical dilemmas and choices raised in relation to the idea of the sustainable society are truly immense. There appears to be no way at the moment to resolve these dilemmas, and it would be cheap Christian ethics and cheap Christian moralizing which would promise a ready solution to our present difficulties.

Yet it is precisely this element which makes the world situation so theologically and ethically gripping. All the hopes based on pure reason, all the plans based on growing human understanding, all the ideological and social theories which assumed some kind of human ability to achieve a certain progress within history seem to be confounded by the realities of our world. Their proponents can maintain their position only by covering up or ignoring important facts. It is precisely the test of the Christian faith whether it can at this moment face the harsh realities of a world which is threatened by the products of its own ingenuity and power.

When today we enter into the discussion of the just and sustainable society, we must therefore have no illusions that we can "solve" any of these problems. This applies especially to the rich countries which are the captives of their own power and the prisoners of their technological achievement. They cannot turn the clock back. The Pandora's box that they opened cannot be closed. And the poor nations are now also the prisoners of the technological world system. The population problems paradoxically reflect the achievements of modern agriculture and medicine. Their economic and social problems are a result of the practically irreversible industrial and urban transformation of their societies. And their political goals reflect their desire to challenge and contest the power of the industrialized nations, which they can do only by gaining access to the secrets of their opponents' technical and economic strength. In the words of an Asian leader, the frustration of the countries of the Third World, faced with the new Western debate about the ambiguities of science and technology, is not unlike that of a person who is attracted by the thrilling pictures he sees outside the movie theatre, and is induced to buy a ticket. But as he waits in line for the next showing, those leaving the cinema tell him, "Don't waste your money — it is a poor show". But he has already purchased his ticket!

It is not surprising then that all nations are perplexed about the direction to take; that some people, and not only youth, advocate stopping the drive towards greater technological power through moratoriums and through a return to simple life styles. Nor is it surprising that others believe that there is no recourse but to go on with technological endeavours, in the hope, increasingly dim, that some solution will turn up, that the scientists and technologists will prove to be wiser than we thought, or that, by a little more popular participation in decision making, science and technology will be magically humanized. And neither is it surprising that still others take refuge in various new religions which promise peace or escape from the confusions and perplexities of this world.

The call to work for a just, participatory and sustainable society is not a call to a crusade but a call to a discernment of the meaning of faith in the sovereign God who said, "My ways are not your ways, my thoughts are not your thoughts". It is a call also to assume the ethical and intellectual responsibility for the future of society even when our freedom of action seems to be almost totally circumscribed, and where we can at best see that future only "as through a glass darkly".

I.

The Theological and Ethical Evaluation of Science and Technology and Their World-Views

2 · Faith, Science and Human Understanding

This chapter is about two human ventures. One meets the world with an inquiring intelligence. It values accurate, testable knowledge. It experiences the sheer joy of knowing, of understanding the world, of making discoveries and the power of prediction and control. This is the venture of science and technology. In its own way it is a venture of faith.

The other venture meets the world in wonder, trust and commitment. It values the relations of persons to each other and to their ultimate source and destiny. It glories in the beauty of holiness and the responsibility of service. This is the venture of faith.

Most people engage in both ventures. Both belong to the gifts that characterize humanity. The famous philosopher, Alfred North Whitehead, described science and religion as "the two strongest general forces (apart from the mere impulses of the various senses) which influence men" [1].

People face many perplexities in relating the two ventures to each other. Whitehead wrote: "When we consider what religion is for mankind, and what science is, it is no exaggeration to say that the future course of history depends upon the decision of this generation as to the relations between them." [2] That statement was published in 1926. Today it is obvious that no generation makes such a decision *finally*. The question is as urgent now as when Whitehead wrote.

Christianity and Science

Christianity has had an especially close relationship, sometimes friendly and sometimes stormy, to the development of science. Many historians have made the case that the spectacular rise of modern science took place in cultures influenced by Christianity, and that the relationship between the

---

[1] *Science and the Modern World* (New York: Macmillan, 1926), p. 260.
[2] *Ibid.*

two is more than coincidental. Christian monotheism denied the reality of the gods, spirits and demons that, in the beliefs of many religions, inhabit the world. It thus secularized the world, removed tabus to scientific inquiry, and made scientific investigation a legitimate human activity.

Likewise Christianity endorsed human labour. It did not, like the Greek philosophers and the teachers of many religions, separate spirit from matter. It started, not among sages who separated themselves from the world's work, but with a carpenter and some fishermen. Its story of creation gave God's human creatures a dominion over physical nature. Hence technology could have a legitimacy and dignity within Christianity.

Only a few years ago, Christian theology was inclined to take pride in this responsibility for the development of science and technology. Theologies of secularization acclaimed the development of science and technology. Theologies of secularization acclaimed the achievement of Christian faith in "desacralizing" nature. Then rather suddenly an impressive number of ecologists began attacking Christianity for its contribution to human destructiveness of nature. Christianity, said the critics, gave a spiritual endorsement to human superiority over nature and to the human exploitation of nature that has brought the world to a state of crisis. We shall come back to this issue later.

But first we must note another side of the story. It is sometimes called "the warfare of science and religion". Science has often attacked specific religious beliefs, and the church has often responded by attacking or even trying to suppress the work of science. Today most Christians regret that effort. They say, for example, that the church was wrong in silencing Galileo. The reason is not that Galileo was entirely right and the church entirely wrong in that controversy. Many of the ideas of astronomers, since the theory of relativity, are quite different from those of either Galileo or his opponents. But Galileo was making a significant advance in the history of science, and he was using methods that have advanced knowledge. Even though many scientists disagreed with Galileo at that time, the church was wrong in opposing his scientific descriptions on the basis of its interpretation of a few verses of Scripture and its traditional beliefs; and it was even more wrong in trying to suppress ideas that it opposed.

A still more momentous controversy followed the work of Charles Darwin. His theory of the origin of species challenged the prevailing views of Christians (and most other people) on two subjects: beliefs about creation and human self-understanding. In some places, people are still trying to prohibit the teaching of evolution in schools. But today most church people would renounce that effort, while they would encourage discussions of the meaning of evolution and would think it important to continue revising ideas about evolution as well as theological traditions about creation.

The tensions between science and religion centre not only on specific scientific and theological ideas — both of which often change — but also, on a deeper level, on what is sometimes called a "scientific world view". We hear that phrase less frequently today than a generation ago, mainly because scientists have become more reluctant to set up world views. But the issue has been, and still is, an extremely important one. In its classical Greek form, the scientific world view sought to explain all happenings by "efficient" causality (that is, causes that were essentially mechanical and measurable in their operation). This led to an entirely deterministic view of the world. When this notion was challenged from within science (particularly by the theory of indeterminacy), the world view was revised to include probability. Then everything was explained by some combination of causality and accident, or *Chance and Necessity*, to use the title of a well known book by the French biologist, Jacques Monod.

This "scientific world view" usually included positivism, i.e. the belief that the only truth is "objective", in the sense that it is verifiable by specific observations and measurements available to all unbiased people — or at least all who are in a position to make the necessary observations. Everything else — including love, trust, commitment, response to beauty — is subjective and emotive. It has no relation to "truth". Science, according to *this world view*, is the final and only arbiter of truth.

This world view, as it was frequently set forth, had no place for God. In the conversation between Napoleon and the astronomer Laplace, Napoleon listened to the scientist's account of the operation of the universe, then asked about God. The famous answer of the astronomer was, "Sire, I have no need of that hypothesis". For many positivists God became not simply an unnecessary hypothesis but a meaningless word. On this level, the church had a real controversy, not necessarily with science but with a philosophical position that sometimes claimed to be scientific.

Technology, as well as science, belongs to this story. The common opinion is that science aims at understanding the world, technology at controlling. But technology also affects understanding and self-understanding. People who make and use machines sometimes think of the world as a machine; thus in the 18th century, the world was often compared with a watch and God with a watch-maker. People who try to dominate nature with technology are likely to have very different impressions of nature from people who approach it with a sense of mystery and dependence. Above all, people who use machines may begin to think of themselves as machines — as in classical behaviouristic psychology or the more recent attempts to understand the human mind as an intricate computer.

We have been looking at some of the historical background for the relation between science and technology, on the one hand, and faith, on the other. We have seen some evidences of Christian attitudes that support both science and technology. We have seen evidences of tension and controversy. Both these historical tendencies influence the present situation.

An Evaluation of the Scientific Situation

Contemporary science, despite its tremendous achievements, is in many respects more modest than the science of recent past centuries. At least in some of the Western societies that have seen the most dramatic scientific accomplishments, scientists rarely claim to discover the ultimate truth of reality. Scientific literature says less than in the past of definitive laws, more of hypothetical theories; less of determinism, more of probability; less of "truth" and more of "models". And the models are not understood as mental or visual replicas of reality, but as effective ways of thinking about reality for certain designated human purposes.

A change has come in the way of thinking about the history of science. Popular thought often sees each generation of scientists building on the assured results of preceding generations in an on-going cumulative process. This conception has its truth: the body of scientific knowledge does grow, and research moves from solution of old problems to investigation of newer, more advanced ones. But there is increasing recognition that the great advances in science are not simply additions to past work. Frequently they involve reorganizing the findings and reconceptualizing the models of the past. The pioneering scientists do not simply add to the work of predecessors, but undo some of that work because they see things in new ways. The great achievements of science are acts of an imagination in some ways comparable to the artistic and religious imagination.

This does not mean that scientific theories are arbitrary or capricious. Two kinds of criteria exist for evaluating new theories. One is a kind of satisfaction in understanding the world. If a theory can relate phenomena that were not related by earlier theories, or if it can organize them in a more "elegant" or "beautiful" or "simple" way, that theory is persuasive. (The words within quotation marks are frequent words in scientific writings and discussions.) The other kind of criteria have to do with functionality. Good scientific theory is testable by experimentation, by success in prediction, by usefulness in spinning off new theories and fecundity in suggesting new questions for research. In popular thought and in some scientific efforts, practical usefulness is the test of scientific knowledge.

There are four other characteristics of contemporary science, especially interesting for anyone who tries to relate science to faith. First, scientists today rarely talk about "scientific method", in the sense of some single universal method of science. They talk about methods, and they devise new methods for solving new problems. Success in prediction is an important method of testing scientific theory, such, for example, as the prediction of the existence of an as yet undiscovered element. But astronomers, working on the origins of the solar system or a galaxy or a universe, cannot determine what happened aeons ago (although occasionally they can predict that a certain designated observation will, if their theories are accurate, lead to certain findings). The methods of mathematicians devising a non-Euclidean geometry are quite different from those of geneticists studying the structure of DNA molecules.

Second, scientists sometimes are ready to use different complementary models to understand the same phenomena. The best known example has to do with the structure of both light and particles. For certain purposes, it is most helpful to think of light as corpuscles or particles moving through space at tremendous speeds. For other purposes, it is more helpful to think of light as vibrations or waves in a field of energy. So scientists use both theories. And they recognize that the language of both, like much scientific language, is metaphorical. Occasionally they combine the language of the two as in the word "wavicle" (wave-particle), but neither theory is reduced to the other. There is something uncomfortable about this use of two differing theories. Many physicists think that some day there will be a break-through to a new conception that replaces the old ones. Meanwhile there is no hesitation to go on using both concepts, with the realization that neither is final.

Third, there is a rethinking of the meaning of objectivity in science. In traditional thought, science gave objectivity, quite independent of the scientist's personal interests. Something of that ideal persists. The value of critical experiment is that it settles doubts and arguments. One of the noblest moral qualities of scientists is the willingness to follow the evidence where it leads and to accept the evidence, even if it refutes the preferences or hopes of the investigators. But there is increasing recognition that scientific investigation is engaged in answering human questions asked by human persons, not questions somehow asked by "objective" reality. And the answers sought are answers to the human questions. Furthermore, especially since the work of Werner Heisenberg, there is an awareness that at least in some delicate experiments the influence of the observer affects the outcome of the experiment. The researchers are not investigating an outside reality totally external to themselves; they are themselves part of the experiment. Their findings are related to themselves, and the resultant knowledge is in important ways relational knowledge.

Fourth, the expanding boundaries of science pose many intriguing questions. Sub-atomic physics is an interesting example. Once the atom was defined as an indivisible particle — the last stage in the human effort to break down nature into its ultimate building blocks. Then the atom came to be conceived as a miniature solar system, made up of electrons, protons and neutrons which were the ultimate particles of the universe. Now there are so many identifiable nuclear particles that some scientists look forward to a major break-through and a new way of understanding the nucleus in a simpler conception. Others suspect that complexity may be a last word. But nobody claims to have *the* last word about the structure of the atom.

The general conceptions about science, described in the last few paragraphs, are widespread today. Only gradually are they affecting the teaching of science in elementary and secondary schools.

The situation is somewhat different in Marxist societies. Traditional Marxism-Leninism gives science, including the physical sciences and Marxist historical science, a more authoritative role. It assumes that science refutes religion. Yet many contemporary Marxist and neo-Marxist thinkers, drawing on some ideas of Marx himself, are leaders in the reconceptualization of science and contributors to the ideas discussed above.

Persons interested in the dialogue between science and faith — and these include some scientists — find opportunities in the new scientific situation. No longer do they see science as the sole arbiter of truth, destroying one religious doctrine after another, and subjecting all of them to a monolithic scientific method that threatens to destroy them one by one. No longer do they see science claiming to possess final truth or piecing together a comprehensive and impervious picture of the world.

But the change must not be exaggerated, nor must the dialogue seem too easy. Although science is a work of imagination, it may not imagine whatever it pleases. If scientists rarely talk any more about ultimate reality, they are convinced that they are working with a real world. Although they are modest in staking claims to truth, they are acquiring knowledge — and it is highly warranted knowledge, meticulously related to evidence and cogent reasoning.

It is sometimes said that the old conflict between science and religion is dead. That is too cheerful a statement. It would be better to say that the tensions and conflicts have changed. Science is less likely than in the past to seem to *refute* religion, although it still refutes many formulations of religious beliefs. It is more likely to challenge religion — to ask people of faith why they believe in God, what they mean by talking of God and of God's action in the world. What even the law calls "acts of God" are now generally regarded as scientifically understandable acts of nature. Science and technology have changed the religious situation. To that change we must now turn.

An Evaluation of the Religious Situation

Religions around the world have gone through many changes because of science. Even the most committed Christians, because of science, for example, read their Bibles differently from Christians in the past. They also live differently. They pray differently. They look to science to explain phenomena that they once attributed to direct activities of God. They look to technology for kinds of help that they once asked of God.

There are, of course, great differences among Christians on these issues. But few Christians, especially in societies profoundly influenced by science and technology, regard faith as an authoritative source of scientific information about the world. They may, for example, take the opening chapters of Genesis as seriously as any of their ancestors in the faith, but they are far less likely to regard these as scientific accounts of the origins of the universe and humanity, competing with the accounts given by astronomers, geologists and biologists.

It is, of course, always possible to find some unsolved scientific problems and to invoke God as the explanation and solution. But this belief in the "God of the gaps", as it has been called, has too often proved itself a losing game. True, there are many gaps in scientific knowledge, and perhaps there will always be. But many of the specific gaps upon which past Christians built their cases have been filled by new information. It is pathetic to think of Christians as people on a constant retreat from one gap to another, never knowing when their latest rationale for God will be taken away.

Hence many Christians have accepted Dietrich Bonhoeffer's idea of a world "come of age", a world in which human rationality has won great victories and will win more. It is as foolish and as destructive to try to keep a world in perpetual childhood as to do that to a human being. Bonhoeffer, who resisted the Nazi fury and lost his life in the cause, well knew the many ways in which this world is not mature. But he welcomed whatever maturity humanity had found and he encouraged the development of more.

Out of such an insight come two changes in common conceptions of faith, both of which have long histories. (1) Faith is not an explanation, competing with scientific explanations, of the workings of nature. (2) Faith is not a supernatural technological tool for manipulating nature and other people.

Both those statements are negations, but they involve affirmations and clarifications. They mean a purging of the concept of faith, a disentanglement of faith from the credulity, fetishism, fiction and magic that have often accompanied it.

Yet there are deep perplexities about this reconception of the meaning of faith. In some ways, it means a recovery of the true nature of faith as the confession of the invisible yet living God, to whom the community of faith responds in trust, commitment and love. The problem is that faith may renounce its contribution to an authentic understanding of the world and humanity. It may retreat to the inner life, fenced off from any understanding of nature or of the purpose and destiny of the world. It may let scientific knowledge and technological power become the sole human ways for coping with the world and other persons. Turning from past mistakes in competitive conflict with science, it may settle for total divorce.

Can it be that respect for the autonomy of science has brought faith to a loss of nerve about its own contribution to knowledge — just at a time when contemporary scientists could be more open to appreciation for faith and when technologists seek ethical insight for use of awesome new powers? Is the time ripe for a new evaluation of the contributions of faith, science and technology to a human world uncertain about the meaning of truth, anxious about its own powers, unsure about the good?

There are historical indications that Christian faith can contribute not only to a richer life but to a clarified understanding of the world. We have already mentioned its insistence on the unreality of the spirits and demons that populated nature according to many common beliefs. Another historical example is St. Augustine's rejection of astrology on the basis of his belief in divine and human freedom. Augustine, though he shared scientific misconceptions that even slightly educated people today can correct, was ahead of his time (and of many people in our time) in a sophistication based on faith.

These examples are not meant to claim that people of faith have pre-arranged solutions to scientific problems or even to the most creative relations between science and faith. We are all of us — all human beings — explorers today, moving ahead with some combination of assurance and readiness for surprises. The church has some right to an expectation that Christians, when they are ready to learn from science and appreciate it as a gift of God, can join with scientists, whether they are Christian or not, in contributing to an enlarged understanding of the world.

A New Vision of Nature, Humanity and God

There is at work in theology today a new stirring, a new effort to think about the relationships among God, humanity and nature. The stirring is in part a response to the ecological crisis (as many theological movements of the past have been responses to crises), in part a reappropriation of biblical themes that have been neglected in the recent past.

The dominant theologies of the past generation, most notably in Protestantism, showed a strong tendency to emphasize the "otherness" of God, the sharp distinction between "history" and "nature", the uniqueness of Christian faith in contrast to the insights of all other religions. There were profound reasons for the accents of those theologies. All over the world there were movements and ideologies — imperialism, Nazism, nationalism — that sought to co-opt and corrupt Christianity. The church, in the name of a judging and redeeming God, had to disentangle itself from the cultural forces that almost engulfed it. It sought to rediscover its true identity in order to declare its Gospel and then engage the world in a ministry of struggle and love.

The reasons for that theological effort must not be forgotten; they still exist. But the specific formulations that became a rallying cry for a past generation are not necessarily the formulations for this generation. Many

Christians today are re-exploring the ties that relate God, his human creatures and his total creation.

One step in this current development was a consultation on Nature, Humanity and God, convened by the World Council of Churches in Zurich, Switzerland, in July 1977. The consultation sought to shape a "unifying vision" of reality. It looked at humanity and all nature as creatures of a God who is transcendent but never remote. It related the human dominion over part of creation to human stewardship. It looked again at the biblical promises of a redemption for all creation, asking what these might mean to Christians today.

The Zurich consultation sought to distinguish the Christian vision from two familiar alternatives. On the one hand, it stated: ". . . the realization that God is One and Supreme, and therefore transcendent, effectively desupernaturalizes the world, ridding it of superhuman personal power, whether divine or demonic, and placing man in a position to use his powers rationally in dealing with nature." On the other hand, it maintained: "Nevertheless, nature is not to be evaluated simply in terms of human needs and interests; and to think that it is, is simply a mark of folly. God created the greater part of the world for its own sake — a point that comes home to us, with our knowledge of the immensity of the universe, even more strongly — and wisdom consists fundamentally in recognizing this and the limitations which it imposes upon us."

Both distinctions are important. The first reaffirms the Old Testament prophetic struggle against nature religions, which identify natural forces and objects with gods. It reaffirms the New Testament protest against the prevalent belief that people are enslaved by a demonic fate. It reaffirms the Christian and scientific protest of the 17th century against magical cults of that time. It is a protest today against the return, within contemporary cultures, of beliefs in occultism and astrology, even though these may be recognized as a defense that individuals adopt against a culture that appears to them to be meaningless and inhuman.

The second distinction is perhaps the more recent one in human history. It is a protest against those human attitudes, often connected with industrialism, that see nature only as an object for human exploitation. It is a protest against grandiose human ambition that values nature only as an arena and object of human action.

The importance of the new vision may be seen by comparing it with the tradition of modern humanism, arising in Europe at the time of the Renaissance and then spreading throughout much of the world. Christians originally welcomed this humanism for its appreciation of human values and potentialities. But increasingly it developed along lines that were anthropocentric and often individualistic. By the 20th century, the word humanism came, in common usage, to carry a non-theistic or anti-theistic meaning. Philosopher Jacques Maritain responded by describing an "integral humanism" that related humanity to God and his whole creation. Karl Barth, writing about "the humanity of God", gave the basis for a humanism centered in Christ.

But the anthropocentric tendencies in modern culture, whether secular or religious, remained strong. When human beings visited the moon and human-directed space ships made some explorations of nearer parts of the solar system — a very tiny adventure within the vastness of the physical universe — people talked grandiloquently about "the conquest of space". Some theologians began to talk about "the humanization and hominization of the universe".

There is something unreal about such talk. It is also unbiblical. The Bible confers an immense dignity upon human beings, who are loved by the Creator God and given freedom and responsibility within creation. But it knows that God's creation is vast and mysterious. Prophetic writings contemplate the Pleiades and Orion (Amos 5 : 8), far beyond human exploitation. The Psalmist affirms: "The heavens declare the glory of God." The book of Job tells with awe about those creatures of God (Behemoth and Leviathan) that cannot be tamed and are useless for human exploitation, but that exist as symbols of divine purposes. Jesus points to the lilies of the field and the birds of the air, not as objects for people to use but as signs of God's universal care (Matt. 5 : 26-28).

God's human creatures have a special place in creation and a special responsibility. They have power to give names to the beasts and birds (Genesis 2 : 19-20) — perhaps a first step in the kind of understanding and description that were to become science. They have a qualified "dominion" over other creatures. The dominion is not power of possession. "The earth is the Lord's and the fulness thereof, the world and they that dwell therein" (Psalm 24 : 1). In Christian faith there can be no such thing as property (whether of individuals, corporations or states) in any absolute sense. Human beings have a privilege and responsibility of stewardship. Their dominion is a right and obligation of caring for and making use of a part of creation. They are of "greater worth" than the flowers and birds (Matt. 5 : 26). Who, faced with the choice, would not save a human life rather than a bird's life? But God values all his creation. And he asks his human creatures to value what he values.

Likewise the biblical vision of the future is a vision for all creation. "The whole created universe groans in all its parts" and "waits with eager expectation" (Rom. 8). The Christian expectation is not only for a new humanity but for "a new heaven and a new earth" (Rev. 21 : 1) in a coming age when Christ will rule over the whole creation (Col. 2 : 10).

Such language is metaphorical and poetical rather than scientific, even though, as we have already noted, much of the language of science is itself metaphorical and poetic. Christian faith does not know precisely how to relate such language to scientific understanding. Faith cannot turn this vision of a future into a pseudo-science. Yet Christians believe that such language expresses a faith that contributes to the understanding of humanity, nature and God — and of the human activity called science.

This chapter began by emphasizing the importance of the relationship between two human ventures — the venture of science and technology, and the venture of faith. It ends in an awareness that the relationship has entered a new era with new opportunities and responsibilities for persons who value both ventures.

3 · Science and Technology — Promises and Threats

Knowledge is not only the object of a human intellectual quest. Knowledge is also power. It is power to create and destroy, power loaded with promises and threats.

The Promises...

The promise of science and technology is overwhelmingly evident to modern societies. Science and technology are achievements of human creativity. Humanity develops them to achieve human purposes. Christians regard them as an expression of God's gift of creativity and responsibility which humanity exercises before God and in relation to the created world.

Science through its contribution to understanding liberates people from many forms of ignorance and superstition. Technology liberates them from many physical constraints and insecurities. Medical technology has removed the terror of many diseases and epidemics. Agricultural technologies increase the production of food; when related to adequate social structures, such technologies can remove the age-old threat of famine. Machines can liberate people from many types of drudgery. They make possible communication, travel, leisure, access to the arts. Civilization is possible only with a technological base; the kind of civilization that most people today desire is possible only on a very elaborate technological base.

It is therefore no wonder that most people in most societies crave for science and technology. The developing nations seek technology to lift the burden of poverty. One of their just grievances against the industrial world is that the latter has kept monopolies of many advanced technologies or has allowed access to them only on terms that favoured the technologically advanced societies. Meanwhile, the industrialized nations seek ever more intricate technologies. The wealthiest and most powerful societies push ahead with business and industrial technologies of automation; with medical experimentation in transplantation of organs, new cures for old diseases, discoveries in genetics that promise to overcome hereditary ailments; with the use of earth satellites to discover new information and transmit words and pictures around the world. Almost as soon as a problem is defined, a R & D (research and development) project is launched to work toward a solution.

... and the Threats

Yet in the face of all these promises, science and technology appear to many people as threats. We must ask why this is so and how persons and societies can meet the threats and realize the promises. A look at the contemporary world shows several reasons for the threat.

1. The power of science and technology is available for many purposes, good and bad. In human experience, power is often the power of some people, some classes, some nations to dominate others. In many societies, the first experience of advanced technologies has been the experience of a military technology of a foreign conqueror or the economic power of a foreign exploiter. For that reason, the developing societies, which have the most reason to want new technologies for their promise, also have the most bitter experiences of the threat of technology. They know well that science and technology, which can be liberating powers, are often oppressive powers. The power of humanity over nature, which is a sign of the human "dominion" discussed in Ch. 2, quickly becomes the power of some people to control others.

Furthermore, there is a strong tendency in social structures to acquire technologies in ways that accentuate inequality. One reason is that new technologies build upon preceding technologies; those who have the most technology are in the best situation to acquire still more. Another related reason is that complex technological innovations, even if they are the means to economic gain, are costly to get started. So those with the most wealth can buy or develop the most advanced technologies. So while the poor struggle painfully to catch up, the rich and powerful are leaping farther ahead.

Even if science and technology are considered to be "value-free" (a frequent and erroneous assumption), they operate within social structures that embody values and organize power. So their use serves the purpose of those with the power to pay for them. Perhaps even more ominous is the fact that much of the direction of R & D is determined by the structures of power in a society. Even the most idealistic researchers are likely to find themselves devising and working on projects that can be funded. The sources of massive funds are corporations and governments. Corporations spend huge sums on R & D to develop new products, then spend more money on R & D to persuade people to buy the new products. They spend very little on research on the social consequences or the value-implications of the new products. Governments are less likely to sponsor R & D for profit. But they direct R & D to goals determined by the government officials, who may or may not represent the real needs and values of the society. Often they merely replace the corporation's goal of profit with the goal of national advantage.

Military technologies are a special case in point. The pacifist, Albert Einstein, went through a real struggle of conscience in deciding to alert President Roosevelt to the possibility of building an atomic bomb. What followed was one of the most portentous R & D projects of all history. Einstein later found himself helpless to prevent the use of the atomic bomb. Many a scientist who worked on the project has done profound soul-searching about the meaning of that work. Some of the scientists have engaged in ethical crusades connected with nuclear weapons and the uses of nuclear energy. One of them, Robert Oppenheimer, said, on November 25, 1947: "... the physicists have known sin, and this is a knowledge which they cannot lose."

The increased awareness of the consequences of scientific power and the evidences of its misuse have brought about a change in public moods. When the World Council of Churches sponsored a consultation on The Ideological and Theological Debate about Science (Cambridge, UK, June 20-26, 1977), one finding was: "It is surely one of the most striking features of our own time that science and technology have come under sharp attack, both in the Western and in the Third Worlds. There has been a shift in science's own self-image, and the authority of the scientist with the general public no longer goes unchallenged."

Christians, who regard science and technology as part of the divine gift of human creativity, have reason not to join the forces that want to demonize either science or technology. But they have equal reason to show concern for the social structures that so often turn the promise of science into threat.

2. It is not only destructive human purposes that turn science and technology from promise to threat. Even well-intended uses of technology have unintended consequences that perplex or frustrate the people who initiated them.

There are many kinds of examples of such unintended effects.

a) Technology affects the natural environment. Many an effort to increase human power in the natural order has ended in destructiveness to nature and, in turn, to human life. Poor people, seeking food and firewood, have not intentionally produced dangerous soil erosion, but the effect has been disastrous. Households and factories may not intend to pollute the air, but the outcome is as bad as if it were intended. Manufacturers of aerosol cans did not intend to endanger people by depleting the protective ozone in the upper atmosphere, but the unintended happened. Sometimes, of course, greed blinds people to the effects of their actions. But innocent ignorance is also blind.

b) Technology affects social structures. Massive technologies have led to the re-ordering of cities and nations, both in their visible physical organization and in their functioning. The automobile, to take a single pervasive example, has influenced human life — including work habits, recreation, housing patterns, sexual practices, the saving and destruction of human lives — in ways far beyond the reckoning of its first builders. Machines, intended to liberate people from poverty, make them dependent on vast networks of mechanical services and energy supplies. Factories organize people in relation to the efficiency of machines and often install drudgeries worse than the drudgery machines were designed to overcome.

c) Technological efforts sometimes develop a momentum that is hard to resist, even when it needs human restraint. Large-scale technology means big investments and organizations. Many people come to have a stake in the success of the enterprise. Government officials, industrial managers, researchers and labour unions may maintain the momentum of dubious or harmful projects. Today many people suspect that this is what has happened in cases of weapons, supersonic transport planes and reliance on nuclear energy.

d) Technology affects even human self-understanding, a point already mentioned in Ch. 2. When people complain that they are merely "cogs in a machine", they show how organized technological production has affected their self-image and even the language they use. Technology originates as a means to human ends. Its unintended effect is often to make people means to the success of specific technologies.

Because of these unintended effects of technology, people sometimes experience it as a fate, even a demonic force, beyond their control. Others reply that technology is a human creation, that it has no will of its own, that people direct it, that the experience of it as fate is illusory. But even if this experience is illusory, it is a powerful experience for some. It points to the necessity of conscious, thoughtful, resolute efforts to subordinate technology to human purposes and to examine those human purposes in the light of the highest human faith.

3. Special issues arise in the transfer of technologies from one society to another. Such transfers are often highly desirable. They can be a means of overcoming great disparities of power and the injustices they mean. Part of the world's technological problem is that too many owners (governments and corporations) regard their technologies as possessions, to be sold only for their own advantage and not to be shared at all with potential competitors. Countries acquiring new technologies sometimes complain, with reason, that other countries sell only their obsolete or hazardous technologies,

retaining the secrets of their best ones. There is an ethical case to be made for increased transfer of technologies.

But again threats accompany the promise. The transfer of technology is never the transfer of technology alone. A technology brings with it something of the culture that produced it. A society adopting a foreign technology adopts something of the foreign culture. To introduce into any society the automobile and airplane, motion pictures, radio and television, even a soft-drink bottling factory is to modify traditional habits, sometimes in unexpected ways.

Since culture is never static, the changes accompanying new technologies may bring genuine benefits. But technology also frequently becomes an agent of cultural disintegration, not only deliberately (as in threat No. 1 above) but also inadvertently.

Hence the transfer of technologies puts an ethical responsibility on all parties to the agreement. A society transferring a technology has a responsibility to offer not simply the devices it no longer wants or those it can sell at a profit, but the devices that the other society really wants. The society acquiring a technology has a responsibility to think through its consequences and to make the judgment as to whether it will really enhance life for all people in the society.

Any healthy transfer of technology is difficult when there are great disparities of power between parties to the contract — as usually there are. Hence this issue raises major questions about the nature of the world's economies and the relations between them.

4. The success of science and technology in solving certain problems has led to unreal expectations. Popular hopes frequently assign to technology a messianic role in the conquest of human problems. People then may be unprepared when technology fails to solve some problems and produces others. There is a need to distinguish what science and technology can and cannot do.

For example, technology has increased economic production and consumption beyond all expectations of past centuries. This achievement has led many to hope that it would eliminate poverty and bring widespread happiness. But human misery, degradation, despair and starvation persist. By this time, it is evident that no quantitative increase in production will solve the problems of poverty without attention to basic moral concerns for justice. It is also evident, in the face of overwhelming alienation and disaffection among affluent people, that extravagant consumption is no assurance of happiness.

A few years ago, two scientists, Herbert Wiesner and H. F. York, took a look at the problem of international competition in nuclear weapons. They concluded that the chief rivals sought security by trying to build armaments that would overwhelm enemies. The result was the contradictory system of increasing armaments and decreasing security. Wiesner and York commented that there was no technical solution to the problem. Their insight has been broadened by other writers, so that today one may read in many places that there are many problems with no technical solutions. That is, there are problems for which the only solution is a reorientation of human purposes, values and ethical practices. That insight should not come as a surprise to a church whose Lord called on people for *metanoia* — a word usually translated as repentance, but actually meaning a basic change in direction. What is new is the increasing insistence from centres within the scientific establishment that no technical solutions can take the place of ethical concern and action.

To believe this is not to disdain the contribution of technology. The meeting of many human problems has both a technical and a non-technical aspect. The church cannot pull out of its storehouse of tradition the concrete and specific answers to contemporary social problems in situations never before experienced by people.

For example, technologies of good production, preservation and distribution are an essential part of the answer to human hunger. But by this time there is overwhelming evidence that increased production will not solve the problem apart from attention to human greed and social-economic organization. Technologies of contraception can contribute to meeting the population explosion. But they will not solve the problem without changes in human desires and social institutions.

To take the most important example of all, technology can contribute to human fulfilment. Think what writing and printing have meant for the expression and sharing of achievements of the human mind and imagination. But technology cannot tell what "life more abundant" is, nor can it provide that life. It cannot tell what a just society is, nor can it produce such a society apart from human insight and commitment.

Opportunities and Problems of Participation

From most parts of the world today, there comes a cry of people who want to participate in making the decisions and exercising the power that affect them. The cry comes from individuals and from groups: from racial and ethnic groups long kept out of power, from women in male-dominated societies, from youth, from the aged, from labour unions, from the poor. In the international arena, it comes from nations which feel dominated by great powers or "super powers".

Long ago, Plato and Aristotle could argue that people were born into a hierarchy and that only a few were fit to govern. The world will no longer buy that. The idea of a universal human dignity, affirmed by the Hebrew prophets, has made its way around the world. Although often violated, it cannot be repressed.

Plato and Aristotle could add to their argument of a natural hierarchy an additional fact. Only people with considerable leisure — not slaves or labourers — could spend their time discussing public issues in the market-place and come to informed opinions about important policies. That argument always had its flaws: the slaves and labourers knew some things about the society that the wealthy did not know. Today the argument is more fallacious than ever. It is not slaves and labourers who have mismanaged affairs on the grand scale.

Technology brings some advantages for informed participation in decision-making. Technologically advanced societies are, for the most part, literate societies. The press, radio and television give to many access to information once available only to the few. Universal suffrage for adults is available in many societies, and public opinion polls report almost daily on the trends of public opinion.

Yet an immense number of people in all kinds of societies do not participate in major social decisions and often do not even know how they are made. They feel alienated from the centres of power. Obviously something has gone wrong. What is it?

There is no single cause. But here our concern is to look for the relevance of science and technology to this situation.

One part of the story is that large-scale technologies may bring desired products and services to people at the cost of dependence on giant organizations (governmental agencies or business corporations) that are remote from the people, hard to influence and governed by other interests than the service of the people. In many kinds of society, people complain about the inertia of bureaucracies. In technologically advanced societies, most people can tell stories about arguments with computers. Large industries — sometimes — produce goods that are cheaper and more efficient than cottage industries can turn out, but most people have seen machines that are idle because of the lack of a spare part that must come from a distance, perhaps from another nation.

In some of these cases, trade-offs are involved. An individual might prefer some dependence upon a distant automobile manufacturer to the independence of going it alone. The trade-off might mean a net gain in mobility, power and freedom. There are advantages, both ethical and practical, in interdependence. But some people get crushed and some get lost in massive systems, and vast numbers feel alienated and dehumanized.

Another part of the story is that science and technology depend upon a technical and managerial elite. Societies come to depend upon "the priest of the machine" (Spengler), who can manipulate the mysteries beyond the comprehension of ordinary mortals. People without sufficient technical knowledge cannot make informed decisions on technical issues. Yet they are not convinced that the experts can either, and they do not want to deliver over to experts the decisions that may help or destroy themselves. Was there ever an era so dependent upon, and so distrustful of, experts as ours?

Contemporary scientific technology shows two especially conspicuous examples of the issue. The first is nuclear energy. Here is a technology that may provide energy to compensate for the dwindling supplies of fossil fuels. Already some societies are using it extensively, and more are seeking it. The hazards connected with it — accidents, diverting of nuclear materials to weapons, sabotage, transportation and disposal of wastes — are real. Accepting risks is part of the venture of human life, but not all risks are ethically justifiable. Controversies rage about the risks. Citizens and policy-makers cannot judge these issues without scientific information, but the opinions of experts will not determine the value that society puts on large supplies of energy. People cannot assess risks without scientific judgment. Unhappily, eminent scientists disagree in assessing risks. The citizen is not entirely sure how far the arguments among experts reflect differing scientific opinions and how far they reflect differences in values and political judgments.

In the spring of 1977, the World Council of Churches, through its subunit on Church and Society, made a presentation to the International Atomic Energy Agency's Conference on Nuclear Power and its Fuel Cycle (Salzburg, Austria, May 2-13). Some people wondered: why should this United Nations agency, dealing with so technical a subject, give time to the World Council of Churches? The reason was a recognition that "public acceptability", which means in part ethical acceptability, is an important element in decisions about nuclear energy. The WCC, in developing its statement, involved some of the world's foremost physical scientists (including both pro- and anti-nuclear physicists). Its statement included its own best assessment of some highly technical questions about advantages of various sources of energy, about comparative risks of different systems, and about human needs in relation to resources. But it put its major accent on the two ethical issues of justice in access to energy and the legitimate concern of the public in decision-making.

The second example is genetic experimentation. The most prominent issue in this vast field is currently the argument over recombinant DNA ("gene splicing"). This new technique may give the means for preventing diseases that have haunted human history. It represents a giant leap in both science and technology. But some scientists warn that it may unleash new diseases for which human beings have no immunity and no remedies. So serious is the scientific concern that geneticists recently agreed to observe a prolonged self-enforced international moratorium on such experimentation, while they drew up guidelines for further work. Now governments, national and local, are legislating on the issue. The normal government policy-maker or citizen does not know much about the issue, let alone have a basis for sound decisions, apart from information that comes from scientists. Yet people, who may be helped or hurt by the experimentation, do not want to turn over decisions to an expert elite, who in their enthusiasm for research may have different values from the public at large.

Many other developments in genetics present important ethical issues. Should genetic science try to prevent the birth of abnormal people? Should science try to increase the intelligence of people by new genetic techniques? What is it to be normal, to be human? These issues are discussed further in Chapter 6. Great scientific-technological endeavours centre on such issues, but science and technology will not themselves answer the questions.

Scientists have long fought, sometimes against superstition and tyrannical restraints, for freedom of inquiry and experimentation. Society, including religious and political institutions, has often restrained science, then has usually lived to regret its restraint. But society has a legitimate concern for the effects of research. Surely society has a right to some control and direction of research. This is most obvious in the case of applied technology. For example, many societies have decided (at least in their public stance) that research directed toward bacterial warfare is unethical. But even pure research has ethical limitations. There are widespread constraints upon experimentation on people without their "informed consent". And now even experimentation on bacteria is restricted for the sake of public safety.

The advances of science and technology make urgent the question of decision-making that affects the public good. There is a role for scientists and technologists in shaping public policy. They cannot simply assert that their activity is value-free and that they have no responsibility for the use made of their achievements. But, on the other hand, they cannot become moral arbiters for society. As the Cambridge consultation (mentioned earlier in this chapter) put it:

> "The relationship between science and war, science and the control of behaviour, technology and the ecological crisis, among others, are facts which every scientist should take into consideration. Responsible scientific work thus demands a rigorous analysis of the socio-political and economic framework of the scientific enterprise. Although science is incompetent to determine values or ends, it can provide an objective clarification as to the means to be used or as to the ends which are actually achieved."

As part of the public, scientists have a responsibility to alert society with candour to the ethical significance of their actions, so far as they can discern them. But then there is a role for the whole public. No matter how able the expert, the people affected by decisions have a moral right to participate in the making of them.

Faith and its Ethical Consequences

Christian faith has consequences for ethical decisions. In Jesus' parable of the Last Judgment, the decisive issue was not what people had said or felt, but what they done for the hungry, the sick, the imprisoned. Faith that is real makes a difference in action. Today it makes a difference in actions within a world of science, technology, and political and economic activities.

Yet Christians are often perplexed about the precise meaning of faith and theology for practical decisions. They may be as puzzled as the rest of humanity, for example, about which precise forms of political and social organization best serve justice or (to recall two cases just mentioned) what to do about nuclear energy or research on DNA. Uncertainties and differences in judgment are to be expected within the church. God does not give the church immunity from the perplexities that haunt the human race.

In such a situation, Christians meet two enticing temptations. The first is to make faith irrelevant to ethical decisions. That is clearly an evasion of the demands of discipleship. It is a denial of the Lordship of God over all life. The second temptation is to try to find in the Bible or theological tradition definite answers to questions never before faced by humanity. That is to avoid the responsibility God gives his people to use their intelligence and follow the guidings of the Spirit.

Christians share a faith that God has met them and showed his judgment and love in Christ; that Christ has called them to share in the Kingdom of God; that God's Kingdom is a Kingdom of grace, justice and peace. Christians have used various methods for enacting this faith in ethical decisions. We list a few examples of ways in which Christians and the church have gone at the task of making ethical decisions:

a) They have seen the Bible as a source of ethical laws to be applied to changing situations.

b) They have located a teaching authority within the church, either in a hierarchy or in a communal body.

c) They have drawn from the Bible general ethical principles, from which they have moved through "middle axioms" to specific decisions.

d) They have emphasized the uniqueness of specific situations and have sought to find the most appropriate response of love to each situation.

e) They have found analogies between biblical and contemporary situations or between biblical symbols and ethical actions, using biblical teachings and events as parables for decisions in later times.

f) They have sought, with the help of the social sciences, to analyze the structures of social organizations and to learn how those organizations serve human needs or oppress people.

g) They have looked for the guidance of the Holy Spirit or the inner light, working through both prophetic individuals and the community of faith.

h) They have discovered in the biblical story insights and illuminations that affect their perception of the world, of human relations and of the meaning of love in human affairs.

Within all this diversity, we may expect continuing conversation among Christians about the best ways to relate convictions of faith to practical decisions. Differences of judgment remind Christians not to condemn quickly those who come to different conclusions on specific issues. The difference is not necessarily a sign of moral weakness or opposite ethical commitment; it may stem from differences in experience or information or practical judgment.

But unity in Christ reminds Christians of a responsibility to learn from one another and to seek fuller insights from the variety of experiences. Above all, it reminds them of a responsibility to avoid the temptation of letting diverse opinions become the excuse for inaction or complacency in the face of evil.

Christians are called to strive for social justice, and in so doing they often work with people of other faiths and ideologies. The problems and opportunities vary greatly in differing situations. In Christian history, the church has often been a persecuted minority. It has been a major influence in shaping some societies. It has been a community of faith within pluralistic societies. The strategies of faithfulness in one situation may be inappropriate in another.

Yet there are some convictions of faith that Christians can carry into social situations. They are not a separate race with specific solutions for the problems of the world. But they are a called people, who look to God for his continuous new creation. They look to Scripture for the story of God's ancient revelation and for clues to his continuing revelation and guidance. They will not seek to limit God's work or influence to their own history and experience, but will rejoice whenever they meet people committed to justice and love. They will maintain an openness for conversation with all who will converse openly. In such conversation, Christians will expect both to speak and to listen, both to testify to their convictions and to learn from others.

Christians will bring to cooperative efforts some distinctive accents, which they will make more or less explicit depending upon the occasion:

— the love they have known in Christ, seeking embodiment in justice, compassion and a special concern for the oppressed;

— a gratitude for science and technology as gifts and responsibilities to be exercised before God and for all creatures, under the guidance of love;

— a conviction that creatures exist primarily for God, just as God exists for creatures;

— a warning against the temptation to use power without restraint for self-affirmation and self-enrichment;

— an interest in a quality of life that includes economic goods and the gifts of technology, incorporating these in a community with more than economic and technical interests.

And Christians will bring to their efforts a hope in God as the ultimate Lord of life. This hope gives a measure of freedom from shifting moods of optimism and pessimism. It is a hope in a Kingdom of God, already active in history, never fully embodied in any human institution, always coming in judgment and love. It is a hope and confidence in the saving power of God for humanity and all creation.

4 · The Biblical Interpretation of Nature and Human Dominion

Nature

There is no semantic equivalent in Old Testament Hebrew for either the modern concept of nature or the ancient Greek concept of *physis*. This is true not only of nature as idea, but also as aggregate. The characteristic Hebrew method is to indicate the totality by listing its main ingredients, e.g. "heaven and earth and sea". We do not even find "all things" as an equivalent for our term "universe".

What we do find is the phrase "all (God's) works". Earth and heaven are never thought of as autonomous entities. They are always seen as inseparably linked with God in the great cosmic community. God is not equated with nature; the Old Testament is not pantheist. But neither is God the wholly other, the remote and transcendent; the Old Testament is not deist. God is intimately and enduringly involved with nature. He is Creator, but not in the sense of a mere initiator. Through his "word", "wisdom", "spirit", "name", "hand", he is continually active within it and responding to it. Likewise no creature is independent of any other or of God. Man *('adam)*, the ground *('adama)*, plants, animals, birds, fish, the earth, the sky — all are mutually involved, mutually influenced.

God's place in this cosmic community is unique. Even the highest heaven cannot contain him, but he fills heaven and earth. His relationship with the cosmos is at once defined and wrapped in mystery by reserving to him the word *bara'*, "create", which is never found with any being but God as its subject. This divine creativity is unique. It is not *ex nihilo* (that is an idea that enters with Greek thought), but it is fundamental in an ultimate way. Thus, God does not work within given frameworks of space and time; he creates those frameworks. Before creation there is only chaos, devoid of either dimension or direction. Again, the time-scale is something instituted only on the fourth "day" of God's creative work.

It is part of God's total understanding of and permanent involvement with his creatures that he relates to each of them in the appropriate way. By so doing he constitutes them into a hierarchy: the hosts of heaven —

the stars — humanity — animals — plants — the earth. Within this cosmic hierarchy the last four levels form the community of earth; and within this community humanity and the animals go together as a distinctive group, that of beings who can be described as *nephesh* (conventionally, "soul"; more accurately "living individual"). Only these are said to be alive *(hava)*. This is not because all others are thought of as inanimate, far from it. The *'adama*, ground, from which man is formed, is itself living and active; plants reproduce their kind, and so on. But animals and humanity have life in pre-eminent fashion; an animal is an individual living being, and as such closer to humanity than any other creature. Even so, it is not an equal partner and companion. Humanity comes distinctly at the head of the earthly community.

This understanding of the earthly community of creatures is possible only because the Old Testament has demythologized nature to a degree unique in the Ancient Near East. The counterpoise to the fact that man is an integral element within the community of earth, himself a part of nature, is that the other creatures are not divinized. They are not, as in Mesopotamia, for example, manifestations of competing spiritual powers. God alone is sovereign and he is one. Creatures are themselves, and subordinate to him at the proper point in the hierarchy. This gives man freedom from *Angst*, so characteristic of Babylonian religion, because ultimately he has to deal only with one controlling power, God, and God's character is known. The relations of all creatures to God are set within the framework of a covenant, made with all flesh and with the earth itself, in which God promises stability to existence.

The Role of Creatures

Covenant in the Ancient Near East and Israel is primarily something unilaterally imposed by an overlord, and carries with it both promise and law. With God's promise of stability go the laws which he establishes in appropriate fashion for each creature: for sun and moon, for migrant birds, for the sea, and so on. But not all creatures unfailingly achieve the goodness appointed for them. Leviathan, the great sea monster, the most magnificent of all animals, may be God's playmate; but he can also be something evil and dangerous. The lion's roar is a prayer to God for his food, a prayer which God answers; but the lion too can be something hostile and demonic, a threat which in paradise regained will become harmless. Of all creatures only the birds seem to get a uniformly good press! And in the primal history, in the age before the Flood, it is not just man whose ways are evil; all flesh has corrupted its way before God and filled the earth with violence, and so all are destroyed.

When, however, creatures fulfil their role, they have two kinds of value. They have value in the community of creation, in their contribution to the interdependence by which the life of all is sustained. But equally they have value in themselves to God, which is quite distinct. For this reason life is sacred to God, and the blood which is the vehicle of that life is reserved to God, and must not be consumed by man. Indeed, it is because of its value to God that it can be accepted by him, on his own permission, as a propitiation for man's wrongdoing. Similarly there are many creatures which have no discernible utility; but God takes pleasure in them. There is here a distinction which seems in some sort to echo our own distinction between instrumental and intrinsic value; but the former in the Old Testament is never merely value to man but always value within the earthly community as a whole.

Within this community man has a special position given him by God. In Gen. 1 this is characterized as "dominion". This term has been the focus of much debate in recent years, and is therefore treated in more detail separately below.

Moral norms concern the relationships between humanity and animals as well as relations between human beings. Thus, the blood of every animal must not be touched, because through blood it is related directly to its creator. There are other laws which in the biblical context are signs of man's responsibility for the welfare of animals, e.g. the prohibition against taking away a bird with its eggs or muzzling a threshing ox (Deut. 22 : 6; 25 : 4). Righteousness is necessary even towards cattle. Christian ethics needs to work out the detailed manifestations of the spirit of these norms in ways appropriate to our own time and place.

Heilsgeschichte, "salvation-history", is something that unfolds within the framework of creation as a whole. The promised land is far more than a mere place to live. It is the ground on which life in *shalom* ("well-being", "peace") becomes possible, the basis of a religious as well as of an economically adequate existence (*menuha*, "rest"). But as a kind of living entity the ground belongs ultimately to God, and Israel must free it from service time and again (Lev. 25).

Sin as Alienation from Nature

In spite of God's enduring creativity, *sin and alienation* have entered human life. They originate with the first man and spread and develop. But to say that the fall of man entails the fall of nature is to over-simplify the biblical understanding. The basic laws of nature are a framework of time and space which mankind can never destroy. Nevertheless the effectiveness of God's blessings and curses is based on the presupposition of an insoluble connection between human behaviour and the "response" of earth, although not in a simple casual way (Deut. 28). The sin of Adam and Eve incurs the lessening of earth's spontaneous abundance (Gen. 3); the ground refuses to give her strength to the sinner Cain (Gen. 4). Sin always involves some kind of loss of "earth". Alienation from God goes hand in hand with alienation from nature.

To break the ban of sin and its consequences, the rites of *propitiation* are conceded to Israel. By the vicarious death of an ox or sheep, its master can be rescued from death. Only in this case man may use the blood for his own purpose.

The prophets, however, maintain that the sinfulness of their fellow-countrymen has been intensified to such a degree that no propitiation will save them. The coming catastrophe will bring not only illness, death and destruction of the human community, it will bring also the loss of the promised land as basis of life and welfare *(shalom)*.

For the prophets, God's aim with his people (and mankind) is salvation and a new *sedaqa*, "righteousness". Judgment is only a transitional stage and may be falsified by Israel's repentance. At last creation will be completed in *a new heaven and a new earth*. Then not only alienation between man and man or man and God, but also alienation between man and animal will come to an end (Is. 11).

Nature in the New Testament

By contrast with the Old Testament, the New Testament has relatively little to say about nature. The reasons for this are partly fortuitous, partly sociological, but also inherent in the nature of the primitive Christian community and its world-view. The fortuitous reasons arise purely from the scale and character of the New Testament material. In volume it is only 30% of that of the Old. The bulk of its contents falls within a period of forty years, and the outside limits of its dating bracket only a century, compared with the nine centuries between the earliest and latest passages in the Old Testament. The New Testament is the work of a relatively small community with highly selective interests, whereas the Old Testament is the product of a whole nation, a minor one certainly, but always much larger than the church in the New Testament period, and inevitably concerned with a nation's wider issues and situations. Hence it is no surprise to find in the Old Testament far greater diversity of types of literature than in the New. There is nothing in the New Testament, for example, to parallel the large collections of "observations on life and world-order" which we call the "wisdom literature" of the Old Testament, or its extensive range of liturgical poetry, or the detailed corpus of its laws on what we would regard as secular matters. The very types of material, therefore, in which an attitude to nature might be most likely to be reflected are precisely those which are missing from the New Testament.

Sociologically, it is hard to escape the impression that most of the New Testament writers are "urbanized", compared with the predominantly agricultural orientation of the mind of the Old Testament. The Gospel material, especially in the teaching of Jesus, with its use of images from nature and husbandry, is nearest to rural society and to the world of the Old; James is thought by some scholars to be addressed to the

Palestinian church. But otherwise there is little sign in the writers of any attention to nature; and their audience, where known, is almost exclusively urban. While it is true that this would not have been as strong a distinction in the Roman world as it is in our own megalopolitan culture, nevertheless it is probably fair to say that nature was not one of the things in the centre of the mental focus of the early Christians; and this is partly related to their sociological classification.

There were, however, other reasons, inherent in the earliest church and its Gospel, which conspired to minimize concern with the question of human attitudes to nature. The first was the approach of primitive Christianity to Scripture. For Christians of the first century, the Old Testament was their Bible, and it alone was the inspired "Word of God". Primarily, however, the first Christians were interested in it as a vast source-book of predictions, some clear, some enigmatic, of the coming of Christ, his nature, life, death, resurrection, redeeming work, and heavenly glory, and of the mission and destiny of the church. Their exuberant and untiring obsession was with the Gospel. They were not, on the whole, interested in the total range of an argument or the total message of a book. These are characteristically modern ways of using Scripture. Given this situation, it can be seen that many of those elements in Judaism which we have been considering were effectively blanked off from early Christian consciousness.

Secondly, there is the fact that the Christian message was initially a gospel of personal salvation. It impinged on ordinary life but primarily at the points of religious belief and personal and social morality. The criticism of much present-day Christian preaching as being still too much concerned with these two things only, instead of having something to say on corporate or global issues, must, if it is to be both honest and helpful, face the fact that in the foundation (and still authoritative) documents of the church precisely these were the overwhelmingly dominant concerns.

The third and perhaps most important of all reasons is, of course, that the earliest Christians felt themselves to be those "upon whom the end of the ages has come" (1 Cor. 10 : 11). Since, therefore, the created order did not have long to run, there was no incentive to develop a constructive long-term attitude to nature as it was.

The Goodness of Creation

It is clear, nevertheless, and must be said with emphasis, that all the New Testament writers assume without question that the Old Testament view of the created order is God's work and therefore good. Inevitably, because they lived in a world of Greek thought and culture, and wrote in Greek, this view was largely mediated to them in the forms of Hellenistic Judaism, which added to the Old Testament conception the notion of *creatio ex nihilo* (Heb. 11 : 3). This is for them, however, little more than an intensification of their sense of God's power and wisdom; there is no sign that they are concerned with any philosophical problems it may raise. Basically, their vision remains that of the great Old Testament themes that any radical dualism is to be rejected, and that God is closely and continuously involved with the cosmic community: "in him we live and move and have our being".

The Graeco-Roman world at this time, however, was afflicted with a deep sense of pessimism and of helplessness in the grip of fate, conceptualized widely as the tyranny of astral powers. Moreover, Stoicism encouraged many to believe in the ageing and degeneration of the world, which was thought of as declining towards the end of the current cosmic epoch. This degeneration was seen as manifest not merely in man but in the realm of nature. The New Testament at many points reacts strongly against this assessment of existence, not by denying the situation it expresses, but by asserting that through Christ liberation is at hand. This is perhaps the major new New Testament contribution to a theology of nature, humanity and God, and may be studied in two main contexts. The first is Paul's brief but densely packed reflection on the state of the creation in Rom. 8 : 19-23, the second the concept of the cosmic Christ and cosmic salvation in Heb. 1 : 22 f., Col. 1 : 15 ff., and the Prologue to St. John's Gospel. Because these are the principal points at which Scripture seeks to relate the Gospel hope to the creation as a whole, it is desirable to discuss them on their own in somewhat more detail.

We may summarize the main indications for *praxis* emerging from the biblical utterances about nature as follows:

a) For the biblical writers the determining factors in thinking about nature, as about every other subject, are the all-controlling rights and power of God. "The earth is the Lord's and the fullness thereof" (Ps. 24 : 1; 1 Cor. 10 : 26) and this can be carried so far even as to have practical consequences for human social organization, as in the principle underlying the law of Jubilee, that no human being can ever "own" land outright but must be regarded as a tenant installed by God (Lev. 25 : 1-34).

b) Under this overall sovereignty of God, man does have a position of control over nature, which is approved by God, and which is meant to be exercised in a spirit of respect and responsibility. Skills and technology of all kinds may be admirable, but the tyrannical or greedy use of human power over nature is a failure deriving from human sin, not from God's intention in creation.

c) Man's proper control over nature is made possible because the realization that God is One and Supreme, and therefore transcendent, effectively desupernaturalizes the world, ridding it of superhuman personal power, whether divine or demonic, and placing man in a position to use his powers rationally in dealing with nature.

d) Nevertheless, nature is not to be evaluated simply in terms of human needs and interests. God created the greater part of the world for its own sake — a point that comes home to us, with our knowledge of the immensity of the universe, even more strongly — and wisdom consists fundamentally in recognizing this and the limitations which it imposes upon us. Technology may explore and exploit nature, but it will never discover the way to "wisdom" (Job 28). The truly wise man never imagines that he knows fully what God was about in creation.

e) Since God, however, has a moral and rational character, man must in the end submit to things as they are, as a genuine revelation, so far as he can grasp it, of ultimate goodness and wisdom. Hence the careful and comprehensive observation of nature will yield indications for human behaviour which were part of God's intention in creating in the first place, and which therefore have the status of moral imperatives for man. We must ultimately be guided by respect for the intricate character and needs of the natural order.

f) If we are so guided, then we may hope even to improve the condition of nature, which does not as yet embody God's character as human beings have come to know this through their communion with him. Nature is not perfect; there is a work of salvation to be done in her, as well as in humanity, as part of God's eschatological purpose, and this salvation is part of man's responsibility for her.

Human Dominion

Among Christians the question of the relationship between humanity and nature used to be a part of the doctrine of creation. The creation story found its classical expression in the first chapter of the Bible. Here the relationship between humanity and nature is established by a blessing of the Creator himself: fill the earth and subdue it, rule over the fish in the sea, the birds of heaven and every living thing that moves on earth. Regarding this sentence and its impact on the Western tradition there has been some dispute in the last decade. Some theologians have stressed the measure of demythologization which lies behind such a commission. In all other cultures, man was restricted in his intercourse with his environment by respect to a lot of mythical entities which were believed to be around him, and by many rituals corresponding to these. In Gen. 1, however, a unique *Weltverantwortung* (world responsibility) is transmitted to mankind. This, together with other influences, lays the ground for the incredible development of natural science in the West in modern times. But others, like the historian Lynn White, believe the contrary and challenge those theologians who have interpreted Gen. 1 as the separation of mankind from all non-human beings and the transfer of a god-like power to human will and exploitation. From whence, says Lynn White, comes a Christian arrogance towards nature. This, it is said, is the historical root of our environment crisis today.

Certainly both positions minimize the complexity of a large historical process. Nonetheless the present crisis calls for a new description of the human ontological position and the ethical values of his scientific and technological attempts to change the surface of earth. In this regard, a new approach to biblical and Christian tradition is necessary, in church as well as in theology.

The concept of the dominion of humanity over earth should not be viewed apart from the corresponding understanding of God. The characteristics of this dominion can be explained only if the relationship of humanity to God is taken into account. The decisive point is that humanity is created in the likeness and image of its Creator. Human dominion over earth is always conceived as a function of God's dominion over humanity. For dominion over earth is another thing than pure administration: it includes creativity. Corresponding to differing doctrines of God there are very different views of human dominion in church history:

a) When God is thought of as a kind of omnipotent dictator who puts his laws on humanity for incomprehensible reasons, then humanity may also be thought of as an unlimited dictator over the beings and resources of earth (cf. Max Weber on the rise of early capitalism in Protestant societies).

b) If God is purely transcendent, observing or judging his creatures only from outside, then it follows that the human essence is its immortal soul which has in principle nothing in common with sub-human beings; God may condemn or raise them up as he may choose to do; the consequence is neglect of the world and all in it (the Gnostic view).

c) If God is considered as working at his creation even "on the eighth day", pushing it forward to its ultimate destiny, then dominion implies human involvement in planning and shaping history (Pannenberg).

d) If the universe is conceived as contributory to the divine life and God behaves sympathetically with all his creatures, humans too should be compassionate to all beings around them (Hartshorne).

Dominion and Ultimate Hope

These are only a few examples. But the selection is sufficient to prove the thesis that there is no adequate statement about man's dominion without a corresponding statement about God's dominion. Reference to Gen 1 : 28 is not enough; this verse must be taken together with 1 : 27 and the whole context of creation.

In Gen. 1 God is thought of as creating by language, and by language he puts his blessing on the course of history. In the hierarchy of space and time, humanity takes a special position because it alone is able to communicate by hearing and speaking with its creator. Therefore it is blessed with the dominion on earth.

This dominion is not the same towards inanimate beings (Gen. 1 : 28 *kibbes*, subduing) as towards animals *(rada,* rule). But in both cases it is a continuation of God's creativity, because humanity rules as image and agent ("vassal") of its creator, and with it starts the process of history.

"Subduing the earth" includes tilling the soil, building houses and changing the surface of the earth. Humanity "serves" the earth and takes care of it; if man works as farmer *(abad, shamar)*, he supports its powers for the use of all its inhabitants. The other kind of human dominion, rulership over animals, includes perhaps using them for labour, but only at a later stage consuming or sacrificing them (in Gen. 9, Exod. 25 ff.). Even then the use of blood remains prohibited. So this rulership is a highly responsible one and by no means dictatorship. Rather it is understood in terms of shepherd-kingship according to an Ancient Near Eastern ideal; perhaps the responsibility of a shepherd, so far as birds and fish are concerned. The totality of humanity's behaviour shapes the course of time and the world, and the sphere of influence of its deeds spreads out for the fortune or misfortune of all the creatures.

The Old Testament notion of human dominion over earth is taken up by the New Testament. Nonetheless there are in the latter some new viewpoints. They result from the new experience of God which Christ has opened. Love is revealed as God's very essence. Under the Old Covenant God was experienced as the one who loves his chosen people. But in Christ he appears as loving the cosmos.

It is not surprising that only in Jesus Christ were the true likeness and image of God seen by New Testament writers. For the history of the people of the Old Testament has clearly shown that the dominion of mankind over earth does function only within limits. The growing prophetic experience with God obliges us, more and more, to suppose that God's aim in history will be to set forth a redemption and salvation which will go beyond all that has happened before. The coming Kingdom of God needs a man as God's vicegerent who has been righteous and can be a model for future human life. In this regard, for early Christianity Jesus becomes the key figure in human dominion too. Through him, God reveals himself as God of love. No wonder that in the New Testament the reference to Christ as the true image of God mentions also the cosmos (Col. 1 : 15 ff., Hebrew 2 ff.). Under the influence of Greek traditions the creation was now considered as *ta panta*. The transition from an agricultural to an urban society resulted in a new sophisticated statement of the relationship between humanity and earth. The dominion over the universe is now connected with the hope of bodily resurrection.

For Christian considerations about the position of humanity within creation the Old Testament framework remains necessary. But the ethical impact of this theme is not to establish whether the love of God is taken into account which is revealed in its fullness first in Jesus Christ. It is told that he "was among the wild beasts" in the beginnings of his ministry (Mark 1 : 22). Some exegetes interpret this as a sign of the anticipation of the coming Paradise (cf. Is. 11). Jesus of Nazareth is not the end of the process God started with his creation: he is the anticipation of a new earth and a new relationship between humanity and nature.

"Many things are terrifying, but none more terrible than man", says a Greek poet. Human dominion over earth is not a mere article of faith; it is a matter of fact since neolithic times at least. Never will this responsibility be taken from us. But to be aware of it in the right way and to act according to it, that will be the consequence of faith.

5 · Rethinking the Criteria for Quality of Life

For more than a decade the question of the quality of life has been cropping up in discussions of development and of the future of technologically organized societies, particularly in view of the environment debate. One reason for concern has been the discovery that increasing affluence does not necessarily enhance the quality of life, especially in the industrially advanced market economy countries.

However the quality of life, which could be an appropriate criterion for assessing human development, remains almost undefinable and unmeasurable. While we want quality of life we are not sure what it is, how to measure it, or how to programme it.

These are in fact the three fundamental questions at the heart of economic theory itself:

a) What is the most desirable quality of life and by what criteria do we decide this?

b) What parameters can be devised for the measurement of quality of life?

c) How does society as a whole plan for a higher quality of life and not leave its achievement to individuals and groups alone?

These three questions may be denoted as philosophical, mensural and operational.

I. Philosophical Considerations

How can economic theory take quality of life into account as a fairly comprehensive category for assessing human development? Where do we find the characteristics of a lower or higher quality of life, and how do we achieve a social consensus about quality of life goals?

It is clear that quality of life cannot be a consequence of state planning alone. Personal choices, group choices, religious influences, cultural factors including educational choices all can affect quality of life. Culture itself cannot be entirely planned by the state. Nor can the leisure time activities of individuals. But the state's economic planning can provide greater support for cultural and leisure time activities.

The way in which the production of goods and services is oriented and structured is a decisive factor in quality of life. The fundamental economic questions in relation to quality of life can be formulated thus:

a) To what *ends* should economic activity be directed, in order to aim at a higher quality of life for all?

b) What *principles* should govern the social organization of economic activity, in order to ensure a higher quality of life?

The two major questions in economic organization which bear on the quality of life are:

a) What is the motivation for economic activity — profit, personal attainment, or social commitment?

b) Who owns and controls the means of production?

Both these questions are ideologically loaded, which makes it very difficult for international groups to discuss them dispassionately. Yet they are of key significance to quality of life. For it can be argued that at the root of the current malaise about affluence are the personal egoism and aggressiveness fostered by a competitive individualistic economic system and culture. The striking of a right balance between the personal and the social aspects of human existence, and provision for personal creativity within a context of commitment to the needs and purposes of society as a whole, are necessary characteristics of an economic and social organization capable of fostering quality of life. Where a desire for personal or group profit and advancement dominates, quality of life for all must eventually deteriorate. A society with a higher quality of life can be achieved only if there is mass education for commitment to social goals and purposes, where major restraints are placed on personal or group acquisitiveness, exploitation and aggression.

Therefore it is clear that there are severe limits to quality of life within both a market economy system, and a socialist system which imposes unnecessary restrictions on personal liberty. But socialist systems, insofar as they are able to ensure certain fundamental possibilities for all (e.g. equality, employment, health care, education, freedom from economic exploitation, etc.) and remove progressively restrictions on personal liberty while safeguarding justice and dignity for all, can be regarded as on the way to achieving a higher quality of life.

The extent to which quality of life can be improved for all within the market economy system seems rather limited. Inequalities persist despite great growth in affluence. Even the affluent become increasingly dissatisfied and insecure. Arguments to the effect that there have been substantial and far-reaching changes in the market economy system, and that such changes have overcome its basic defects fail to carry conviction.

Questions of economic organization, the motivation for economic activity and the ownership and control of the means of production are therefore fundamental to any discussion of the quality of life. But these economic questions lead to deeper philosophical questions:

a) What sort of an animal is man, and what, if anything, is normative for humanity as such? Here questions of freedom, community, society, history, etc., have to be approached at a level deeper than the socio-logical or economic one.

b) How can society achieve consensus about social and economic norms? How can it provide for the possibility of dissent?

c) The philosophical question about quality is the most profound question in human existence. For the effort to define quality inevitably leads to the philosophical-ethical question of the nature of the good, which is a perennial and basically unanswered question in the history of human existence. The question about the good inevitably leads beyond the limits of critical rationality (read, for example, that piece of American literature called *Zen and the Art of Motor-Cycle Maintenance*).

The philosophical aspects of quality of life are somewhat daunting. But should they for that reason be avoided?

II. Measurability Problems

How can the good be measured? In terms of utility, pleasure, need, satisfaction? It is not necessary to resolve this philosophical question in order to enter the discussion about parameters for measuring quality of life. While not everything about quality of life can be quantified, it is certainly possible to measure more than the aggregate volume of goods and services produced.

The following list is offered only as a provisional attempt to denote some areas of social development that could conceivably be measured with some focused effort at devising parameters. Justice, participation and sustainability are involved in almost all the ten categories listed.

1. *Quality of Goods and Services Produced:* Some major quantifiable elements are:

a) The proportion of goods meeting basic needs to luxury goods. The criteria for distinguishing between these two classes will vary from society to society, but some basic elements are food, clothing, housing, transportation, health care, education and culture for the masses, though in each of these areas it is difficult to separate luxury from need.

b) The quality of education or health care is somewhat difficult to measure, but parameters could be devised which might help to promote quality in education and health care in all countries.

2. *The Distribution Pattern:* The ratio between the average per capita income and consumption of the upper ten-percentile and the lowest ten-percentile groups. This should include such items as per capita protein consumption and housing space. Equally important are distribution patterns between regions within a nation, between linguistic or cultural groups, between urban and rural populations, etc.

3. *The Employment Pattern:* The proportion of the population that is unemployed or under-employed is a clear parameter of the quality of life.

4. *The Environment:* While pollution volume is a negative indicator of the quality of life, the relation of investment for pollution prevention and control to the volume of pollution can be a useful parameter. The carbon-dioxide level, impact on ozone layer, total amount of heat produced, etc., can be used as negative indicators. Resource utilization patterns can also be measured.

5. *The Dependence Pattern:* To what extent is the pattern of development increasing self-reliance on the part of the nation as a whole and on the part of groups within the nation in relation to each other? (This is a criterion that is both difficult to measure, and impossible to absolutize, since certain aspects of inter-dependence in society seem to be healthy rather than negative factors.)

6. *The Participation Pattern:* The degree to which participation by the people in major decision-making related to production, distribution and government has been maximized seems to be measurable, and can be used as a criterion of quality of life. However, imagination is required to .devise adequate parameters, for people's participation is often formal rather than actual.

7. *The Quality of Motivation:* The quality of human attitudes is the hardest to measure, but they are basic to the quality of life. Selfishness, greed, acquisitiveness, exploitation and domination of others — these are certainly indicators of negative quality. Love, service-mindedness, willing-

ness to contribute one's labour for the welfare of others, in short a social motivation for labour itself, seem to be essential elements in quality of life.

In every society, positive and negative motivations are mixed in various proportions. The same people who are driven by the profit motive to accumulate property and power contribute generously to charitable causes. All people make their contribution to society through the payment of taxes. The difference arises in the basic motivation for labour. Is it personal profit or a desire to serve their fellows? It cannot be both: one of them has to be basic.

A related question, which motivation is encouraged and reinforced by the pattern of social and economic organization? Is it personal egoism and advancement, or the desire to serve society? This is very important in the long run. Personal egoism is used even in socialist societies as a spur to production. It is not on that account to be justified. A society has a responsibility to integrate with its system of production and distribution a system of social education which will eventually overcome personal greed and make it possible to provide everyone with an opportunity to contribute his labour to society and to have all his needs provided for by that society.

It is not totally impossible to measure the extent to which economic organization encourages social motivation which seems to be of central importance for the quality of life. In any society, justice and sustainability imply, in addition to this social concern, at least two other important factors: concern for future generations, and concern for the integrity of nature. All three have to be provided for in the structures of the society, and some of their aspects should be measurable. A society deficient in all three can hardly be considered to have a high quality of life.

8. *Human Rights and Human Freedom:* Any effort to devise parameters for measuring human rights in a given society comes up against the problem of the priority given to various human rights. In some societies, the right to dignified labour and to a truly human life worthy of man seems fundamental, with personal rights of dissent and protest being accorded only second place. Other societies regard freedom of opinion, of the press, and of protest as primary. Agreement on a scale of priorities is a prerequisite to the shaping of adequate parameters which can be used universally. Despite these difficulties, human rights constitute one of the essential characteristics of a dignified life and need to be incorporated into the set of quality of life parameters.

9. *Cultural Freedom and Creativity:* UNIDO has already had some success in the extremely difficult field of devising parameters to quantify cultural development. Factors like per capita investment in culture, the variety of cultural forms and international recognition are not totally reliable, but they are helpful in evaluating cultural quality. Scientific and technological creativity can also be considered aspects of cultural creativity. Many societies which are far behind others in industrial development may be ahead in cultural variety and quality. Appropriate parameters can contribute to a more balanced evaluation of the degree of development of a society.

10. *Some Negative Parameters:* Development can also be measured by certain negative parameters, such as:

a) prevalence of contagious diseases;

b) prevalence of mental disease, cancer and cardiac ailments;

c) accident rate;

d) crime rate;

e) suicide rate;

f) number of alcoholics per thousand;

g) number of drug addicts per thousand;

h) number of people in prison per thousand;

i) prevalence of bribery and corruption;

j) estimates of blackmarketing and smuggling.

This list is not meant to be exhaustive. In some cases, parameters may take a long time to develop, but this should not prevent a beginning in the use of a set of criteria wider than GNP. This will change the evaluation of some societies which are now classified as "least developed" on the basis merely of the aggregate quantity of goods and services produced.

The concept of "diseconomies" may be incorporated into the quality of life discussion. Many of these are quantifiable. Others are more difficult to compute — ugliness, urban sprawl, other features which jar the nerves or impair human health without people being conscious of it. E. J. Mishan [1] lists some of these basic "external diseconomies" in terms of property rights; in terms of noisy or polluting neighbours one has not chosen (factories, airports); of built-up areas, when our cities expand in patterns

---

[1] *The Costs of Economic Growth* (Penguin, 1975), p. 82.

beyond the control of the residents; of separate facilities (smoking or non-smoking, etc.), of the derelict city, of tourism, immigration, racist conflict, etc.

Growth itself has unmeasurable consequences; for example it encourages a passion for a fast pace, for new experiences, for gadgetry. There seems to be some conflict between the demands of technology-based growth and those of our own instinctual nature. Alienation itself is part of the deteriorating quality of our life. There is need for work on measuring the element of alienation in our social life as a negative parameter for quality of life.

III. Operational Problems

How can we operate with these parameters in economic planning? Not all economies in the world are centrally planned, but even in the most traditionally free enterprise societies the level of government or central regulations is increasing. It is not necessary to subscribe to any convergence theory to recognize that structured relations are becoming more and more decisive in human life everywhere. In many market economy societies, however, there is a growing suspicion that both the machinery of the state and the machinery of industrial production are badly alienated from the people.

In such situations, it does not seem reasonable to expect initiatives for improving quality of life to come from above. People feel helpless about "the system" and seek to improve their own personal quality of life by adopting alternate life styles with less consumption and ostentation, more simplicity and spontaneity. Or they opt out of organized society to live in communes. Certainly such pioneering has intrinsic value, and may produce patterns of life to be emulated by others. But experience of the past 20 years or so would seem to indicate that such individual and group efforts do not have a decisive impact on the quality of life of organized society.

The problem is rather one of national economy and of global structural relationships. The attempt by individuals to solve it for themselves is itself part of the problem of egoism. Each person is responsible for all and not just for himself or herself. If this is recognized and acknowledged, the struggle will be to improve quality of life not for the individual but for the whole of society.

A new society cannot, of course, be made of whole cloth. We do not build society as we construct a building, with plans and blueprints made from scratch. Society is an existing and dynamic reality, and planning simply means the controlling and channelling of social dynamics.

But there does not seem to be any evidence of the existence of an invisible hand operating to steady and guide the chariot of history. Humanity is called to gain as much control as possible over the forces of history. National and international planning seems to be an integral part of that effort. No nation can continue to escape the responsibility of planning its economy. The question is the extent to which quality of life considerations are taken into account in national policy and planning. If there is a genuine desire for a higher quality of life for all, there must be planning in which all sections of the community have an opportunity to participate.

6 · Ethical Dilemmas in the Biological Manipulation of Human Life *

The advent of new understanding and new technologies in genetics and in the control of behaviour raises important ethical issues about how people ought to influence one another. The new knowledge produces new problems on which much new thinking is needed in ethics by theologians, ethicists and scientists meeting together. When such a group was recently brought together by the World Council of Churches to discuss the ethical problems arising from the application of modern genetics to human welfare, they formulated an important principle for such discussions. They said: "Churchmen cannot expect precedents from the past to provide answers to questions never asked in the past. On the other hand, new scientific advances do not determine what are worthy human goals. Ethical decisions in uncharted areas require that scientific capabilities be understood and used by persons and communities sensitive to their own deepest convictions about human nature and destiny. There is no sound ethical judgement on these matters independent of scientific knowledge, but science does not itself prescribe the goal." [1]

I

There are two ways in which genetic knowledge can now be used to control the genetical constitution of people. A third way, genetic engineering, is as yet only a possibility. The first is *negative* eugenics, the elimination or reduction of deleterious genes. Programmes of negative eugenics are now in practice in many countries. They involve the identification of the genetic patterns which produce defective children, and discouraging the couples from reproducing, or from marrying at all.

---

* Prof. Charles Birch, Australia, and Prof. Thomas Sieger Derr, USA, collaborated in preparing this chapter.

[1] Report of the Ecumenical Consultation on Genetics and the Quality of Life, *Genetics and the Quality of Life*, edited by Charles Birch and Paul Abrecht, p. 203.

Abortion following the detection of a defective foetus is also part of negative eugenics. *Positive* eugenics, the deliberate increase of "desirable" genes, aims at improving the human genetic constitution by, for example, selective breeding. These programmes are possible, but for the moment largely hypothetical. Genetic *engineering* is the direct manipulation of genes. It has been achieved in micro-organisms but not as yet in higher organisms. Some scientists believe it will be possible to apply these techniques to people within a decade or so.

Negative Eugenics

The object of negative eugenics to reduce the incidence of genetic disease is a rational and laudable one. It can be regarded as an extension of what happens without human intervention already. One out of every 130 conceptions ends before the mother realizes she is pregnant because the fertilized egg (probably defective) never attaches itself to the uterus. Some 25% of all conceptions fail to survive to birth, and of these a third have identifiable chromosomal abnormalities. More than 1,600 human diseases caused by genetic defects have been identified. Some are very rare. Others, such as cystic fibrosis and sickle cell anemia, are relatively common diseases. About half of all cases of congenital blindness and about half of all cases of congenital deafness are due to defective genes.

What can be done now about reducing the incidence of genetic diseases? Quite a lot. It is now possible to identify some of these diseases in the foetus by means of the technique amniocentesis, the analysis of fluid drawn from the sac surrounding the unborn child. Selective abortion may then be practised. Secondly, for an increasing number of genetic diseases the "heterozygous" carriers of the defective genes, though themselves normal, can be identified by appropriate biochemical tests or in the case of chromosome abnormalities by chromosome analysis. The list of genetic diseases for which the heterozygous carriers can be detected increases at the rate of three or more each year with over 60 already that can be detected. It is thus possible to identify the critical marriages in which two carriers are wed. That would involve massive screening programmes which would hardly be practicable except where the disease had a high incidence, as in the case of phenylketonuria where carriers constitute 1% of the population. In this example the disease can also be detected by appropriate tests at birth enabling the immediate treatment of the new born.

When something is known of genetic diseases in family histories, it becomes feasible to screen suspected carriers of the defective gene. "Genetic counsellors" in increasing number are doing this work. For example, the female carriers of haemophilia and the Duchenne type of muscular dystrophy can be detected by appropriate tests. The sons of such women have a fifty-fifty chance of being affected. Since identification of the sex of the foetus *in utero* is now possible, abortion can be offered if the parents are unwilling to take the high risk of having a male child. Conversely, if a male haemophiliac married, he might wish for a female child to be aborted, since she would be a carrier, whereas his sons would all ben ormal. The objective of screening heterozygotes is to reduce the number of children born with a particular disease. Such a programme may be effective in this objective, but that is not to say that it will be very effective in reducing the incidence of the deleterious recessive gene in the community. The eugenic programme would have to be extremely severe (e.g. no reproduction of heterozygotes) to reduce greatly the incidence of the gene. Some programmes may achieve a considerable reduction in this direction; however, it is totally unrealistic to imagine that eventually negative eugenic programmes would eliminate deleterious recessive genes. Most of us carry on the average several of them. If we were to eliminate all of them, we would eliminate mankind in the process.

Positive Eugenics

The hypothetical schemes for "improving" the human genetic constitution by positive eugenics, selective breeding and other means, are a matter of concern but do not have the urgency of the issues that are raised by negative eugenics which are now well and truly with us. The geneticist H. J. Muller was one of the prime proponents of positive genetics. He advocated the development of "sperm banks". Sperm would be donated by donors with "desirable" qualities — "outstanding gifts, intelligence, moral fibre and physical fitness". Married couples would be encouraged to choose artificial insemination with sperm from desired donors. Or eventually ova may be fertilized by desired sperm and implanted in the uterus of the foster mother. The more hypothetical programme of "cloning", reproduction from the body cells of only one parent (already developed to quite an advanced stage in amphibians), would, if practised, result in any number of individuals with identical genetical constitutions. This would provide a much faster route to any chosen goal. In positive eugenics in general there is a negative correlation between the degree of acceptability and the efficiency of the practice in reaching desired goals of change. That is, a programme which would really be effective in improving the genetic stock would doubtless run into a lot of public opposition, because it would involve extensive curtailment of human freedom.

Genetic Engineering

Genetic engineering is the direct manipulation of deoxyribonucleic acid (DNA), the chemical carrier of "genetic information" in cells. DNA is the molecule which stores genetic information and passes on hereditary traits. Direct manipulation means changing, subtracting from, or adding to the genetic "instructions" in the cell. That it has been achieved using bacteria raises the possibility that it could be done with higher organisms.

Current interest centres on the possibilities — and dangers — of recombinant DNA research. In this process, segments of DNA from cells of one species are inserted into another kind of organism, there to be reproduced. The potential practical benefits are enormous, for example the synthesis of insulin for diabetics, or new antibodies that can be administered by mouth. Opinion is divided as to whether it will ever be possible directly to attack deleterious genes that cause disease and replace them with normal or desired genes. More plausible is the possibility that crops could be improved by genetic engineering; perhaps wheats could be given genes to enable them to fix nitrogen, i.e. produce their own fertilizer.

One much discussed danger of this research is the chance that experiments on micro-organisms may accidentally produce new organisms pathogenic to people. Should these escape from the laboratory, their spread in the environment might be irreversible and the consequences disastrous. For this reason, strict safety guidelines are now advocated for laboratories doing this research. Some people fear, however, that the strictures can never be safe enough. A related fear is that even when new combinations are approved for human use, we cannot predict their consequences over the long term, given the fact that they have not been derived by the usual evolutionary processes. Furthermore, if genetic engineering were ever applied to man, it might alter the human "gene pool" in deleterious ways and could be used for nefarious purposes.

Because of these fears, some advocate a moratorium or alternatively an outright ban on all research in genetic engineering. From a practical point of view, the enforcement of a complete ban presents considerable obstacles, perhaps insurmountable ones. Even the enforcement of safety guidelines is difficult. There is enormous commercial interest in the possibility of "recombinant DNA", and in private industry trade secrets are a way of life. Any enforcement procedures will have to be such as to reassure privately owned drug companies and other commercial ventures that their work will be kept confidential.

Genetic engineering thus raises questions which seem to be without real historical precedent. The positive possibilities are spectacular, but then so are the dangers; and the process for coping with them is not at all clear.

Behaviour Control

Human behaviour can now be controlled to some extent by a number of means: administration of psychotropic drugs, electrical stimulation of the brain, psychosurgery and psychological conditioning (e.g. aversion therapy). There is much controversy about the effectiveness of any of these procedures for controlling specific sorts of behaviour such as aggressive activities. Most of the research is strictly empirical, and sometimes one or other procedure is advocated when all else has failed. What is not in doubt is that people using one or other of these means do have some power to alter the behaviour of other people. Medical interest centres on the use of such procedures for reducing distressing symptoms, as in certain forms of mental illness. There are, however, other applications, notably alteration of the behaviour of criminals or of dissidents.

To a certain extent, of course, behaviour control has always been practiced through education or propaganda. The brain is invaded by ideas regularly and systematically. Furthermore, the techniques of such invasion have become in this century fairly sophisticated and have scored some remarkable successes. Yet there does seem to remain a difference between this kind of control, which is indirect, and which in theory at least leaves the individual free to reject the alien ideas, and direct invasion of the brain by chemical, electrical, or surgical means, whose results cannot be evaded. The latter procedures attack the person's centre of decision and thus alter the person himself, so that he becomes really another person. These newer techniques leave little possibility of an idiosyncratic response from their target. Thus they are critically different from education or propaganda, and have accordingly roused ethical challenge and outright fear.

II

A large number of particular ethical questions are raised by the possibilities of genetic and behaviour control, questions which have received varying amounts of attention from ethicists. One concerns the decision-making process. It is not simply that the contribution of experts must be kept in perspective, but that the level of decision must be identified. What decisions properly belong to the individual, to the family, to the ethnic community, to the nation? And which transcend nations and become matters for global agreement? A related issue concerns risk evaluation, the difficult process of balancing potential benefits and dangers in deciding upon a course of action.

Another issue, raised especially by eugenics, is the relation between present and future generations, whether and to what extent existing people may be obligated to sacrifice for the welfare of those yet to be born. Still another issue is resource allocation, the development of criteria to distribute scarce and expensive new medical technology among many claimants.[1] Sperm banking and cloning, for another example, raise questions of the relation among parentage, marriage, and procreation. And this list could easily be expanded.

---

[1] See Annex to this chapter, "Who Shall Live?", for one example of this.

One fundamental and critical issue which underlies questions of genetic and behaviour control is the definition of essential human characteristics. What is human? Is there a core which we are obliged to protect from the gene controllers and the brain invaders, however worthy and plausible their motives? There has been a lot of conversation in ethics about this point, and interest tends to focus on the search for that core of inviolable individuality. It is found in certain forms of brain activity, and defined rather carefully by specialists. If, then, the brain is altered so as to impair the critical functions, the unique person is destroyed. So the alteration is ethically forbidden except in such extreme circumstances as would give us the right (if such a right exists) to destroy another person.

But there is a prior question, fully as critical. It is not in *what* human uniqueness consists, but *whether* that inviolable core exists at all. It is an article of faith in the Christian tradition that individuality is sacred, holy to God, and ought to be protected, defended, revered. No wonder that Christians — and not only Christians — fear the implications of some of the new biological techniques, which suggest that man is a machine to be manipulated at will — at someone else's will, usually. There is some justification for this fear insofar as the methodology of behaviour control is aimed at altering some "brain mechanism" in its function.

In many respects, we should fear even more the images of man implicit in the philosophy of certain "behaviourists" which put the emphasis on man the machine rather than on the subjective aspects of behaviour such as feeling and purpose. Some popular writings on ethology (animal behaviour) leave the impression that people are no more than naked apes or conditioned ducks and chimpanzees. The logical conclusion of this approach is that human behaviour could be controlled if we could learn how to control ducks and chimpanzees, as though the "higher" human faculties play little or no role. So-called "sociobiology" hardly commits this fallacy but it does emphasize the deterministic (genetic) aspects of human behaviour (as an evolutionary heritage) and soft peddles the role of culture (environment) and social conditioning on human behaviour. This is one reason it has aroused such hostility among social reformers of various ideologies who see sociobiology as a threat to the calls for social and environmental change to improve the human lot.

The Christian image of what people are or might become can be — needs to be — articulated against mechanistic visions. It is an open challenge to traditional Christian opinion when certain apostles of the new biology claim that the relevant question today is no longer "What is man?" but "What kind of person are we going to construct?" The supposedly sacred individual, they say, even now scarcely exists at birth, but is formed, constructed, a product of various kinds of input.

The contrary view, certainly more congenial to Christian thought, is that the brain has a genetically determined structure which unfolds in interaction with the environment. A person is not to be "constructed" but nourished, so that individual potential is actually realized. The uniqueness of the individual is always the start of the value system.

This distinction, however, is not as neat and clear as it may appear. From the traditional point of view, centred on inviolable individuality, it may not be bad that man is apparently randomly programmed, beyond the control of other men. But one might also argue a Christian responsibility for human destiny, the use of our God-given intelligence to do rationally what is now done by "nature" chaotically. Natural chance is full of flaws, it may be said. Human beings, who are the summit of creation and stewards of nature, have a mandate from their creator to improve the world they were given to start with — by such means, for instance, as genetic and brain control.

At any rate the issue is joined. Large questions of human freedom and responsibility within the natural world are raised urgently by this new biology. Their resolution will not come easily, within the Christian community or anywhere else.

Perhaps the dominant problem raised by the biological manipulation of human life is the conflict between individual and community rights. It is, of course, an ancient problem, the persistent theme of political philosophy; but it is raised here in a new way, with particular force. On the one hand, there is, again, the theme of individual worth. The Christian concern for the weak, the poor, the sick, the forgotten and despised, has been interpreted — rightly — to be a defense of the ultimate value of every single person no matter his contribution to society or social standing or state of health. God loves and cares for each one. Every individual has rights by virtue of being a child of God. No other reason need be given.

On the other hand, the community also has rights. The "people of God" are a community of mutual love and obligation where service of the neighbour means active concern for the welfare of others, even to the point of denying oneself. Even without considering the secular foundations of civil society, powerfully compelling in their own right, the Christian is bound to take into account the welfare of all, of the whole community, and indeed of all mankind.

Thus in matters of public health it is common and ethically defensible to require the individual, for the sake of the health of others, to submit to procedures which he might be privately unwilling to accept. Compulsory vaccinations are an example, or the blood test for syphilis required of couples planning to marry. But the borderline between what is acceptable for the sake of the common good, and what is an unacceptable violation of individual rights, is never very far away. It is, moreover, an indistinct and ill-defined frontier, much subject to argument. For instance, the insane have been sterilized in the name of the health of their (otherwise) potential offspring; but this practice does not commend itself to every conscience. Now that many defectives can be detected in the womb, it is strongly urged in many quarters that these foetuses be aborted not only to spare them lives of pain, but to spare society the high cost of caring for them. Not surprisingly this argument has been challenged, too. One may question the reasoning by which a "right" to health becomes a right not to be born defective, which in turn becomes an obligation to abort defective foetuses.

The line between individual and social rights is also easily blurred for the genetic specialist. When the medical professional, who has his traditional allegiance to the individual, engages in genetic counselling, he is likely to put his patient's interest ahead of other considerations. A population biologist, on the other hand, who thinks of the whole species and its collective future, would be likely to emphasize eugenics and recommend compulsory policies. Scientists used to dealing in abstracts could forget that mutations are carried by individuals, and that programmes whose aim is to reduce the incidence of genetic abnormality may compel behaviour against the individual's will.

Such compulsion runs against the tradition of human rights favoured in Christian culture and enshrined in such secular codes as the United Nations Declaration. So it is not surprising that the weight of common moral judgement so often favours the individual over the community. Human rights are less often violated that way. Yet the conflict remains, and is not so easily resolved.

The tension is particularly poignant in matters of mental health. People who are severely ill mentally are usually institutionalized and become wards of the community, as much to protect the community as for their own supposed good. There they are "treated" in an effort to reform their behaviour so they can function "successfully" in a normal social environment. Most people approve this pattern and consider it humane. But there are critics who say that the mental health practitioner in this system is violating the responsibility of a doctor for his patient. He has become instead a social agent programming so-called deviants to make them conform. The individual, the critics argue, has a right to maintain his deviant behaviour, which is an attempt to manufacture significance for his particular life in the face of a rejecting world.

This argument becomes acute when the reform involves incursions into the brain. The programming is absolute and there is no appeal from it. Recognizing the extreme nature of the procedures, most of their defenders appeal for justification to the need for desperate measures. The patient may be in intolerable pain, or prone to behaviour genuinely dangerous to himself and others. Here the justification seems clearly therapeutic. But note that it excuses, by appealing to the extreme or exceptional circumstances, what would otherwise be ethically unacceptable.

What worries many people today is that these "exceptions" can be too easily extended. What is genuinely dangerous behaviour? Are all criminals prospective subjects for the aversion therapists and brain manipulators? What about political dissenters in a closed and highly structured society? Chemical "therapy" has indeed been used on them. It is easy enough to see how these new and decisive methods of behaviour control could become frighteningly effective weapons in the hands of a powerful state or group within the society.

Sensitive to the dangers, interested people have suggested criteria for permitting these rare incursions into the human brain. Respect for the integrity of the person would be fundamental, and would be expressed at least in a requirement for the patient's informed consent to any procedure. Unfortunately even this criterion can be unclear in cases of mental illness, and other proposed guidelines have even more obvious shortcomings. If the test is that the individual's state after the brain incursion must be more valuable than his condition before it, one is bound to ask who would judge that value? If the protection of society and social cost are admitted as criteria (e.g. for the "criminally insane"), the door to possible abuse of the individual is opened yet a little further.

Apparently not only these newer biological manipulations of life, but all medical interventions in general, are affected profoundly by the reigning social philosophy. Social conditioning of biology and medicine is inescapable. Studies in the history of medicine have shown that each age has its own view of madness, which reflects the social concerns of the time. Diagnosis and treatment have always been based on unstated ethical and social judgements, hidden behind a claim or intention of diagnosing and treating objective structures. Psychiatry is thus a social institution, and mental illness a social construct. In our day, so-called "radical" psychiatrists have called "treatment" a form of totalitarian control repugnant to conscience. What could not be done in the name of morality has become acceptable in the name of health. "Health" is *imposed* on people who do not fit the power structure's definition of normality.

Whether or not one goes this far with the critics, it is apparent that mental illness is subject to social definition. This is true also of genetic control, which is biological intervention in defense of a socially-defined interest. Not everyone may share this interest, least of all those people who are the objects of the control programme. People tested, perhaps against their will, for defective genes, and found to be carriers, may be subject to difficult pressures, particularly if the information is public. Eugenics, and the possibility of genetic engineering, mean collective choice of the traits to be perpetuated in future generations, with resultant peril for bearers of unfavoured traits.

We might say, in fact, that *all* illness is socially conditioned, a human interpretation of natural events which in themselves are value-free, apart from the meanings human beings attach to them. They acquire the negative connotation of "illness" only when people do not like them, define them as abnormal, and wish or try to eliminate them. Illnesses are conditions we do not wish to tolerate if we can help them; and, as medical skills increase, we tolerate less and less. We hardly tolerate death any more, pushing back its arrival as if immortality were the only acceptable outcome.

The inevitable result of this process is that illnesses increase as health *expectations* increase, as there are fewer conditions we are willing to tolerate by not thinking of them as illnesses. Expectations take wing on the advance of the biological sciences. The concept of "health" expands to the optimum possibility: "a state of complete physical, mental and social well-being", as the famous World Health Organization definition puts it. And when health, so broadly understood, becomes the "right" of every individual, then we are entangled in the political question of distributing the community's resources for health care, since there cannot possibly be enough to bring everyone to that optimum, ideal condition. One thinks of the discussions, in the Christian Medical Commission, for example, on the relation among curative medicine, primary health care, and distributive justice.

The history of medicine shows, then, a close interrelation with social philosophy in both diagnosis and treatment. The new techniques of biological manipulation will surely intensify that involvement. The increasing power of medicine means greater power for its social controllers, and a greater danger that the rights of individuals will suffer as the community extends its own legitimate rights. In order to avoid a tyranny of a narrow power group, or of the "experts" ("Who will guard the guardians?"), we cannot leave problems of ethics in social policy to leaders or specialists alone. An informed public is a vital element in the decisions, and within that public, Christian opinion can make a significant contribution. The medical techniques before us here are not solely the province of the biologist and the doctor; for they involve the problems of competing rights and social priorities whose resolution is for the whole body politic.

* * * * *

ANNEX: WHO SHALL LIVE?

"We have 10 to 25 years — at most 50 — to set up new decision-making apparatuses and answer some profound questions which previously we have left to God."

> *Leroy Augenstein (1969) in the preface to "Come Let Us Play God".*

More than 20,000 people are alive in the world today who at any other time would have been dead. They have lost their kidneys and are kept alive with an artificial kidney, the renal dialysis machine. This machine extracts from the blood harmful substances that are normally excreted by the healthy kidney. Until 1960 artificial kidneys were used only in cases of reversible uremia, that is to replace defective kidneys, functioning for a few days or weeks until the patient's own kidneys could function normally again. There were technical difficulties in using the machine for longer periods. These were overcome, particularly by the invention of the Scribner vascular shunt which establishes a permanent short-circuit between an artery and a vein in the forearm. This device can be safely left in place and connected whenever necessary with the artificial kidney. From then on all that was necessary was an eight to ten hour dialysis session two to three times a week either in hospital or in the patient's home. This new treatment raised a series of ethical, social and economic problems for patient, family and doctor.

In 1960 when the artificial kidney was first used, there were only a few such machines in France, the United States and Britain. But there were thousands of potential patients. Who were to be the fortunate ones? Who would be the unfortunate ones who would be allowed to die? Hospitals set up committees to sit in judgment on who should have priority for a scarce resource. They had to make agonizing choices. Should the brilliant academic without a family be spared or the labourer breadwinner of a large family? That particular problem fortunately no longer exists. In industrialized countries at least, there are now enough kidney machines for everyone needing treatment. But there is a second problem. In France the cost of an artificial kidney treatment is about $20,000 per year per patient. Every year 2,000 new patients swell the number of those undergoing treatment. Given that the average life expectancy of a patient is ten years, 20,000 people will receive treatment in the ten-year period. This involves an expenditure of $4,000 million. As a country's health budget cannot be increased indefinitely, the $4,000 million must be taken from some other part of the health expenditure (Crosnier, 1974). Priorities have to be established and decisions must not be left entirely to the bureaucrats and economists. Difficult ethical decisions have to be made when we have to choose whether to spend money helping this patient rather than that.

In 1959 the first successful kidney transplant was done. Removal of a kidney from a healthy donor involves some risk, about one in 2,000 in young healthy people. So it is small but not negligible. The only other source of kidneys is deceased patients. Obviously there are limits to both sources and in most western countries there is now a shortage of kidneys for transplants. So the problem of who is to benefit from a short resource arises in another form. Patients who are kept alive with an artificial kidney machine tend to look on a transplant as their great hope. But if the patient is managing to lead a more or less normal life with the aid of a machine, there may be little claim on the short resource. So medical criteria will exclude some applicants. Are there any other criteria on which to base a selection? Helmuth Thielicke contends that any search for "objective criteria" for selection of patients for "scarce life-saving medical resources", SLMR for short, "is already a capitulation to the utilitarian point of view which violates man's dignity". Furthermore, he thinks that a decision based on any criteria is little more than one arrived at by casting lots. Others too argue that random selection is the only way to determine who shall live and who shall die when not all can live. Childress (1970) argues for random selection on the grounds that it alone provides for equality of opportunity. To use any other method is to threaten trust which is inextricably bound up with the respect for human dignity and is an attitude of expectation about another, in this case that of the patient toward the doctor. A threat to this sort of trust was demonstrated in the billboard that was erected after the first heart transplants: "Drive carefully! Christian Barnard is watching you." Not very different from the lottery system is the "first come first served" approach which tends to be the way the lottery system would work anyway because applicants make their claims over a period of time and not all at once.

A kidney transplant is considerably less expensive than the use of a kidney machine. Even so the question arises as to what medical resources of a country should or should not be devoted to this. The operation is performed in some hospitals in India provided the patient pays. To be able to pay you either have to be well off or you have to borrow, if that is possible. A person borrows and is helped by friends and charitable appeals, has the operation and pays for it. The patient then finds there are heavy expenses each year for the drugs necessary to keep the new kidney functioning. So again there is an appeal to friends or charitable groups to defray these heavy costs. The person who is well off, or has friends who are, or who has the ability to collect from various resources manages to get a new kidney. The poor person without connections goes without. How should the scarce resources of a developing country be used in its medical services? Who is to be helped and who is to be left without major help? The ethical problems are no different in principle from those in a rich country. They are only more severe.

The dramatic forms of scarce life-saving medical resources such as transplants have compelled us to examine the moral questions that tend to be concealed in many routine decisions in medical care. The distributive injustice in health services throughout the world is a very vexing problem, both within and between nations. A rich country may spend a lot on transplants and sophisticated medical techniques while a poor country still lacks the most basic health care. Preventable diseases, especially those that occur in women and children, are much more common among people who are poorly educated, poorly nourished and poorly housed than among the comfortable middle and upper classes. Within the United States, for example, diseases that hit the poor the hardest include vitamin deficiency diseases, iron deficiency anemia, protein deficiency diseases, metabolic toxaemia of late pregnancy, tuberculosis, pneumonia and rheumatic fever. And between nations there is no clear ethical foundation for orienting the thrust of international health schemes. And as Dan Callahan says, "It is fundamentally wrong that so much avoidable illness exists in the world."

Questions for Discussion

General

— Is the human essentially something that is given and cannot change or may we direct evolution to the point of creating a fundamentally new creature?

— Should the human person always be given priority over all other creatures?

— Are medical personnel primarily responsible to their individual patients or to the larger community?

— To what extent may "health" be defined and treated objectively, apart from socially affected perceptions of "illness"?

Behaviour control

— Can the criterion of "informed consent" be adequately applied to incursions into the brain?

— Would any circumstances justify alteration of brain functions without the subject's consent?

— In whose interest is brain control advocated or practiced?

Eugenics

— Should society take any hand in deciding who should or should not have children?

— Are there permissible and unpermissible means of eugenics? What is the difference?

Genetic experiments

— How do we balance the possibility of great danger against the possibility of great good in genetic experiments with DNA? What are the criteria for risk evaluation and choice? On whom is the burden of proof — the proponents or the opponents of risky experiments?

Individual and social decision-making

— The Ecumenical Consultation on "Genetics and the Quality of Life" (1973) concluded that in matters relating to foetal diagnosis and selective abortion "the parents must remain the principal decision-makers". What is the role of the experts, the Church, the community and the state in advising the parents of their responsibilities to society?

— In the 1973 Consultation it was also said that
"Where science has brought new possibilities of modifying the human genetic make-up, parliaments and governments should take the responsibility of looking into the relevant social and ethical issues, not leaving them entirely to the doctors, counsellors, parents or other people directly involved. It is not fair to let them bear this burden alone, and society does not expect this of them in other fields. Furthermore, governments should bear much, if not all, of the cost of care and treatment of the unfortunate victims of genetic disease and should support research on further advances in treatment." What discussion is taking place in your country on the way in which governments seek to fulfil this responsibility?

— Where this takes the form of proposed legislation, what are the major ethical issues posed?

II.

Energy for the Future

Until recently the question of energy was considered a predominantly technical problem, and by definition not an area in which the churches would have anything to contribute. Today on the contrary it has become one of the technological problems around which there is an intensive social-ethical debate, even within the churches, so much so that it was impossible to get agreement on any one analysis for this book. We begin by presenting two essays, and their titles indicate their major point of difference:

— *Energy : The Argument for Keeping All Options Open —
Including Nuclear*

— *The Argument for Conservation and the Fullest Possible Use of Renewable Energy Sources*

Behind these two arguments there are considerable divergences of views: about energy requirements for the future, about alternative energy possibilities and their social consequences, and about the technological risks of different energy options and our evaluation of them. Nothing could better illustrate the difficulties facing all societies when they must make technological choices for a just, participatory and sustainable society, now and in the future.

The chapter on the churches and the debate about nuclear energy reveals the way in which the churches have been drawn into the consideration of this controversial technology.

This section closes with questions on each of the energy options.

7 · Energy: The Argument for Keeping All Options Open — Including Nuclear

The Role of Energy in Human Affairs

The most revolutionary changes for the improvement of societal life became possible when the energies contained in coal, oil, and natural gas were made to serve human needs and appetites. Invention breeds invention, with the result that societal demands for energy spiraled to astronomical magnitudes. The effects have not been uniform around the world, however. For while in "developed" Western Europe the yearly per capita energy consumption in 1972 was the equivalent of 4,000 kg of coal (and nearly three times that in the United States and Canada) the consumption in most of the rest of the world (the "developing" societies) was one-tenth that or much less. While happiness and human progress are not determined by magnitude of energy consumption, extreme energy disparities usually indicate unacceptable living and health conditions in some areas.

Recently the energy spiral suffered a jolt from the realization of the constraints affecting the oil and natural gas resources of the world. This coincided with an awakening to the serious damage to the environment caused by not only prodigal but also thoughtless energy production and utilization. Thus while coal remains in substantial supply, the fear of the high cost in human lives and in damage to the environment caused discourages too great dependence on that energy option.

The effect has been to direct attention to renewable energy alternatives presumably less harmful to the environment and to human health. These include solar radiation, geothermal gradients, the energies of winds, waves, tides, ocean currents, and biological materials. But the technologies for use of these resources have yet to be developed to meet the needs of either communities or industrial centres. Hereafter energy will not be derived as cheaply as it has been through combustion of hydrocarbons piped from the ground. Clearly we have entered a new phase in the economics of energy utilization, a phase in which industrial, agricultural, and military interests, national prestige, environmental husbandry, human progress, human suffering, moral issues, and the interests of generations yet unborn, vie for consideration.

Nature of the Energy Crisis

Up to the present more than 90% of world energy has been provided by fossil fuels, with the ancillary sources of hydro-electric, geothermal and nuclear power relegated to a comparatively minor role. During the past 25 years, world energy demand has continued to grow at an aggregate rate of around 5% per year. At present the International Energy Agency and other international and national groups are searching for strategies to reduce this growth substantially, but adequate specific actions to accomplish this goal are still to be taken. It is anticipated that rising prices may depress the increase in the overall demand to 4% per year, but beyond that matters are unclear.

An appraisal of the current prospects for world energy supply and demand suggests the following general conclusions:

  (i) World oil production will reach its peak by about 1990 and decrease slowly after that; the peak for natural gas production may come somewhat later than for oil but this cannot be precisely defined at this stage. (Figure 1)

  (ii) Oil will remain the most important marginal fuel to meet expanding demand in the period up to and including 1985-1990, if there is high economic growth (3.6-4.0%), and for five to ten years longer if low economic growth (2.5-2.8%) prevails in the period up to the year 2000. (Figure 2)

  (iii) It is unlikely that alternative sources of energy can be developed fast enough to permit energy demand linked to either high or intermediate economic growth to continue after 1990; in case of low economic growth, the potential scarcity of energy may be postponed until nearer the year 2000. (Figure 3)

  (iv) While evidence accumulates that increasing energy use and economic growth can be decoupled, especially in the most developed and energy-intensive countries, the rate of separation of the two trends is tied closely to the rate of replacement of energy-intensive capital equipment with energy-conserving equipment. This is a slow process, which may limit the rate of separation to about 1% per year. Over several decades, that leads to substantial improvement, but no easy change is achievable in the short term.

  (v) The higher oil prices that will result from constraint on world supplies may be substantially above the cost of the long term alternatives, of which coal, nuclear power and solar are likely to be the main contenders during the next 40 years. (The high oil prices will largely reflect the long delays encountered in the expansion of coal and nuclear power production and distribution, and the development of newer energy forms, including solar and geothermal.)

It follows from these conclusions that if additional investment in energy supply and conservation is not made well in advance of the potential energy scarcity implied by the assumptions about the level of economic growth, then the transition from unconstrained increase in the use of energy could be extremely difficult for both industrialized and developing countries.

The estimated potential for energy conservation without resort to emergency demand constraint in industrial countries is 15-20% of the consumption levels now forecast for 1985. The effort required to achieve this would be much greater in some countries than in others. Since major shifts in consumption patterns, from non-commercial to commercial energy sources, are expected in many developing countries, the impact of conservation in these countries is expected to be much less than in the developed countries.

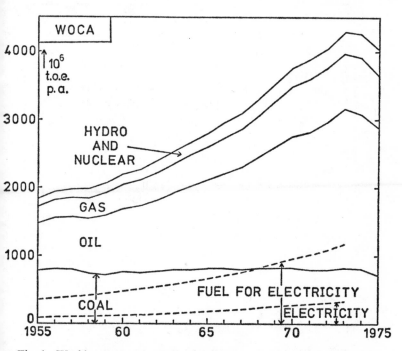

Fig. 1 World energy consumption (outside Communist areas), 1955-1975

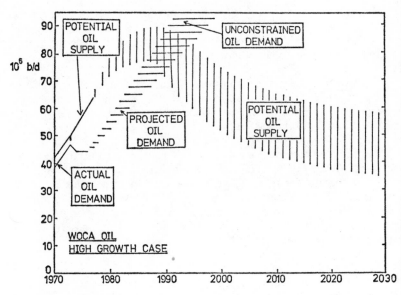

Fig. 2 World (WOCA) oil supply and demand projections (high case)

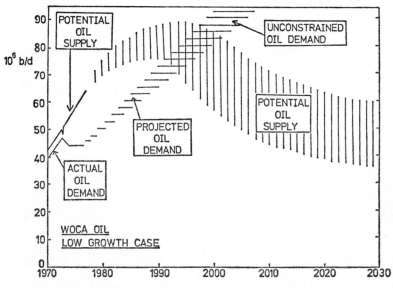

Fig. 3 World (WOCA) oil supply and demand projections (low case)

Both industrialized and developing countries are consequently approaching the edge of a precipice. Present systems of energy production based on non-renewable resources are not sustainable. The conventional social indicators of energy use per capita and of energy intensity (energy generated per unit of land area) do not reveal the concealed dependencies on available energy resources as these are currently distributed between industrialized and developing countries. The changing pattern of energy supply is central to the whole issue of resource management and control beyond the constraints of the international market place. A balanced society offering a basic minimum standard of living demands a satisfactory energy quota for each person. This means that the present-day predicament caused by the rising costs of energy must be resolved in an equitable fashion. Otherwise, the distribution pattern will be exacerbated in the future, with the industrialized countries acting in concert to protect their own domestic energy markets.

The movement towards an energy economy based to a large extent on more lasting and less vulnerable energy sources has started, and in some areas of the world is well underway. These sources include nuclear fission primarily, thought of either for the long term or as a transition resource, with increasing emphasis on solar in various forms, geothermal in selected areas, and (more speculatively) controlled fusion. The transition to suitable mixes of these sources will last several decades at least. During this transition period, existing fossil fuel reserves and higher grade uranium deposits will be exploited increasingly heavily.

This transition will be governed by the following constraints: (i) the limitations on proven reserves of oil and gas; (ii) the limitations on reserves of low-cost uranium; (iii) the limited industrial capacity for the construction of nuclear power stations; (iv) the drain on capital resources that full implementation of the nuclear option would entail.

Scenarios for the Intermediate Term

A scenario, in the sense we use the term here, is not a prediction of the future or a vision of an ideal society, but rather an intellectual enlargement built around a specific set of assumptions. The assumptions may be reasonable or outrageous, even illogical. The proximate purpose in constructing the scenario is to explore the developments that stem logically from such assumptions; indeed, if the initial assumptions are internally inconsistent, a proper development should bring the inconsistency to light. The eventual purpose of constructing a set of scenarios is to examine the consequences of various initial decisions. A set of scenarios chosen judiciously will cover the range of major circumstances likely to prevail, so that even if real life situations turn out to differ in detail from all of them some general insight can be gained. Conversely, study of the scenarios helps us to judge which social decisions are likely to lead to better conditions at some later time.

In covering the energy field, scenarios must be chosen to encompass the range of most likely important uncertainties and possible societal decisions about them. Thus we choose four:

1. Nuclear fission power is generally (but not necessarily universally) rejected.

2. Nuclear fission power, including eventual adoption of breeder reactors, is generally (but not necessarily universally) accepted.

3. There is almost universal agreement that it is unwise to continue to burn fossil fuels at or near the present rate.

4. There is an organized decision among the developed nations substantially to assist the developing nations with their energy problems.

Reasons for choosing each of these will be given as the scenarios are outlined. The discussion covers a transition period lasting until about AD 2010.

Scenario 1.   Nuclear Power Rejected

This is not a remote possibility, but could quite possibly come about. The electric utility companies and manufacturers in some countries are beset with a myriad of uncertainties related to nuclear development: future uranium supply, the climate of regulation of nuclear power, future governmental attitudes towards nuclear power in general, storage of spent fuel, the effectiveness of public intervenors — all of them problems that the electric sector cannot resolve internally — and they decide that uncertainty carried so far becomes unreliable. So in seeking to reduce their own uncertainty and to increase future reliability, the electric sector moves away from nuclear power. This outcome has little to do with whether the reactors run well or not, or whether nuclear power is cheaper. The trend is already well established in the USA in favour of doing nothing until public pressure forces the electric sector to install coal or oil-burning plants on short notice, with federal government support to reduce the sector's uncertainty.

Developed nations other than the USA face a new dilemma: while they are under increased pressure to abandon nuclear power they also recognize the great danger of doing so, especially in view of the increased petroleum demand likely to develop in the US. That demand could be met by the OPEC nations only at the cost of denying it to other developed and developing nations.

In any event, the consequences are likely to be along the following general lines.

The sudden dramatic upward movement of the economic base supporting future investment in oil and gas exploration activities will be accentuated, bringing into operation several sources of these fuels that had been previously discounted as non-commercial; thus there will be an upward shift in the estimates of world oil and gas reserves.

The expected additions to the statement of oil and gas reserves are attributable to four major factors:

(i) intensified exploration in relatively high cost areas;

(ii) the massive use of resources in new oil production areas;

(iii) improvements in recovery techniques;

(iv) the development of techniques for producing oil from offshore areas at ever-increasing water depths.

Under these circumstances, the price of crude oil and gas will surely double before the end of the period, and probably go even higher. Overall energy consumption will probably continue to increase, via massive switching to coal in the industrialized countries, especially in the USA.

— Energy conservation will become much more widespread in all developed countries, as a result of increased price and governmental stimulation. Measures will probably exceed anything proposed, let alone enacted, in most countries, at present.

— The developing countries will be highly motivated to pursue the use of a mixture of solar and nuclear energy, other routes to development being generally economically unavailable to them.

— The atmospheric carbon dioxide problem will become acute (see scenario 3) and general environmental quality would be hard to maintain.

— The industrialized countries will set goals of more energy independence via use of solar power and coal where applicable, but Europe and (especially) Japan will still be almost completely dependent on imported fuels before the end of the transition period. On the other hand, there seems little motivation for the OPEC nations to feed their own inflation by supplying more than about 30 million barrels of oil per day.

The broader economic and financial implications of these strategies for energy planning are difficult to ascertain. But two can be identified as follows:

1. The rapid expansion of high cost domestic energy production, together with continued high import prices, will add substantially to the overall costs of production in industrialized countries.

2. The higher cost of oil imports from oil exporting countries will result in large financial transfers, although the proportion of these revenue flows that will be exchanged in goods and services is highly speculative.

The principal effects of much higher world prices for petroleum on the share of total primary energy provided by different forms in 1980 and 1985 will be:

1. Coal will reverse its declining trend and increase its share relatively sharply.

2. Natural gas will increase its share temporarily, reflecting an increase in use in Europe and many developing countries and a fall in the United States. However, by AD 2010, its continued greater use appears very uncertain.

3. Electricity consumption will show little significant change in absolute terms.

The political implications are also interesting. National programmes geared to the political goal of "self-sufficiency" will require a very large shift of capital investment to the energy sector, particularly for countries rich in fossil fuel resources. Exploitation of this potential, therefore, conflicts with other economic objectives.

While the opportunity exists to create new ground rules for the introduction of alternative energy technologies, a real dilemma surrounds the present pattern of reinvestment in conventional fossil fuels. Accelerated erosion of this resource base can be expected if the policy decisions already outlined are implemented. If energy consumption continues its present growth rate, there will be a serious overall shortage of world fossil fuel within the next two decades. The production schedule for petroleum fuels will become very much more unpredictable as accelerated programmes of oil and gas extraction from conventional sources are combined with the production of synthetic fuels, especially from coal. The advent of economic coal gasification and liquefaction processes will obviously hinge in many countries on revitalization of the coal mining industry, although a much higher degree of mechanization may be a necessary prerequisite to such action. Although the technology is available, this path to the future is clouded with uncertainties, and the prospect of a sustainable supply of basic primary energy is nowhere in sight.

Finally, this scenario presents political opportunities unparalleled in history for any larger developed country that has substantial fossil fuel resources *and* decides to develop nuclear power during this transition period.

Scenario 2. Nuclear Power Accepted
Even though nuclear breeder reactors could not be built fast enough to affect appreciably the pattern of energy generation before AD 2010, never-

theless a decision not to close off the breeder option is necessary; otherwise the major manufacturers of present-day reactors (mainly light-water) are likely to curtail manufacture. This general view prevails among governments and manufacturers in Europe and Japan, and among manufacturers in the US.

Such a continuing role for nuclear fission requires some prior ancillary decisions, among which the principal are:

— Development of a stronger international programme of inspection, safeguards, etc.

— Probable development during the transition period of multinational fuel reprocessing and fabrication centres.

— Exploration of different reactor types. For example, the high temperature gas-cooled reactor may supply process heat for the production of non-electric secondary energy, e.g. in the form of hydrogen. The use of such reactors and of hydrogen in a later post-transitional stage will be extended. These reactors work best in principle in a different fuel cycle using thorium and uranium^{233}.

— Exploration of different nuclear fuel cycles, not only to minimize the risks of weapons proliferation and fuel diversion, but also in view of the needs of advanced reactor types.

Since the availability of thorium in the world is as great as that of uranium and the fuel reprocessing technology for separation of U^{233} is viable with further research and development work, from a long-term radiological hazards point of view the U^{233}-Th^{232} breeder cycle has some advantages over the Pu^{239}-U^{233} cycle. Some disadvantages also exist, but a proper comparison has still to be made. The planning of the nuclear power programme of any country through either cycle, however, is dependent on the initial plutonium inventory.

Many of the broad economic implications of the previous scenario carry over into this one, but with substantial modification:

1. Electric power increases its share of the energy market, especially in developed countries. By AD 2000, nuclear electric power may account for more than half the total in many of these countries.

2. There will be less financial transfers to oil exporting developing countries; however, financial transfers within the industrialized countries installing nuclear power plants will be expected to increase substantially. However, it is not clear whether these amounts will exceed the capital and other expenses of new mines required for equivalent capacity using coal.

3. While the share of coal will increase, it will not do so at as fast a rate as with the first scenario.

4. The share of oil will decline at a much faster rate.

5. The emphasis on conservation will continue, but not as strongly as in the first scenario.

6. The tendency for developing countries to emphasize a combination of solar and independent nuclear power is lessened. However, the cost of nuclear power and petroleum will still provide substantial incentive for solar power in all nations except those exceptionally plagued by clouds.

Scenario 3.   Carbon Dioxide Recognized as a World Hazard

This scenario could just as well be named "low fossil fuel", but the present title suggests a possible and perhaps a principal cause for its adoption. Any large-scale use of fossil fuels becomes unattractive in the long term, because of the build-up of carbon dioxide in the atmosphere, and a consequent increase in the global temperature due to the trapping of an ever-larger portion of the earth's reradiated heat. This "greenhouse effect" appears to be long-lasting, and without any reasonable technical fix. The carbon dioxide takes many centuries to be absorbed in the deep ocean waters. If present energy trends continue, the carbon dioxide concentration will double early in the next century, leading to substantial climatic effects. Other reasons to be interested in a low fossil fuel scenario could be political events that shut off Mid-East oil, or *(mirabile dictu)* an ethical decision to leave coal, oil and natural gas in the ground as a chemical resource.

Eventually of course the world must go onto a low fossil fuel diet, and that transition will be difficult enough even with other energy options developed. An early, essentially unplanned transition as contemplated here will have profound effects, principally:

— Energy conservation far surpassing that assumed in any of the other scenarios must be adopted in the developed nations, for the simple reason that about 80% of their energy supply is to be banished.

— But (perhaps surprisingly at first sight) the problems of many developing countries may be eased during their critical transitional growth period. This is because *a)* the developing nations as a whole do not use very much energy (about two-thirds of Africa presently uses fossil fuels at about 1% of the US rate) and their continuing development by the use of fossil fuels would not affect the world-wide cutback very much; *b)* the price of petroleum and other fossil fuels will fall drastically. Of course this brings in a dilemma between economics and politics — economic theory would indicate that the political decision to refrain from use will be self-limiting, because it will erode as the price falls.

— The transition will be very difficult, because of society attempting almost at one leap to use only "sustainable" energy resources. The rate at which solar energy can be developed becomes critical. The most detailed estimates which we know are made for the US. Solar power optimists state that with an "all-out" effort as much as 30% of present US energy use (i.e. 22 quads of energy per year out of 75 total) could be produced by AD 2010, but the cost of such a programme has not been documented. Others put solar power in AD 2010 as low as 5% of US energy (3.5 quads), with it being just one of several sources (e.g. coal, fission, fusion, etc.). Under the political conditions imposed by this scenario, a figure approaching the upper limit may be possible for the US, and probably for certain other countries. However, the world as a whole could not make such a rapid transition. Hence the heavy pressure on nuclear power and on draconian conservation measures.

— The environmental improvement will be enormous, because (e.g.) the vast majority of air and much water quality degradation arises from the transformation and combustion of fossil fuels.

— The generation of energy from urban wastes (approx. 2% of US energy needs, at most), animal feed hot wastes (approx. 2-3%), forest and food crops residues (a larger but unknown fraction) figure as part of the sustainable strategy, broadly classified as "solar". The provision of the necessary facilities and institutions makes the transition long.

Scenario 4. Decision to Assist Developing Nations

Admittedly idealistic and perhaps unrealizable, this scenario nevertheless is included in order to cover a wide spectrum of possibilities. It is less traumatic for the developed nations than scenario 3. The main difference is that the developed nations do not attempt to give up fossil fuels in one great convulsion, but plan to phase them out over a longer period; a small per cent of the energy used by the developed nations would suffice for the present stage of most developing countries. Other principal differences are:

— The price of fossil fuels remains high, so that developing nations *a)* find much more incentive to develop renewable resources (or nuclear power), *b)* must be economically aided by the developed nations to a greater extent than in scenario 3.

— The assistance policy will not remain inexpensive for more than a decade or two, because at adequate rates (say 5-8%/year for developing countries) the energy needs double every 9-14 years.

— The developed nations probably must be convinced that the energy restraint required of them will not hurt them economically. This re-emphasizes the importance of establishing by example as well as theory the actual extent and rate to which welfare and energy use can be decoupled

Scenario 5.   Combination of Scenarios

One can of course imagine various combinations of scenarios, because many are not exclusive, or can be adopted in part. Scenarios 1 and 2 (nuclear power rejected or accepted) are incompatible if either is adopted fully, but regional acceptance of nuclear power would create situations of supply, shortfall, etc., lying between the two extremes.

To reject both fossil fuel and nuclear power seems entirely unrealistic for the transition period. The capital stock which would supply the sustainable energy or would use energy sufficiently sparingly could not be installed at anything like the necessary rate. The only option would be to abandon a large fraction (probably more than half) of the energy-using capital stock. In a few sectors this might be done under extreme duress (no personal cars, for instance); but 42% of US energy goes into industrial processes, and 31% into residential and commercial heat, light, and similar services. The capital equipment used for these can be improved or replaced only gradually.

Sustainable Energy Strategies

If we consider the prospects for a sustainable energy supply on a 100-year (or preferably longer) time-scale, it is reasonable to suppose that more natural energy utilization, increased efficiency and other energy-minimizing strategies will dominate the scene. We must recognize that nuclear energy, embracing both fission and fusion breeder systems, and solar energy, including ocean, wind, and wave energies, are the only potentially viable sources capable of matching the level of anticipated demand. Solar power seems assured of a significant permanent role because of its general environmental and social attractiveness. The remaining energy requirements (which are liable to be very large) will to some extent be competed for by fission breeders and controlled fusion. Some of these technologies lend themselves naturally to electricity production; therefore we anticipate a general trend towards a more electricity-oriented society. Indeed, one of the problems in this post-transitional society will be providing adequate supplies of transportable fuel. This might be hydrogen produced by electrolysis or other methods, by methane from various forms of biomass, or from other less likely sources. Basic research on producing such fuels from "renewable" or "inexhaustible" sources is underway now.

The words "renewable" and "inexhaustible" need to be put in perspective. "Renewable" as applied to burning wood and growing more trees superficially seems straightforward. But, as Plato remarks in *Critias* and as Roman records show, the Greek and Roman civilizations cut down their trees for firewood, and by not taking proper care of the soil, lost it, thus destroying the agricultural productivity of much of the Mediterranean littoral. In our time, we face more subtle disasters through gradual loss of farmland top-soil, forest top-soil and sub-soil, and so forth, via faulty agricultural and ecological programmes. At the same time, we might imagine uranium or thorium to be a wasting resource, if used in nuclear reactors. But the supply is so vast that if used in breeder reactors it would last for perhaps many millions of years.

The long-term resources will now be reviewed in turn.

Nuclear Fusion: A Comparison of Fission Breeder and Fusion Breeder Systems

For the long term, controlled fusion must be included, although even with the best of luck, it will not be generally available before the year 2000. Technologically speaking, it will be as much more difficult to develop than any fission technology as fission technology is more difficult than simple burning of coal.

Several points need to be made about the concept of fusion energy, i.e. the combining at stellar temperatures of light nuclei to make heavier nuclei.

1. The basic fuel, deuterium, is virtually inexhaustible and is obtainable at relatively low cost. The most promising nuclear reaction also requires lithium, which is in shorter supply, but still sufficient for millennia.

2. The by-product of the fusion reaction is helium, which is non-toxic, non-radioactive, and hence causes no problem of radioactive waste management.

3. There is no possibility of a runaway nuclear reaction and consequently no danger of a large scale reactor accident.

4. Fusion normally produces nothing of use in nuclear weapons; however, some of the intense flood of neutrons from a fusion reactor could with considerable and visible effort be diverted to irradiate thorium or uranium to make U^{233} or plutonium, respectively; these could then be used in nuclear weapons.

Despite major national programmes of fusion research, controlled thermonuclear fusion under reactor conditions is not yet technologically feasible. Fusion, if achieved, promises to be environmentally and societally much more acceptable than nuclear fission, but not ideal.

Some comparisons have been made of the risks and the potentialities of fission breeders and fusion breeder systems.

— Essentially inexhaustible supplies of energy would result from the successful development of either system.

— The danger to future generations arising from the need to store radioactive wastes is different in kind and degree. In fission, large quantities of waste require storage with very high integrity against exposure to the biosphere for centuries, and more moderate care thereafter. Fusion produces no radioactive waste in its primary cycle, but the structure becomes radioactive to a degree depending on its composition.

— The fast-breeder power excursion that the fusion reactor avoids is a limited risk and can be entirely accommodated within present designs.

— There is substantial heat generation which necessitates continuous cooling of the fission core even after the reactor has been shut down, but this situation would not arise with a fusion plant.

— The inventory of volatile radioactive material present in each reactor circuit would be roughly comparable; however, the volatile fission product activity (iodine 131) derived from the plutonium-based fuels would be very much more significant in the period following a reactor shutdown. This would equalize with the tritium activity in the fusion plant about a month after any shutdown, and beyond that period the volatile radioactive material in the fusion plant would exceed that of the fission plant. However, the relative biological hazard of tritium is very low, and in general the hazard from tritium in a fusion reactor is a very small fraction of the hazard from other radioactive sources in either a fission or fusion reactor.

— The largest inventory of radioactive material in either system comes from non-volatile things (fission products and actinides in the breeder, a radioactive structure in the fusion reactor). The fusion system poses less hazard, by a factor of three or four in the most pessimistic fusion case, to a factor exceeding 1,000 in the most optimistic.

— The present focus of concern over safeguards for strategic nuclear weapon material is undoubtedly the plutonium generated in the fast breeder reactor fuel cycle. The projected movement towards fusion systems does not eliminate this type of hazard; a fusion system could be modified to produce plutonium or U^{233} for weapons, but not surreptitiously. The safeguards problem is therefore ameliorated but not eliminated. Combined fusion-fission hybrid systems have been proposed as more efficient energy generators and better breeders of fissionable material. They would rank with breeder reactors in terms of diversion or perversion to produce material for weapons.

It should be clear that it is the breeding characteristics of both fuel cycles, one based on plutonium and the other on tritium, that promises the enormous supply of energy. The plutonium breeder system is now quite far advanced, and is only about one developmental step from practical deployability. Fusion is much further behind. The research and development programmes will continue to go forward under the pressure of world events. Although any economic comparison would be premature, it is already evident that more than 90% of the total generation costs of either system will be directly related to plant capital costs.

Present expectations are that commercial fast breeders may become available in the early 1980's, but since the successful demonstration of technological feasibility in fusion engineering is not expected within the next decade, the reactor concepts appear to be widely separated in terms of large-scale availability. While many nations have aggressive development plans and hopeful guide-dates for controlled fusion, we cannot now predict the outcome.

Solar-Related Energy Resources

Of the various energy alternatives that are available, world-wide solar energy is both the most naturally attractive and the most enduring. The energy comes in many forms, including that of winds and waves and of temperature variations of the environment. Most remarkable is the photosynthetic process that produces plant life, which some scientists in the Soviet Union believe should be studied for clues to our energy needs in the future.

Attractive as it is, it cannot, under present circumstances, compete economically with the burning of fossil fuels to obtain heat energy. (This is only partly because the cost of energy obtained from the burning of fossil fuels fails to take into account either the loss of chemical values of the fuels, or the permanent loss of those resources to generations yet to come.) As a result we have based our economies largely on the consumption of oil, natural gas and coal, to the neglect of the more abundant solar-related resources. Technologies that might have made the use of solar energy more attractive have been neglected. There are many ways in which solar-related energy can be used. But even in the industrialized nations there has not yet developed the technological or the public informational base through which to take advantage of these alternatives.

The potential use of solar energy to supply part of the residential energy requirement is receiving increasing attention. In many regions, the sunlight energy that falls on buildings is sufficient to meet a substantial portion of their requirements. At the present stage of the technology, however, solar energy costs range from two to five times the current costs of fossil heat energy.

The costs would be substantially "reduced" through better insulation. Many building designs have demonstrated that improved insulation can reduce heat losses to one-tenth the average. Some of these incorporate energy storage facilities in the form of beds of sand, rock or water, which collect the heat of sunlight and almost eliminate the need for other heating. The same storage facility can often be cooled by the night air to retain a pleasant interior during the heat of the day. Ordinary home and hot water heating can be provided through collectors and exchangers that usually operate well below 70°C. The efficiencies decrease as temperatures are raised above that range, although 3,000°C temperatures can be reached at high cost. The conversion of sunlight to electric energy through photovoltaic cells is presently too expensive except for special applications as in space ships.

Large-scale production of solar electric energy is in an experimental stage in many places, the largest being a pilot plant in New Mexico, USA, which may achieve a capacity of 10 megawatts.

While there is uncertainty today about the use of solar energy for large-scale energy production in industrialized countries and in the energy systems required by large urban communities, there is a serious need to examine the possibility of solar energy conversion for those areas where this source has been largely discounted. Both small-scale installations (e.g. small water heaters) and large-scale (e.g. solar electric power plants) will be important in the future. There are many specific technical parameters which must be re-examined, including the availability of unused land, the levels of insolation (or solar flux, dispersed as well as undispersed incident solar radiation) and the overall environmental impact of the collection and conversion process.

The challenge is not so much in producing a watertight economic argument but in integrating solar energy systems into existing energy systems. A serious problem will be energy storage for periods of predictable nighttime and unpredictable overcast conditions. Hydrogen production is one possibility (with the hydrogen then being stored and used as a fuel), and other schemes such as pumped water storage or compressed air storage have been proposed. Work continues on this problem.

Many large and small experiments are also underway around the world aimed at converting the energy of winds and of waves into electric energy. Research and development effort is also underway for large-scale production of hydrogen gas through the dissociation of the water molecule. The production of methane gas through bio-conversion is also receiving increasing attention in the developed as well as developing countries. If successful, these gases could help to make up for the depletion of natural gas. These remain expensive possibilities, but improved technology and unavoidable rises in the cost of fossil fuels will make them more competitive and generally attractive.

What might be the ultimate gain from the new technologies and these renewable resources? If the world continues its current prodigal waste of energy, and homes and commercial buildings continue to be "energy sieves", the ultimate gain will remain more symbolic than real. But with conservation improvements through insulation of buildings, higher efficiency of power consuming equipment, redesign of commercial heating and ventilation processes, introduction of energy-recovery equipment in production plants, and the practice of recycling of wastes, it is conceivable that the solar-related energy resources can account for as much as 20% of the needs of industrialized societies and for even larger portions in regions where sunlit days are the rule.

It is clear, however, that the gains will be realized only as there is adequate support of research and development in the new technologies, with full and free exchange of information in the new technologies between nations. There is the additional need to give due attention both to the differing regional needs and to the needs of developing nations whose economy may gain more quickly from these developments than is possible to highly industrialized nations.

Policy Choices and Initiatives

In the face of any future energy crisis, national governments can be expected to respond with the customary level of expediency and self-interest. If these same governments were now to address themselves to the immediate task of preparing energy policies in anticipation of severe changes in the pattern of supply and demand, the transition to a sustainable energy future would undoubtedly be better managed and fewer people would suffer directly as a consequence of these changes. The difficulty in industrialized and developing countries alike in persuading governments to respond in advance of this well-defined crisis state is already recognized. Major barriers of a conceptual and an ideological nature must be overcome before the necessary policy initiatives will be taken, but it is worth defining where these barriers can be found. The guidelines or consultative documents on energy policy prepared by individual governments should wherever possible be examined against the following recognized social and ethical criteria for developing energy policies at a national level.

Centralized versus Decentralized Systems of Energy Production and Distribution

In response to the energy crisis, a government may choose to explore the option of changing the balance in its investment in energy generation from concentration on central power stations serving large urban areas to the inclusion of more total energy schemes incorporating combined heat and electricity production at a community level. The losses in the economies of scale associated with large turbine generators will be offset by the overall increase in thermal efficiency associated with better heat management. A further shift in the degree of decentralization to the level of the individual householder may also be practicable in certain countries where access to solar energy is particularly favourable for economic and enviromental reasons. There will be considerable prejudice against such a shift in those countries where a substantial investment in the "all-electric" economy has already been committed through the construction of expensive high voltage transmission and distribution networks. Resistance to the move towards decentralized production can therefore be anticipated and it is not realistic to imagine that this commitment will be easily abandoned. These developments also bring into the open the entire system of investment appraisal whereby public utilities make significant choices on behalf of large numbers of people without explicitly stating the values on which the final decisions are based. The real tensions of the decision-making process are never properly exposed and the debate as to whether a more desirable balance of centralized/decentralized production can be achieved is never joined. Electricity dependence thus emerges as a yes/no point of decision, but with the scales heavily tilted in favour of electricity as a clean, convenient and all purpose system of energy transfer.

High Personal Mobility versus a Reduced Need for Transport
The outlook governing the supply of alternative liquid fuels to replace petroleum fuels in transport is not encouraging. Several of the substitute fuel systems that are being examined, including methanol and hydrogen, would require massive inputs of electrical energy in order to achieve production on anything approaching the scale of a substitute for liquid petroleum. This investment in electricity production is causing certain countries to review their strategies on liquid fuels for the transport sector. The move is once again towards fuel cells with easily interchangeable electrolytes rather than to the replacement of electrical storage batteries with unfavourable power/weight ratios. Such changes are marginal in an organizational sense as it is always implied that the motor car is the most convenient and most socially acceptable form of transport. The failure of public engineers to demonstrate new technology at reasonable cost and low environmental impact has to be acknowledged, but changes will have to come at a more fundamental level if a transport network is to become sustainable. This will involve planners together with politicians in evolving strategies for new settlements that minimize the travel-to-work problems and peak capacity costs of all inner city transport. Once again nothing short of an ideological shift will generate constructive change, and the number of examples where goverments have so far responded to this need are few and far between.

New Concepts in Building Design — Low Energy, Long Life, Loose-Fit
To provide homes for more and more people, to build more work-places, schools, hospitals — here is a real challenge to designers, architects and planners to respond sensitively and creatively to all the demands made upon their professional skills. This challenge has generated a new concept in building design which brings the resource constraints into the area of social decision-making. Patterns of energy consumption are closely allied with community housing needs, and buildings will always play a major part in conditioning the attitudes of people to their environment. The new design concepts in low-energy, long-life, and loose-fit housing demand that the

occupants be responsible for good housekeeping, particularly with respect to the heat balance and insulation properties of the buildings. The transition period to a new sustainable society will have to be accompanied by a real change in social attitudes, and policy initiatives in the housing field will hinge on the ability of governments to advance these concepts with the consent of their electorates.

Land Use and Energy Planning

Attempts are underway in industrialized and developing countries to reconcile the conflicting claims on land use that come from all sectors of an economy. The coordination of energy planning with land use is already a matter for immediate concern and must constitute a key policy area, again incorporating a large degree of public participation. Systems of public enquiry into land use will have to be further developed at a local level to achieve the necessary degree of public scrutiny. It is only under these conditions that the social and ethical choices of a particular community can be openly debated. Apart from national guidelines relating to strategic or other defence issues, governments should be persuaded to let the community decide, providing only the necessary means of arbitration if a consensus view fails to emerge.

8 · The Argument for Conservation and the Fullest Possible Use of Renewable Energy Sources

Questions Arising

In the last few years in particular, both within nations and on the world scale, the energy problem and energy politics have moved to the centre of the stage. The search for adequate energy policies continues to grow in importance, swayed this way and that by the multitude of forces and interests involved. The present fierce debates about the effects of oil price rises, promises and dangers of nuclear power, the environmental impact of increased coal use, and prospects for alternative sources of energy such as solar all illustrate different aspects of the world-wide energy problem. Thus it is good and timely that we should ask, "What does it mean to speak of energy for a just, participatory and sustainable society?"

1973 is regarded as the year in which the world really woke up to the fact that it faced an energy problem. For then the OPEC countries decided to quadruple oil prices in a short space of time. For the Arab countries the rise was a weapon in the war against Israel, but also a means of achieving both greater control over their own resources and a larger share in the profits taken by the transnational oil companies. In the West, inflation mounted and balance of payments problems were aggravated, with severe economic and political effects. Undoubtedly the poorer countries of the Third World were hit hardest of all, as regards their energy and fertilizer needs, financial dependency and disrupted development plans.

But it is not just a matter of the end of *cheap* oil. Actual production of this major source of energy for Western economies is approaching its peak. If a continued exponential growth in demand is met, the reserves of oil may not last much into the next century. Thus the time available to solve the energy problem is not great.

Alongside this realization of overdependence on oil coupled with depleting reserves, the great nuclear energy debate has been gathering force around the world. The nuclear future embraced with enthusiasm during the 1950's and 1960's is now being seriously questioned as the hazards involved are coming to be recognized more clearly. Similarly, there is concern about greater use of coal because of the potential impact on the global climate of dioxide gas in the atmosphere, as well as its local environmental effects.

Some of the questions raised by the energy debate are as follows:

— What can the energy future be? What energy policy and individual choices are required now in order to assure that future? What are the different prospects locally, nationally, globally and how do we evaluate them?

— What risks and hazards are acceptable or not acceptable, and on what basis do we decide?

— As we seek solutions, what is our responsibility: to ourselves? to the world at large? to the earth? to future generations?

— Can we make energy choices that improve social equity and the economic situation, reduce international tensions and promote justice?

— What type of society can we hope for, globally and nationally? What decisions on energy will move us in that direction? What are our goals for community life and for the quality of that life?

— What are our real needs, and what are merely wants?

— Who does and who should own and control energy resources? Who should be involved in the decisions to be made, and how should they be made? That is, what do democracy and participation mean in relation to energy?

Clearly these questions have scientific and technical elements, but they also extend to issues of global outlook, social vision, ethical responsibility, political reality and economic impact. The whole community ought to have an opportunity to participate in the discussions, debates and decision-making processes on such matters. They cannot be left to scientists or bureaucrats or politicians alone. They are matters on which the ethical and social choices have to be set out clearly, and which call for commitment and action.

Our own stances will be formed in light of our understanding of what precisely the energy problem is, of the role of energy in our societies and of the alternative possibilities, and of a dialogue with those of different points of view. We shall now attempt to define the energy problem and some alternative approaches to it.

What is the Energy Problem ?

a) *Resource Depletion*

In recent times, more than 90% of world energy has been provided by fossil fuels, with hydro-electric, geothermal and nuclear power taking a minor role. Over the past 25 years, world energy demand has continued to grow at an aggregate rate of around 5% per year. This means a doubling in total energy consumption about every 14 years.

If we assume continued exponential growth in the demand for oil, then we see the demand probably exceeding the potential supply by 1990. The peak for natural gas may come a little later. Generally speaking, there are good world supplies of coal for at least the next century, but such a statement hides the difficulties of distribution and the dangers of making such predictions. How long coal lasts will depend, of course, on the uses to which it is put; if it is to be used to synthesize oil for transport as well as for electricity generation, then the known reserves will not last nearly so long.

At present oil meets 45% of world energy needs, and is used mainly for transport. It will not last much longer. One way or another, the world must enter a post-petroleum era.

But oil is not the only energy resource in short supply. For many millions of families in the Third World, the energy crisis is already manifest in the daily extended search for firewood for cooking and heating — it is becoming increasingly scarce as forests are destroyed, and there is no obvious replacement as oil prices have risen beyond reach. Forest depletion has been a factor in the spread of deserts and in soil depletion through erosion and the removal of nutrients. Where cow dung is substituted for firewood as a fuel rather than being left as fertilizer, the latter process is worsened. Here then is a first connection between the world energy problem and the world food problem.

b) *Unsustainable Directions*

In the richer societies energy is all-pervasive — it may be thought of as the universal currency of all activity. Each technology and each use of materials has its energy cost in manufacture and its energy cost in use.

Western societies are characterized by the progressive replacement of human and renewable energy by fossil fuel energy, and a continuing exponential growth in the use of the latter. In brief, men and women are being replaced (automation) or absorbed into machines (for example, the car); there is an energy cost of doing this. Natural sources of energy (plants, vegetables, natural fertilizers, fresh foods, fibres) are being replaced by synthetic materials (plastics, synthetic textiles, artificial fertilizers, frozen, processed and convenience foods), produced at a large energy cost.

In these senses we may claim that Western life-styles have become increasingly energy-intensive, a trend which has been associated with increasingly wasteful and inefficient energy use in all sectors. We choose energy intensive, which usually means energy inefficient, transport modes, architecture, industry, settlement patterns, and technologies.

The questions that arise about present directions are, then: Can such inefficiency and wastefulness and exponential of growth be countenanced in the light of the resources situation? And more profoundly, should they be countenanced in light of the type of society desired, quality of life considerations and environmental impact?

In this last question we have pinpointed two related issues: the issue of the environmental impact of high rates of energy use, and the issue of energy use and social well-being.

High rates of energy use imply high environmental impact. By the ineluctable laws of physics, energy cannot be created or destroyed, but it is always degraded, in any process, into waste heat. Whatever we do — generate electricity or process food or drive to work — some useful energy is converted into unusable waste heat. Where fossil fuels or uranium are dug from the ground to provide this energy, there is an inevitable addition to the earth's natural heat balance. Here is the problem of thermal pollution and its subsequent effects on climate, the ultimate limit to energy use. There is also the environmental impact of the energy industry itself: mining, oil spillages, air pollution from fossil fuel burning, radioactive pollution from nuclear leaks and waste disposal. And there is the environmental impact of other energy intensive activities: car driving, packaging, synthetics manufacture, etc. *Thus high energy use and high environmental impact go hand in hand.*

Obviously that is one aspect of a relationship between energy use and the quality of life. The question of the full connection between energy and social well-being is now under investigation. Thus the car-based sprawling city, an energy intensive city of necessity, is also criticized for its stultifying effect on community and creative life. So too is the progressive replacement of small-scale activities, crafts and natural materials by production lines, automation and synthetics. And many of the epidemics of Western society — heart disease, road accidents, diet- and pollution-based diseases — are related to energy intensive activities. Here then is another critical connection that must be examined further.

Present growth in energy use in the richer societies is not sustainable indefinitely. Not only are they running up against resources depletion, but also against the demands of energy efficiency, ecological balance and social well-being. The post-petroleum era must become an energy conservative era.

c) *Global Need*

There is a global dimension to the energy problem beyond the global availability of resources. For energy is intimately connected with the other world problems of population growth, food needs, resource limitations and environmental impact. The maldistribution of fossil fuel resources on the one hand, and energy consumption on the other are aspects of the world poverty situation. In 1972, the richer nations, with about 30% of the earth's population, used about 83% of the earth's fossil-fuel resources, leaving 17% for the two-thirds world, where basic needs are greatest. Population growth at the same time places continuing new strains on direct energy resources and on food, land, services, shelter and other resources, all of which require energy inputs. There is also the problem of increased energy needs for food production now and as the population grows, and increased energy needs for mineral extraction as resources dwindle. The overexpenditure on world armaments continues to take energy and other resources that could be directed to the challenge of world poverty.

The global situation of poverty and population growth therefore warrants increased growth in energy supply for basic human needs, coupled with a more equitable distribution and a transfer of energy resources from some uses to others.

d) *Some Principles for the New Era*

The energy problem is a crisis of resource shortages, of unsustainable directions and of unmet global need. It is a crisis of too much and too little: too little in the way of firewood and available oil reserves to meet the continuing growth of demand; too little in the way of energy resources where they are most needed to meet the essential human requirements for food, shelter and materials in poorer countries.

On the other hand, the peoples of the richer countries are using too much energy for there to be a just distribution of energy resources, and too much for the earth to continue to sustain this rate of use for long. Too many strains are appearing in the earth's capacity to supply energy resources at present rates of growth, and to absorb the waste that results.

We seem to have here an illustration of the global ethic proposed by one of the working groups at the 1974 WCC Bucharest Conference on "Science and Technology for Human Development": It is both immoral and self-damaging when some peoples consume resources and pollute at a rate greater than the earth could stand if all peoples did likewise.

What seems to be required then is a cooperative world effort to find suitable and sustainable energy resources, and to ensure a fair and just distribution of them. This aim could be partially met by increased energy growth in the poorer countries and a reduction of energy use growth in the rich. The major task for all countries is to find energy efficient growth pathways which eliminate the wastefulness of the rich and which direct the growth to where it is most needed. The interests of rich and poor coalesce in the exploration of less wasteful patterns of use and increased efficiency.

Their interests also coalesce in the search for sustainable energy sources. The urgency of this task has already been emphasized. The necessity of taking a long-term perspective, so that short-term decisions do not lessen the chances of long-term solutions, has been underlined by the WCC Energy Advisory Group. Above all, there is the need to put people first; to find energy sources and technologies which are appropriate to real human needs, to community goals and to social well-being, and appropriate within the overall global context. Such a statement implies the participation of people in energy decisions and actions. So we add the word "appropriate" to justice, participation and sustainability as a criterion for the energy future.

We shall now attempt to apply these criteria first to possible patterns of energy use, then to possible sources to meet that use.

Energy Demand: The Challenge to Existing Patterns of Consumption

Energy conservation — saving energy, eliminating waste, and using energy more efficiently — is often left out or given only lip-service in the discussions of energy experts. Yet there are profound possibilities here. Some nations are beginning to recognize them. For richer countries, in fact, energy conservation is one of the most immediate, promising and safest of the energy "resources".

One prerequisite to saving energy is becoming aware of how it is used. Energy being all-pervasive, this involves analysis of energy flows and energy costs in all activities. The science of energy analysis is a young science which has already produced some important results and will produce more guidelines in the future. Meanwhile energy awareness in societies might involve:

(i) Energy budgets at the government level, whereby the total flows of energy in the economy, both supply and demand, are presented in the light of available resources.

(ii) Energy impact statements incorporated into public sector and industrial decision-making, whereby the total implications for energy requirements of proposed new developments, new technologies, new consumer goods and alternative ways of doing things are examined in detail.

(iii) Energy consciousness at the individual level, whereby energy is taken into account in the decisions of individuals and families and community groups. This calls for information and education along with other measures such as testing and labelling consumer goods for energy efficiency.

With energy awareness as a prerequisite, the stage is set for societies to choose their energy pathway to the future. Studies such as those of the Ford Foundation Energy Policy Project in the USA, the International Institute for Environment and Development in Europe, and the Open University Energy Research Group in Britain help to clarify the choices that are possible. Basically five potential growth pathways merit serious consideration. So far three of them ((ii), (iii) and (iv) below) have been the subject of the detailed studies mentioned above.

Note that we now consider the *rate of growth* of energy use, not simply the total energy consumption itself. Both increased and reduced rates of growth mean increased total consumption over time. Hence pathways (i)-(iii) below all mean increased total consumption to different degrees.

(i) *Increased Growth Pathway:* This is the only option for many developing countries for, say the next 50 years, and is not an option for richer countries. It involves an increase in the *rate of growth* of energy use through the development of appropriate and sustainable energy sources. What counts is the quality and direction of such growth under the demands of equitable distribution, increased local self-reliance and energy efficiency, together with international cooperation to help achieve it. In addition it should not be forgotten that there are already prospects for energy conservation in regions where increased growth is warranted. Arjun Makhijani, for instance, has pointed to the large potential savings in current firewood use in Third World rural villages through the design of more efficient stoves and cooking implements.

(ii) *Continued Growth Pathway:* The energy rich could allow energy use to continue to increase as now, and attempt to meet it by aggressive development of all possible supplies. Envision massive increases in the use of oil, gas, coal, and nuclear energy over the next 25 years. Hope for a new source, the fast breeder reactor or nuclear fusion or large-scale solar energy, to take over eventually.

The advantage of this pathway is that it is "business as usual" for the rich, requiring the least change in the short-term. The disadvantages lie in the continued depletion of fossil fuel and uranium reserves, increased atmospheric pollution, all the risks attendant on nuclear energy, massive capital investments required for energy supply alone, and that overall the direction remains unsustainable. For high energy using countries this would be a "fragile" energy policy, in the sense that if success were not achieved on all fronts at once, then the goal of high growth could not be maintained.

(iii) *Reduced Growth Pathway:* Try to reduce the *rate of growth* by say one-third or one-half by planning over the next 10-20 years. This would involve application of energy-saving technologies and policies to reduce demand by improving the efficiency of things we do at present. Little change in life-styles would be called for; the measures are more in the nature of a "technical fix". The sorts of measures that could be used include insulation of houses and buildings, heat pumps and combined heating schemes, encouraging a shift to smaller cars and reducing the shift from public transport, direct use of fuels rather than electricity for appropriate purposes. Other possible measures will be mentioned later.

Such a policy could be instituted immediately in richer nations, and would immediately begin to ease the mounting strains on resources and the environment. It lengthens the time of transition and sets the stage for further possible reductions in the future. In the short term, the demand could be met by several possible mixtures of resources; in this sense it is a robust and flexible policy. Disadvantages relate to the structural changes in employment and investment (this is opportunity as well!) and to investments already made assuming continued high growth (for example, tooling for large cars). In the long run, growth, although reduced, is still exponential and so ultimately unsustainable.

(iv) *Zero Energy Growth Pathway:* Aim to level off the use of energy by, say 1990, so that there is a zero growth rate and constant demand after that date. This would require certain life-style changes which could be advantageous on other grounds. Measures might include extensive use of small-scale solar energy equipment on houses and buildings, a shift towards public transport, slow down in *the growth* of plane travel, recycling of materials, reduction in the use of plastics and packaging, and a shift of employment from industries producing consumer goods to quality, craft, service and creative activities.

Zero energy growth does not necessarily imply zero economic growth. The relation between these is complex, but evidence suggests they can be uncoupled. Nor does it imply a reduction in total employment; in fact quite the reverse because many of the new measures are based more on labour than on machines. The advantages of this pathway are a great easing of the strains on resources, greatly eased environmental impact, greatly increased flexibility in the choice of the mixture of resources, and potentially improved quality of life in communities and in the workplace. Disadvantages include the pains of restructuring, the penalties of mistaken investments, and the outcry of vested interests. Nevertheless all countries must move to very low or zero energy growth eventually; the question is whether it is desirable in the short-term or in the long, and whether it is to be planned or haphazard.

(v) *Negative Energy Growth Pathway:* The transition to a negative energy growth pathway has not been the subject of consideration by any government so far! However there may be a moral obligation on some countries to consider this path in the interests of world justice, where the global ethic is being violated. And it may be worthwhile for some in so far as it leads to better use of resources, increased self-sufficiency, lessened environmental impact and improved quality of life. Economic effects of such a course of action have yet to be studied. Negative growth could be achieved by a combination of technical fix and life-style changes, using most measures mentioned above and below. It, too, is worthy of investigation as one possible choice of the people.

Potential energy savings are enormous if a rich country chooses to follow one of the lower growth pathways. The US and UK studies are in agreement in showing potential savings of about one-third — 33% — by 2000 if the reduced growth pathway is followed, rather than the continued high growth. If reduced growth leads to zero growth, the savings could be almost one-half — about 48%. In either case the energy saved is far more than could be provided by a crash programme of development of any one resource in the same time.

Energy Conservation Measures

There are more possibilities for energy savings than can be listed here. The keynotes, though, are care of the earth and stewardship of resources and a willingness to think about doing things differently. Regional differences of culture and climate and present patterns of energy use (some peoples are already more energy conservative than others) make sweeping statements dangerous. But we can give some ideas as to what is possible.

a) *Housing and Buildings*. Architecture and siting for best heating and cooling, coupled with proper insulation, are initial steps in the right direction. Direct burning of fuels for heating rather than the use of electricity is energy saving. It is estimated (US figures) that savings in operation could be 30-50% in existing buildings, 50-80% in new ones. The lower figure in each case is for optimal insulation and most efficient heating, lighting and air conditioning. The higher savings are with the addition of solar devices, heat pumps and total energy systems.

b) *Transport*. The single-occupant car is a most energy inefficient mode of travel. Of course one could work on improving the car itself: a switch to smaller cars, abandoning automatic transmission, using radial ply tyres, increasing the life expectancy and recycling old cars. Car pools and employer-run van pools would help.

Immense savings are possible in the long run by planning cities more around public transport, walking, bicycling, and intercity rail, that is, by moving to more efficient city patterns and transport modes. Again a combination of improving the present system with altered life-styles carries the greatest promise.

c) *Food*. Food is an interesting case study, for here is the intersection of two of the great world problems. Both are problems having the two faces of overconsumption and underconsumption.

In Western countries, for each calorie of food arriving on the dinner table, something like five times as much energy has been expended in getting it there. The majority of that goes in processing, packaging, transport and preparation beyond the farm-gate.

On the farm the mechanization of agriculture is a substitution of fossil fuel energy for labour. Similarly fertilization is a substitution of energy for more land. The mechanization and chemicalization of agriculture are a change to high energy agriculture. In many cases more careful energy use is possible and would be beneficial.

But we must look to the post farm-gate processes for even greater savings. Refining, processing and overconsumption of foods are not only energy intensive but are also being linked to many diet-related health problems. Over-refining, over-processing and over-packaging of food should be removed altogether, with benefits for both energy and health.

d) *Technology*. Many people are now urging a new look at our technological society with the aim of finding, in the words of E. F. Schumacher, "a technology with a human face". In fact, the term "appropriate technology" has come to speak to our time. One of the great tasks of society is to implement technologies and to produce goods that are at once more humane, more in harmony with nature, enhancing community life, energy and resource conserving, and based on quality and durability. Energy conservation has to be built into the search for appropriate technologies. As far as new energy technologies themselves are concerned, small-scale solar and other renewable units satisfy many of these criteria.

From the energy conserving point of view

— attention should be given to materials used; for example, it costs 2½ times as much energy to make a can from aluminium as from steel;

— attention should be given to waste and unnecessary consumption, unnecessary packaging and advertising;

— attention should be given to the scale of industrial activity and to the improvement of existing processes;

— recycling is generally energy conserving compared to the production of the same material from scratch.

Production processes at the moment are mainly linear: resources → production → consumption → waste. Hence there are the dual problems of resource depletion at one end and increasing pollution at the other. Yet metals, glass and paper can be recycled at a fraction of the energy cost. Replacement of the linear by the circular would therefore save energy, resources and pollution. The sooner the move is made to a fully recycling economy, the better.

Summary of the Arguments for Energy Conservation

Energy conservation does not mean reduced standards of living. Rather it means doing some of the things we now do more efficiently, doing other things differently, and creating some new activities. It means doing more and better with less. The arguments for energy conservation in the high energy using nations are a very powerful set:

1. The potential for savings makes energy conservation one of the best and most immediate of the "resources".

2. It is a necessary component of a sustainable energy economy.

3. It is necessary anyway, whatever else is done, to see us through the next 25 years.

4. It is necessary in a global sense as a prelude to a more just distribution of energy resources.

5. It is necessary in reducing the rate of use of other limited resources.

6. It would lead to reduced environmental impacts.

7. It would lead, if properly planned, to better quality of life in terms of health, community, work experience and opportunities for diverse social arrangements.

Energy Supply: The Challenge of the Sustainable Future

a) *Matching Supply and Demand*

We have considered the present dependence on oil and firewood, and seen that an inevitable transition must take place. The transition calls for energy efficient growth in developing countries and at least reduced energy growth in the rich. The time for action is short, but action must be taken with a long-term perspective of sustainability in mind. What sources of energy supply, then, are appropriate for the short and the long term? Again different prospects arise for different countries based on culture, national goals and patterns of living, population growth, geography and climate, internal resources and external relationships. So the framework here can only be general and imprecise.

In energy terms what resource is best depends on what use is required. Most fossil fuel energy goes to either heat, electricity or transport. Heat for buildings, houses or industry is provided by the direct burning of gas, oil, coal or wood, to a limited extent by the use of waste heat from other processes, or by electricity (which is poor energy matching of source and use). Electricity comes from the combustion of coal, oil or gas and also from hydro and nuclear power. Transport depends almost entirely on oil, and so is the most immediate problem. We need to examine each possible energy source as to its capacity to meet requirements in the three areas of heat, electricity and transport.

The choice of energy futures depends firstly on the choice of an energy growth pathway and only then on the mixture of sources to achieve that pathway. It is clear that lowered energy growth in richer countries leads to greater flexibility in choosing sources of supply, as well as to social and environmental benefits.

b) *Fossil Fuel Futures: Strategy for Transition*

As oil prices continue to rise, intensified exploration for oil and gas and the tapping of presently non-economic deposits, especially off-shore, are likely to occur. Nevertheless the contribution of oil to the total energy picture must begin to decline. The economic changes that price rises set into effect are likely to be far-reaching. Questions of control and social equity ought to be paramount.

Coal is seen by many as the chief transitional fuel. Reserves are sufficient for coal to act as a "bridge" to a longer-term future. Coal liquefaction and gasification could provide substitute oil and gas respectively to continue present social tendencies, especially in transport, for a little while. But at what costs? Capital costs of immense works, environmental and health costs of air pollution and mining, energy costs of using a fuel less efficiently by converting it to other fuels. And a non-renewable resource is still being depleted, its lifetime drastically reduced.

There is scope for a more careful use of fossil fuels. It would be a great improvement if waste heat from power stations was used for town heating — the heat waste is more than two-thirds of the energy released from the fuel. Small-scale power plants at industrial or housing sites or large buildings could provide both electricity and heating on the spot, thereby conserving large amounts of coal and oil. Newer technologies such as fluidized bed combustion also show promise of greater efficiency and lower environmental impact.

c) *Nuclear Futures: Breeding in Doubt*

Rising public concern and economic difficulties of the nuclear industry make the future of nuclear power uncertain. The claim that nuclear power is necessary in the rich countries to fill the energy gap to be left by oil over the next 25 years is usually based on the assumption of the continued growth pathway. Nations could apparently choose to limit their nuclear programmes by following a reduced growth pathway. While nuclear power could help meet the demand for electricity, it could only help on the heating side through more electric heat, which is inefficient, or through the use of waste heat generated at the plant site. It could only be of assistance as regards transport, if its use allowed coal to be diverted to oil production and/or if all-electric transport is envisaged. In either case, the proportion of a nation's capital and energy assets that would go to expanded nuclear power facilities plus coal liquefaction plants, or greatly expanded coal and nuclear power plants in order to add more transport to the electricity load, looks daunting.

Furthermore if the growth of nuclear power were to be based on the present generation of nuclear reactors, known uranium reserves may be depleted in little more than the expected time of depletion of oil.

That is not the case, however, if the fast-breeder reactor were to be included in the programme. For this reactor operates on almost all of the uranium (U^{238}) in the ore, converting it to plutonium, whereas the present reactors use U^{235} which is only 0.7% of naturally-occurring uranium. An alternative type of fast breeder uses thorium which is equally plentiful. So we are beginning to talk about an energy supply which would last into the long-term future. At the same time there is greater uncertainty about fast-breeder reactor safety and widespread concern about any move to a full-scale "plutonium economy" with its radiological hazards, waste storage problems and opportunities for nuclear weapons proliferation. The commercial viability of the fast breeder has yet to be demonstrated.

d) *Nuclear Fusion Future: Science Only, or Social Hope?*

Some physicists see in nuclear fusion the promise of inexhaustible amounts of cheap energy. That is because the basic fuels, such as deuterium, are present on earth in virtually unlimited amounts for this purpose, and are readily obtained. Others are more sceptical, or openly dismiss this possibility. That is because the scientific feasibility of fusion on earth has yet to be demonstrated, let alone the technological and the economic feasibilities. On a large scale the capital and energy costs could be immense because of the materials required to shield the reaction and the need to replace them regularly, and because of the solar temperature conditions under which the reaction takes place. The environmental (radioactive substances are still being produced) and social costs (for example, the social implications of very large-scale capital-intensive fusion systems) have yet to be fully evaluated.

Thus we can say about nuclear fusion: there are aggressive research plans with hopes of finding whether the experiments are to be successful within 10 years. But as an energy source, we cannot now predict the outcome nor base firm plans upon it.

e) *Renewable Energy Futures: Shining Strongly or Limited Light?*

The word "renewable" or "income" is used as opposed to "non-renewable" or "capital" to indicate energy sources that are always present and enduring. In tapping renewable sources, we are making use of natural energy and material flows rather than taking resources which, once used, are gone. They are the in-flowing energy means. Of the various renewable sources that are available world-wide, direct solar energy is both the most naturally attractive and enduring. We include also the indirect solar sources, the energies of the winds and waves and inland waters, energy stored through the remarkable photosynthetic processes that produce plant life, and the energy of temperature variations of the environment. Further, we include the potential energy in urban and rural wastes.

There is a range of opinion about the prospect of the solar future. The reasons for the differing views are various. Some on the pessimistic side have vested interests in present directions, are unaware of the range of renewable energy possibilities and available technologies, or are sceptical about the social and political changes required. To others the possible difficulties are paramount: economic costs, storage problem, possible strains on the supply of materials such as copper for solar absorbers, and competing land uses which place constraints on growing crops for energy. The proponents assert that such problems are more manageable than those of the fossil or nuclear alternatives, and that there are several other factors to take into account. We shall now consider some of them.

Renewable sources have several unique advantages apart from their very renewability. In fact solar energy technologies qualify as appropriate technologies — they can be dispersed rather than centralized and on a small or large scale. They can be matched to a diversity of settlement patterns and life-styles. By and large they are simple technologies and easily understood, are safe and have low environmental impact. Climatic impact, too, is lower. Renewable technologies may, in the words of Amory Lovins, "help to redress the severe energy imbalance between temperate and tropical zones". Many developing countries are well placed climatically to exploit solar and biomass energy.

Some valuable lessons are being learned from work by research and community groups on self-sufficient housing through renewable energy technologies. It turns out that an integrated use of small-scale technologies is required for complete autonomy: solar absorbers for hot water and space heating, methane digester to produce gas and fertilizer from the family wastes, a windmill for electricity generation, and perhaps a slow combustion stove for supplementary heating. The principle of the integration of renewable energy technologies so that they work together is capable of application in many other areas.

The claim is sometimes made that solar energy is good in principle, but that the technologies for operation do not yet exist. A more correct statement is that renewable energy technologies which could take up a substantial portion of the energy load are already available, and that others are in the pipeline. Renewable energy technologies in fact have a very long history.

For heat, solar absorbers are available for hot water, space heating and some industrial processes, that is, for low grade heat less than 70°C which constitutes a substantial proportion of heat needs. Solar drying of foods is well-known and techniques are improving. Solar absorbers, reflectors and focussing lenses for higher grade heat are being developed. Supplementary heat is obtainable from methane gas generation by digestion of wastes, and simply from furnaces burning urban and plant wastes.

For electricity, there are some prospects for almost immediate use. Some cities already generate part of their electricity by burning urban wastes in conventional power stations. Wind energy should not be underestimated, either for electricity or for mechanical work. Tidal power has some limited applications. Small-scale water powered units are being used with success in rural areas. There are large-scale hydro-power possibilities in the developing world. Solar photocells, which generate electricity from sunlight directly at the site where the electricity is required, show promise. Their presently high costs are falling rapidly whereas costs of other means of electric power generation are rising rapidly. For the future, there are prospects of electricity from wave power, and of large-scale solar-electric plants — the solar farm based on chemical processes, the power tower based on reflection by mirrors to a central tower, and solar sea-power based on differences in ocean temperature at different depths.

Transport remains the most difficult problem. As mentioned, the problem would be greatly reduced by and may become manageable through energy-conserving transport modes and city design. Further progress may come through alternative engines such as the steam engine and techniques such as the fly wheel. Fermentation of plant materials to yield alcohols which could almost directly replace petrol in engines, or be added to petrol, is known and somewhat promising. The destructive distillation of plant materials could yield hydrocarbon fuels. The idea of the hydrogen economy, whereby hydrogen gas is generated from solar- or wind-powered electrolysis of water for direct use as a fuel, has been studied and preliminary results suggest that the economic point of breakeven is close at hand.

Given such a range of possibilities and such interesting diversity, one cannot help but ask why more has not been done. For one thing the days of cheap oil have hidden other possibilities from us; the awakening has only been recent. Huge government subsidies and large investments in the nuclear industry have given this a momentum to the virtual exclusion of alternatives. Renewable sources of energy have no military implications. Large-scale thinking has neglected the potential of the small, simpler technologies which have been classed as unsophisticated and old-fashioned. The ideology of progress has blinded us to the potential of what is already available. Now the solar challenge is worth taking up.

Seeking Strategies for the Transition

Clearly the aim of energy policy locally, nationally and globally ought to be to achieve a long-term sustainable energy economy fashioned under the canons of justice.

In each case there is the need to take into account

1. the present situation, including present patterns of energy use, resource dependencies and inequalities;

2. long-term aims, formed with social well-being, resources and the environment in mind;

3. the intermediate term — how to move from the present to the long-term over the next 25 years.

Our discussions suggest energy policies that are much more comprehensive and imaginative than the largely piece-meal efforts of the past. There is now a new urgency and some new elements involved. We must ask that energy policies give equal attention to energy demand (especially inefficiency and waste) and supply. This requires a shift of thinking on the part of energy planners. If we are to move towards a just world, then national energy policies must recognize global need and global effects of energy use. They ought also to incorporate a long-term perspective lest decisions taken with only the short-term in mind lead to further crises later on, and foreclose better courses of action. There has to be a recognition of both the social consequences of energy decisions and the environmental impact of growing energy use. Few nations have yet proposed an energy policy which is as comprehensive as this.

At this stage we may foresee some of the major matters that governments and peoples will have to face as the attempt is made to find such energy policies.

First there is the question of where to place the main thrust of energy research and development; whether to keep all options open with less funds for each or to concentrate on certain chosen areas. There is also the task of devising mechanisms for energy budgeting by governments and energy impact statements by firms. This is complicated by some lack of reliable information on energy resources. For example, information on oil resources is provided largely by the oil companies themselves and there is presently no independent method of verifying its validity.

If a vigorous energy conservation policy is to be pursued, then several matters arise. The social desirability of the many possible conservation measures has to be established, including whether to concentrate only on "technical fix" measures or to promote life-style changes as well. Desirable economic restructuring to implement energy conservation may include devising new systems of taxes and subsidies, removing existing institutional barriers to conservation (for example the barrier of reduced rates for large-scale electricity use), and redirecting employment where people are involved in unsuitable, high energy activities. Energy conservation programmes will have to be mounted in the face of political opposition from vested interests — those whose "reason for being is endless energy growth", in the words of a recent report.

As oil prices rise, measures will also have to be taken if social equity is to be ensured. For here we have questions of possible windfall profit together with the effects of price rises on the transport and heating budgets of poorer members of societies. This also points to the question of the ownership and control of energy resources and technologies (including small-scale renewable energy units). Governments will have to decide how to encourage some developments such as energy conservation and renewable energy industries, given the momentum of existing high energy, fossil fuel and nuclear industries.

The debate over whether to move to further centralized energy systems — large-scale power plants — or whether to emphasize decentralized systems — small-scale power plants, industry and home sized solar units etc. — is now well under way. Underlying it are different visions of a desirable society. Allied to it is the question of whether to aim for an increased or reduced dependence on electricity, given on the one hand the possibility of more large-scale power plants and on the other the greater energy savings and efficiency if electricity use is restricted only to those ends for which it is particularly suitable.

Among the many environmental considerations which come to mind is that of competing land uses. Land required for mining, disposal of wastes, growing energy crops, or large-scale wind or solar operations may be in competition with land required for agriculture, urban growth, recreation, or preservation.

When we think about how the decisions might be arrived at, there are two important aspects: structures of participation and structures of international cooperation. Internally, participation raises questions of how to open the opportunities for public involvement in energy decisions; what means for local-national cooperation are appropriate; how to achieve a fair representation of interests in policy-making bodies, and how to ensure a fair public presentation of information and all sides of the debates. Externally, international cooperation for a just distribution of resources and technologies is clearly required — what bodies, institutions and methods can achieve this? We need cooperation and support at three levels: international — national — local.

These are some of the challenges for energy policy today. How they are answered depends on the context we give to the aim of a long-term sustainable energy economy. Let us consider a strategy towards this end.

Some believe that the only truly sustainable energy economy would be one based on energy conservative ways of living and optimum use of renewable energy resources. According to this view, sustainability would mean not using energy beyond the energy income. Then resources could not be outrun, environmental damage could be limited and social well-being enhanced.

This is the "fossil-fuels — conservation — renewable resources strategy". Policy based on it would include:

1) the more careful use of fossil fuel reserves and firewood as a bridge to the longer term future;

2) promotion of energy awareness in all sectors;

3) a vigorous energy conservation programme;

4) a planned shift to renewable energy resources.

According to this strategy, the high energy using nations should make a transition to low energy growth in the intermediate term (between now and the turn of the century) and then to zero or even negative energy growth in the longer term. Energy needy countries, on the other hand, should seek to achieve high energy growth in the intermediate term and eventually begin a transition to lower growth when basic needs have been met.

This strategy would involve a combination of measures. Energy conservation is a first priority. Efforts should be made to extend the expected life-times of oil and gas reserves through more exploration, development conservation, a shift to other resources and more careful use. There would be increased use of coal, at least in the short term while the transition gets under way, but with greater attention to its environmental impact. Where firewood is the dominant source, reforestation and more careful use might be coupled with efforts to place its use on a renewable basis. Where nuclear energy is already used, there might be an initial small increase in nuclear electricity supply as existing plans are fulfilled, but large-scale commitment to this source could be avoided. An immediate phasing-in of existing solar, wind, waste and biomass technologies would be undertaken, with an emphasis on further research in these areas.

The stage would then be set for the longer term, when energy conservation requiring greater structural change could come into force. The use of oil and gas will have begun to tail off. Coal could be progressively replaced by existing technologies (such as solar absorption), technologies which have become economic in the meantime (such as solar photocells), and newly developed technologies (such as wave power and large solar-electric plants). Firewood may come to take its rightful place as a resource used renewably along with solar, wind and waste under the management of local communities.

Here in broad sweep is one possible strategy for which there is much to be said in terms of sustainability and its potential for greater justice. The idealistic picture of a world living mainly from its energy income with basic energy needs met is a very attractive one from all points of view. This strategy offers many challenges to local vision and ingenuity in establishing desirable directions of conservation, developing appropriate renewable energy technologies, and devising the institutional structures to affect them in an equitable manner.

The main long-term alternative strategy appears to be that based mainly on coal and nuclear power, with or without the possibility of nuclear fusion. Energy conservation is emphasized but with modest expectations. Renewable resources are usually relegated to an insignificant role in the intermediate period (to the turn of the century) and an important but minor role in the long term.

The discussion of this fossil fuel — nuclear strategy leads us back to the centre of the debates about energy growth, the social and political will for conservation and renewable resources, and especially the vexed question of nuclear energy itself. Numerous reports and studies have pinpointed the difficulties and hazards of nuclear power — nuclear weapons proliferation, specific hazards of the fuel cycle itself, the unsolved problem of radioactive wastes, biomedical ignorance and risks, extra dangers of "the plutonium economy", fast-breeder reactor safety, possibilities for terrorism, and uncertainties about nuclear economics. One may be forgiven for thinking that it is a topsyturvy world that puts the development of nuclear energy ahead of energy conservation and renewable resources.

Our broad sweep should not obscure the actual range of choice nor the unique situations of different countries and regions. Whatever choices are made, considerations of justice and sustainability should be foremost.

We have seen that the central issue in striving for justice is to stop the growth in energy consumption in the industrialized world. This is also the first requirement for sustainability. An orientation towards renewable energy resources could help serve the interests of both rich and poor countries.

It is clear that the questions, social visions and values underlying the alternative energy strategies are so important for the future that they should not be left to energy experts and politicians alone. When ways of living are at stake, then all people have a right to participate. Concerned persons, families and churches may take the lead by self-examination and by acting in society at large, in the interests of a just and sustainable energy economy.

9 · The Churches and the Debate about Nuclear Energy

The experience of the churches as they have participated in the debate about nuclear energy illustrates the problems they face in trying to relate their faith and ethics to contemporary issues of science and technology. They are: (1) the difficulties of arriving at judgements on questions in which ethical and technical issues are closely interrelated and where they have limited understanding of the technical aspects; and (2) their lack of an agreed method for approaching ethical-technical issues, and the resulting division and confusion about Christian responsibility in relation to such issues. Because the problem is more generic than specific, the experience of the churches in dealing with the nuclear issue is instructive for other areas of technological controversy.

This paper seeks to show how the churches entered into the nuclear debate and the conflict of theological and ethical opinion which has developed around it.

I. The Churches Welcome the Peaceful Atom

The first development of nuclear power during the late 1950's and the 1960's aroused no opposition in the churches. On the contrary, the peaceful use of nuclear technology seemed to offer a way of redeeming a technology which had previously been used only to make weapons. Moreover the nations were proceeding slowly and tentatively in the construction of nuclear power facilities. Industrialized countries were assuming a long-term development; and the developing ones, with a few exceptions like India, Japan and Argentina, were assuming that for them the serious use of nuclear technology was some distance in the future.

The public accepted the assurances of the scientists concerning the safety of nuclear reactors, and did not, at that moment, reflect on the large social costs associated with nuclear energy which were being emphasized by the scientists themselves. Dr. Alvin Weinberg, one of America's leading administrators and philosophers of science and technology, said in an essay in 1966:

"If in order to produce energy cheaply a nuclear reactor must be much larger than can be accommodated by existing economic and social organizations, then, unless these organizations are merged and enlarged, we shall have to forego the economic advantages of bigness." [1]

In his view, world society would have no choice. To obtain the energy for survival, its social and political structures would have to meet the requirements of living with big technology. The social responsibility of the scientists and the technologists was to remove the technical imperfections from such new, large and potentially dangerous technological systems. "Humanists" and theologians should give their attention to the social and moral problems of the new technological systems, resulting from the increased human freedom, the opportunity for leisure and added knowledge, and which posed in a new and striking way the ultimate question of the meaning and purpose of life. To quote Weinberg again:

"We scientists, even as we set about correcting the physical defects of our technical revolutions, can only pray that the humanists will supply those deeper values which, up to now, Western man has had no time to cherish, but which in the future he will have too much time to survive without." [2]

In other words, science and technology were to perfect the tools; religion and humanism were to give the meaning and purpose.

The churches offered no challenge to such a simplistic division of labour. They tended to accept the promise of atoms for peace, and like the public at large, "failed to perceive the implied future scale of dependence on nuclear energy and were generally apathetic to its social and ethical implications."

II. Problems Appear

With the passage of time, the extension of the nuclear industry, and growing public awareness of its implications, the benign acceptance has turned into mounting questions and astringent debate, with resulting confrontation between the opponents and proponents of nuclear energy. Doubts about the acceptability of nuclear power *per se* have been coupled with a growing criticism of all large technology, its apparent lack of access and its insulation from public participation. The energy debate itself has led the churches to a profound unease about what options are best for the future, and to the realization that the assessments and predictions are unbalanced and incomplete on all sides.

---

[1] *Reflection on Big Science*, M.I.T. Press, USA, 1967, p. 33.

[2] *Ibid.*, p. 37.

In the debate regarding nuclear power itself, a number of factors seem to be influential:

1. As nuclear power becomes more widely used and dependence upon it increases, public awareness of the problems of reactor siting, security and safety grows. The prospects of trying to maintain the rigorous standards required for the safe operation of nuclear power systems seems daunting even under conditions of social stability. Under conditions of serious social instability, maintenance of such standards appears highly improbable.

2. Phrases like "the Faustian bargain", another of Weinberg's trenchant and pertinent images, startled the public and has been used by nuclear critics to increase fears of a technology whose utilization seems to introduce a new and cosmic dimension of uncertainty and anxiety.

3. The perceived link between nuclear power and nuclear weapons persists, and no sharp distinction between "atoms for peace" and "atoms for war" can be maintained. The fear that the expansion of nuclear power would inevitably increase the risk of proliferating nuclear weapons in the world arouses anxiety in many quarters.

4. The environmental protection campaign which gained importance in the early 1970's affirms that nuclear energy poses an immense new and long-term threat to human beings and their environment, and argues the case for developing alternative renewable and ecologically safe energy sources. The existence of long-lasting nuclear wastes appears to foreclose unnecessarily the options for future generations. The waste storage problem will get larger and larger; the time scales involved have few historical parallels. People, governments, and even the nuclear scientific community find it hard to measure the dimensions of this threat to the future.

5. Disillusionment with both the technological basis of Western civilization, and the scientists and technologists themselves has become widespread. Has technology gradually become the master rather than the servant of mankind? Have technologists, through extravagant claims made in apparent self-interest, lost — or worse still, betrayed — the trust placed in them by an overly naive society? Nuclear energy, with the stigma of its violent birth, accompanied by unfulfilled predictions of energy too-cheap-to-meter, and highly publicized accidents and near-accidents, surrounded by an air of mystery and élitism reinforced by specialized industrial and governmental nuclear development groups, has inevitably become a lightning rod attracting criticism from many sides.

With regard to the place of nuclear technology among other various possibilities for future energy production, increasingly broad assessments, starting for the most part in the early and mid-1970's and scheduled to continue for many more years, show clearly that:

1. The days of cheap energy from petroleum, natural gas, and coal are not only over, but in fact never existed. The energy appeared to be cheap only because no account was taken of the finiteness of its sources and because they were used at a much more moderate rate in the past than they are today.

2. The use of "new" resources, such as coal used in more environmentally acceptable form, nuclear power, controlled fusion, and the many forms of solar power, is made difficult by high cost, availability in time, environmental hazards, or some combination of these.

3. The new resources — especially the non-nuclear ones — have received insufficient critical attention, and the consequent lack of information is likely to lead to unbalanced public judgements and administrative decisions.

Several consequences have flowed from these various considerations. One has been an increasing awareness that the nuclear problem cannot easily be separated from other energy problems, nor indeed from those of the application of science and technology in general. As a result, the churches' participation in the debate has become correspondingly more complex. Another has been the realization that energy use itself has limits, depending both upon location and upon its technological form. If, then, energy use is to be expensive, limited, and unlikely to be environmentally benign, strategies of conservation and more efficient use become increasingly attractive. Acceptance of those strategies adds new ambiguity to the nuclear energy debate. On the one hand, are those who see conservation, solar power, and careful use of other resources as permitting more limited use (or even phasing out) of nuclear power, to which the same objections are still applied. On the other hand, we find those who are increasingly alarmed by the difficulty of developing other new options, either at all or in time, and who see nuclear power as a necessary thing and a conditional good.

Thus the stage was set for the beginning of "a vibrant debate" as governments were made aware of the decline of public confidence in the existing institutions for maintaining and securing the nuclear fuel cycle.

It was at this point that the churches began their first tentative entry into the debate. The first ecumenical discussions at the World Conference on Science and Technology for Human Development in Bucharest, Rumania, June 1974, led to a difficult and inconclusive discussion of "the nuclear power option" at the close of the meeting. The issue could not be resolved and the Conference report simply observed that:

> "It remains an open question whether the widespread proliferation of nuclear power plants is a desirable choice for society to make. Yet throughout the Western world there are already clear signs of a growing

dependence on this form of energy production. Since national energy policies are prepared in isolation, it is doubtful that the collective international impact of these rapidly expanding construction programmes has been systematically assessed." (Report of the WCC Conference on Science and Technology for Human Development, *Anticipation*, Nov. 1974, p. 9.)

The Conference agreed to recommend that "the WCC should initiate a study of the major moral, economic, social and scientific implications of the extension of atomic energy plants in the world", a recommendation endorsed by the Central Committee of the WCC in August 1974. This was the start of a programme of ecumenical enquiry and encounter about nuclear energy, which began with the first Ecumenical Hearing on Nuclear Energy in Sigtuna, Sweden, in June 1975. The work was reviewed by the Nairobi Assembly of the WCC in December 1975, which noted that "the ecumenical discussion of these issues has just begun and needs to be continued".

Some churches felt that this was a technical issue primarily for the countries with nuclear capability, and questioned the importance attached to its discussion in ecumenical circles. In other situations, as in the USA, National Councils of Churches became convinced of their responsibility to challenge national nuclear power programmes, especially the use of plutonium fuel.

As more and more countries entered the debate about nuclear power, people began to ask about the attitude of their churches. Thus many church leaders found themselves increasingly caught up in the moral and social aspects of an issue on which they had little or no technical experience or understanding. At the same time, Christian action groups in many countries began to commit themselves to the struggle against nuclear energy, contributing thus to greater awareness of the problem and also to polarization on this issue in and outside the Church.

Many more churches and Christian councils have now entered a period of intense activity, seeking to discern in their own situation what the Christian responsibility might be. Reports have been or are in the process of being prepared by church-appointed Study Commissions in Sweden, France, the Federal Republic of Germany, the Netherlands, the USA, the UK, Canada, Denmark and Italy, and by the end of 1978 the extent of Christian agreement and disagreement may become clearer. However, in many other situations, Christian opinion is only becoming aware of the problem and has not yet reacted. (It is noteworthy that the Roman Catholic Church has offered no opinion on the nuclear issue, though individual Roman Catholic leaders have expressed their concern.)

Some of the reports already received stress the difficulties of formulating Christian opinion on issues of such ethical and technical complexity. Most of the churches have no system for analysing the ethical problems of nuclear energy. And while churches often have within their own membership large numbers of scientists and technologists competent in this field, they lack an organized method of communicating with them, and are unable to make effective use of their insights. The churches' efforts to undertake a careful evaluation are also complicated by the pressure from interest groups strongly for or against nuclear energy, pressures which, for reasons already described, lead to an oversimplified polarization.

III. The Moral Dilemma Deepens

Despite the campaigns to try to halt the use of nuclear power, it is spreading to more and more countries. An increasing number of nations — capitalist, socialist, developing and developed — are making plans to initiate or enlarge a nuclear power programme. Even in countries like the USA, where the programme has been slowed by public opposition, the question of energy resources for the future has not been resolved and the present government policy is to maintain the nuclear power option while pressing forward with research on alternatives. And despite the obvious risks associated with nuclear technology, governments are convinced that they cannot run what they feel is the greater risk of leaving their peoples without the power it provides. Hence, while the development of nuclear energy in certain areas may be slowed down, the possibility of stopping its use worldwide, despite the widespread fears about it, appears slight.

How are the churches to interpret this paradoxical situation of national governments maintaining and even extending their commitment to nuclear energy despite widespread opposition to it? And how are they to evaluate the ethical position of the anti-nuclear movements which include many of their members? By what criteria shall the different arguments, pro and con, be measured? These are questions which give the nuclear debate its special theological and ethical significance.

If nations today feel obliged to enter the nuclear age the reason is two-fold: (1) Nuclear technology as human knowledge gives power over nature. Like all knowledge it is ambiguous in its ethical consequences, but for many scientists it is no more ambiguous than many other forms of technological power already employed. To try to stop entirely its further development would be an arbitrary action and difficult to maintain on the basis of accepted technological and social practice. The challenge to it must therefore be discriminate and specific, not general and absolute. (2) Nuclear technology is also political and economic power. The great industrial nations and some small ones already depend on it for their national economic welfare and military security. In a world in which practically all international relations are based on power, other nations cannot be expected to reject such an important source.

For these reasons the ecumenical evaluation of nuclear energy is not able to produce a simple "yes" or "no" response. The churches are not in a position to resolve the unresolved technical disputes and dilemmas around which much of the ethical uncertainty arises. As the WCC paper on "Public Acceptance of Nuclear Power" presented to the International Conference on the Nuclear Fuel Cycle (Salzburg, 1977) makes clear:

> "Religious traditions offer no ready made answer to the right use of nuclear technology... A critical attitude towards technological reason must not lead to social confusion, to delight in the irrational, to the veneration of simplistic and utopian solutions to human problems... The churches and religious leaders are not in a position of moral superiority but share the uncertainty which afflicts our contemporary culture." (*Anticipation*, No. 24, p. 15.)

And the WCC statement adds:

> "We cannot live as though nuclear energy had not been discovered... We shall find no quick solution to our dilemma, either by abandoning nuclear energy entirely or by devising fool-proof means to control it. The technological system has brought us great benefits but it has also led into new dangers. Nuclear energy epitomizes this dilemma."

In a more recent statement by the WCC Energy Advisory Group it is said:

> "The assumption at this stage of the exchange is that nuclear technology is a fact and the world is faced with the problem of developing appropriate institutions for the just distribution of its benefits and the control of its dangers."

This is not a counsel of despair or fatalism. Nor is it based on exaggerated confidence either in the ability of nuclear technicians to solve all the problems of nuclear power, or in the ability of technology in general to resolve social dilemmas. It is a form of Christian realism which assumes that history cannot be suddenly reversed, which accepts the ambiguity of all human endeavour and which recognizes that a thin line often separates humanity from disaster in the use of what its technological ingenuity has unleashed. As the Central Committee of the WCC said in its statement on nuclear energy in 1976:

> "The validity of underlying presuppositions of faith and values that appear in the debate over the future role of nuclear energy needs to be acknowledged and examined. The paradox of nuclear energy in offering the prospect of immense potential and many incalculable risks remains totally unresolved."

This emerging ecumenical approach is in contrast to other views held within the churches.

1. *The Anti-Nuclear Movement — Theological Objections*

One segment of the Christian anti-nuclear movement argues on theological-ethical grounds for an absolute "no" to nuclear energy, whether for civil or military use. From their perspective, nuclear energy is a technology which is against God's will and must be totally rejected. A recent expression of this point of view is to be found in the statement of the Christian wing of *Mobilization for Survival*, a movement launched in the USA in 1977 with the support of some American religious leaders. Their statement proposes four objectives for 1978, the year of UN emphasis on disarmament: Zero Nuclear Weapons; Ban Nuclear Power; Stop the Arms Race; and Fund Human Needs. In a "pastoral letter" this group declares:

> "Sisters and brothers... the nuked conscience of political, military and economic interests has seized on the lives of our people, with astonishing arrogance — would seize on the sovereignty of our God. The spirit of money, the spirit of violence, symbolized in the boiling frenzy of nuclear weaponry mocks the spirit of the Lord, blasphemously anoints not the servants of the Lord but the nuclear idols and their benighted adorers. They bring bad news to the poor, they proclaim enslavement of the free, they inflict blindness on insightful people, they tread underfoot the freedoms of all, they proclaim a demonic Year of the Neutron." ("A Pastoral Letter on Human Survival", *Engage/Social Action*, published by the Board of Church and Society, United Methodist Church, Vol. 6, No. 1, January 1978, pp. 27-28.)

The statement maintains that no compromise is possible with nuclear technology in any form and denies any capacity of governments to distinguish between its military and its peaceful use.

There have been other and more theologically developed critiques of the human employment of nuclear energy, which do not reject its use absolutely but which argue that the nuclear scientific community has been operating on the basis of doubtful myths concerning the human use of technological power. Lacking clear criteria of judgement, nuclear scientists and governments are tempted to accept uncritically the promises of such technology. A recent paper asks:

> "Are we not at the parting of the ways? We can take the road of Faust and Prometheus or we can take the road that the truly wise men among our ancestors have indicated. We can go ahead with every possible application of scientific knowledge without having seriously reflected on the consequences for society and for man's environment, in the hope that somehow everything will come out all right. Or we can choose a truly responsible course of action which would mean that we carefully count the cost, not only for ourselves, but for future generations, and not only

in terms of the welfare of men, but also in terms of the integrity of the cosmic order." [3]

However, this does not answer the question of how the limits to the use of nuclear science and technology are to be set.

2. *The Anti-Nuclear Movement — Technical Objections*

Another body of Christian opinion rests the case for stopping the use of nuclear power primarily on technical grounds: there are safe and workable alternative sources of energy like solar and wind power. Even if they are not entirely workable yet, they will be shortly. It would be wise therefore to conserve energy radically and press forward with the development of these alternative sources.

This viewpoint, in combination with some elements of the theological argument, also underlies most of the movements for a moratorium on the future development of nuclear energy.

IV. The Dialectic between Ethic and Technique

Ecumenical reflection on nuclear energy tends to be in conflict with the views of those who assume that there is a clear separation between ethical and technical judgements — and that while the technical issues of nuclear energy might be difficult and unresolved, the ethical questions at least have straightforward "yes" or "no" answers. The ecumenical consensus thus far is that since ethical choices depend in part on technical possibilities, they cannot be resolved by theologians or other Christians working in isolation from those with technical knowledge. Hence the ecumenical approach assumes the necessity for a dialogue of scientists of differing views with theologians and with the public.

Unless we absolutely exclude the human use of nuclear energy on the basis of some *a priori* ethical principle, we are challenged to determine the extent and the conditions of its use. In his presentation of the WCC paper to the international conference on nuclear energy at Salzburg in 1977, Dr. John Francis of Scotland made this point when he observed that "the harnessing of nuclear energy is not an unnatural phenomenon, but rather an exceptional phenomenon, capable of setting a unique challenge to the ingenuity and moral courage of people everywhere". This means that the outcome of the disputes between scientists and technologists are crucial to the further ethical evaluation of nuclear energy whether it is concerned with the measurement of risk, the security of the reactor, the reliability of the nuclear waste disposal system, or other technical issues. The churches have no answers to these technical aspects "but they are aware that most of the technical judgements involve some assumptions about human good. Since

---

[3] See essay by W. A. VISSER 'T HOOFT on "The Nuclear Mythology", *The Tablet*, March 25/April 1, 1978, a Roman Catholic bi-weekly magazine in the UK.

such technology also poses new social and ethical consequences, the values that guide technological processes require constant scrutiny and discussion. The question must be raised whether technological processes are actually serving the ends intended or whether they are proceeding by a momentum of their own that overrides human values."

The WCC paper on *The Public Acceptance of Nuclear Energy* addresses itself to the subtle relation between technical matters and our concern for human values:

> "It would be convenient, if it were possible, to separate neatly goals and values from techniques and means, to assume that societies decide their goals, then enlist scientific technologies to realize them. But in fact technology influences goals. Sometimes it suggests or makes possible new goals not previously envisioned. At other times the technical means used to achieve some goals destroy possibilities of achieving other equally important ones. Any sharp separation of technology from human values greatly over-simplifies the dialectics of the relation between technology and society... The problem is to devise new ways by which technological developments (like nuclear energy) can be examined... in creative dialogue between technical experts, governments and the public as part of a responsible decision-making process."

V. The Proliferation of Nuclear Weapons

An important part of the Christian evaluation of nuclear power relates to the danger of the further proliferation of nuclear weapons. This fear underlies the present campaign against the reprocessing of nuclear waste (which could put the plutonium in the wastes into more readily available form, for use in bombs or as more reactor fuel), and to halt or severely control the export of nuclear technology, or the mining and sale of uranium.

The debate about nuclear proliferation is beset with contradictions. In the interest of stopping proliferation, some Christians favour stopping the export of all nuclear technology. However unless the present nuclear powers halt their own nuclear energy and weapons programme, this would only lead to greater disparity of power between the countries already possessing nuclear reactors and weapons and those without. As another example, the campaign against the mining and the sale of uranium (as in Australia and Sweden) might, if successful, actually encourage reprocessing of spent fuel and the development of breeder reactors in countries which have embarked on a nuclear programme, and which would be short of fuel if the embargo on uranium mining were achieved. This therefore is another area where, with the best of intentions, the campaign against nuclear energy may end up achieving the opposite of what it seeks.

Fortunately up until now little commercial reprocessing of spent reactor fuel has taken place and some time exists to reflect upon the problems. It is clear to all that if nuclear fission power is to be an energy resource for the long term, then breeder reactors will be needed. Those reactors that now exist, as advanced experimental devices or early commercial prototypes, generally turn the non-fissionable species of uranium into fissionable plutoniom, which can then undergo fission to provide energy. But the nuclear fuel must be reprocessed from time to time, to remove various nuclear wastes, to purify the uranium and plutonium, and to reconstitute the fuel. All this set of activities is generally known as the full nuclear fuel cycle. A difficulty with it is that unless very particular precautions are taken, plutonium can be made available for weapons.

The decision whether or not to engage in the full fuel cycle with breeders is the central point now in the nuclear debate. The dilemma posed by this development of the breeder reactor will be even more difficult to resolve, since its use promises to provide a way of resolving the energy problem almost indefinitely. The immediate question here is whether nations should continue to experiment with breeder technology in the hope that a reasonably safe technology will be discovered; or whether all further experiments in this direction should be banned on the grounds that the temptation to use a less safe form of the technology (if nothing better is forthcoming) will be very great once it exists. Some countries, especially those without domestic supplies of conventional energy fuels, and having to depend also on import of fuel for nuclear reactors, feel they have no choice but to develop as quickly as possible reprocessing technology and the breeder reactor. Other countries, especially those with their own sources of uranium (USA, Canada), have urged that commercial reprocessing and development of the breeder be postponed! The debate is thus complicated by a series of political and technical factors which make it difficult to distinguish the self-serving arguments of the nuclear haves and the nuclear have-nots from those which have validity in the search for a just solution for all. The challenge posed to the churches is twofold: to demand careful examination at the international level of the security of reprocessing and breeder technology; and to help develop the international institutions and agreements which would be needed if it is agreed that this additional nuclear technology would serve world energy needs in the long run.

VI. The International Sharing of Nuclear Technology for Peaceful Uses

Closely related to the concern for proliferation of nuclear weapons is the issue of "sharing" nuclear technology, especially in view of the relatively modest international machinery now deployed to safeguard against nuclear materials being diverted into weapons. Those opposed to nuclear power are naturally against its export to more countries. In this they believe they are working also in the best interest of those countries whose governments seek access to nuclear technology.

This argument assumes that the countries without nuclear technology will accept to remain nuclear have-nots while the nuclear haves are being persuaded to abandon the use of nuclear energy in terms both of nuclear weapons and of civilian reactor programmes. Not surprisingly, this argument does not at the moment have very much credibility with the peoples of the non-nuclear nations. They tend to believe that the sincere intentions of the anti-nuclear movements within the nuclear "have" countries will be exploited by the leaders of these countries to maintain their present monopoly of nuclear technology, without any guarantee that the "have" nations will diminish their own reliance on nuclear power. In the words of a recent report of the WCC Energy Advisory Group:

> "... it is fair to say that the position of groups opposed to the use of nuclear power, especially in industrialized countries, fails to meet the criterion relating to the right of access of all countries to nuclear technology. Their credibility in the eyes of countries seeking access will therefore continue to be limited unless they prove capable of altering the course of nuclear energy development, both military and civil, in the industrialized countries."

A just international method of sharing nuclear technology would, in the view of the Energy Advisory Group, necessitate bringing the sensitive areas of the nuclear fuel cycle under international control. "This would be an alternative to a policy of denial, and assure access to the technology with non-discriminatory guarantees. Even if this is not yet politically possible, it is the goal towards which we must work and the only basis for overcoming the present distrust." However, at the moment the countries having nuclear technology very largely determine who shall receive it and on what conditions. They have formed a nuclear suppliers club which has set out the conditions for the transfer of such technology. This is an intolerable situation from the standpoint of the nations seeking access to nuclear technology, and can in the long run only provoke them to greater efforts in this direction. The first ecumenical consultation on nuclear energy in 1975 was very much aware of this problem and expressed itself unequivocally:

> "It is difficult on political and moral grounds to deny countries without nuclear technology the right to obtain it because of a fear that they might use it for the development of nuclear weapons. The proposition that the appropriation of nuclear technology would forever be a limited right, to be doled out by the present nuclear countries according to rules determined by their interest, is unacceptable. This would be an intolerable situation for many developing countries seeking to benefit from the peaceful application of nuclear energy and throw off technological domination by the already industrialized countries." (*Facing Up to Nuclear Power*, p. 193.)

None of the present solutions to the access question is satisfactory. All reflect the political interests which prevailed when the present forms of cooperation were developed. They must now be amended to conform with the interests of more people. Since knowledge and use of nuclear technology will inevitably spread, it is in the interests of the nuclear nations to use their advantage today to overcome resentment and distrust before it is too late.

VII. Nuclear Energy and the Participatory Society

The churches appear to agree on one point — that there should be the widest possible discussion of the issues relating to the use of nuclear energy. Decisions governing its utilization have to be taken in a new context. Or as the current ecumenical formula has it, it must be measured by its contribution to the search for the just, participatory and sustainable society.

This means that scientists and technologists have to overcome a tendency to ignore or treat lightly the public questions. This will not be easy. The WCC position paper presented to the Salzburg conference in 1977 noted that:

> "Within each country already possessing a basic capability in nuclear technology, certain assumptions have already been made governing the scale, availability and general disposition of their future nuclear development. Such assumptions are now open to challenge. The days of great expectation arising from the birth of nuclear technology have now been foreclosed by the days of decision under uncertainty that presently characterize nuclear power developments in many countries. Surely few are politically naive enough to suggest that nuclear technology could be abandoned; but a new sense of realism is undoubtedly abroad and challenges to a high level of nuclear dependence must be answered. If public confidence in the future deployment of the technology is further eroded, then re-establishing such confidence will prove undoubtedly to be even harder."

The same paper notes that the churches and the public also have to learn a new discipline if they are to participate responsibly in the public debate:

> "The churches share the temptation to reach a verdict quickly, influenced as they are by a great variety of pressure groups and so-called experts on one side or the other. Pronouncements of this type usually over-simplify the point on which the churches might have something to say: the ethical or theological dimension..."

The "informed public examination of these issues" which the churches should encourage will oblige them to give more careful attention to the social and technical implications of the technological situation in which we live. It is a long-run enterprise where categoric ethical answers may be few but where discriminate ethical judgement may be decisive for the human future.

In the interest of gaining time for such public participation and to answer the need for more information and continued dialogue, there is often the demand for a moratorium, especially on such further technological developments as reprocessing and the commercial development of the breeder reactor. The WCC study statements and papers emphasize that much then depends on the good faith of those demanding the moratorium: "Is it a tactic to avoid making a decision or to delay a decision without regard to the consequences?"; or is it providing "an opportunity for an informed public discussion and the communication of continuing research on the technical problems..." essential to a responsible public decision?

It would appear from the nature of the problem — its centrality in future plans of many industrialized countries; the difficulty of finding alternative energy sources; the absence of simple, absolute solutions; the polarization of the debate; the existence of moral and ethical dimensions so far largely unperceived (or if so, selectively unattended) — that the churches can and must contribute.

Questions and Themes for Discussion

1. Define energy, energy cost, energy conservation, fossil fuel, nuclear power, renewable energy resources.

2. Discuss the questions listed on page 89. How have they entered the local/national energy considerations in your own country?

3. Find out the percentage dependencies of your own country on the various energy resources: oil, gas, coal, hydropower, wood, renewable, nuclear.

4. Find out how energy is used in your community. What proportions are used for heat, electricity and transport? What proportions are used in the various sectors: domestic, commercial, industry, service, transport?

5. What is the energy growth rate in your country, how does it compare to the world average of 5%, and where is the growth occurring?

6. Are there sections of your community whose basic energy needs are not being met?

7. What steps have you taken or could take to modify your own energy use?

8. List the measures that seem appropriate for a national energy conservation programme in your community, in the immediate future and in the longer term. Refer back to question 4, and consider potential savings within each end use and each sector.

9. Which of the renewable resources and technologies are most appropriate in your country? What is being done to develop them? What more could be done? Is there opposition to their development and where does it come from? What are the arguments for and against?

10. List some of the environmental impacts of energy use. How do present ways of using energy affect the quality of life in your area, and what improvements are possible?

11. What are the present energy policies of your national and local governments and political parties? Are they adequate in the light of the world energy problem? Do they take into account: a global perspective, a long-term perspective, demand as well as supply, social equity and quality of life, environmental impact of energy use, participation? Are there better alternative strategies?

12. What are your conclusions as to the meaning of justice and sustainability as they apply to energy? Discuss the personal and public actions which could be taken to further the aim of a just and sustainable energy economy.

III.

Food, Resources, Environment and Population — Key Areas for New Technological Policies

10 · Food: The Prospects

Hundreds of millions of people in the world today are not getting enough food to lead fully active healthy lives. The UN study in preparation for the World Food Conference in 1974 found 460 million people to be undernourished in 1970. In July 1974, world grain stocks reached their lowest level in 20 years. Whereas in 1961 we had a 105-day reserve, by 1974 this had dropped to 33 days and has not recovered since. The decline in stocks has been accompanied by a sharp increase in prices. Those who go short of food are those unable to pay.

A poor harvest in any major food producing country such as the USA and USSR sends shock waves throughout the food sector of the world economy and even beyond. A poor harvest in developing countries inevitably results in starvation and malnutrition. This happened in six countries bordering the southern end of the Sahara desert in the early seventies, where the drought is believed to have killed 100,000 people. In India, in 1972, in the three states of Bihar, Orissa and Uttar Pradesh, hunger probably claimed 929,000 lives. The brunt of global food scarcity is borne by the poorest people in the poorest countries, and among them it is the very young and the very old who suffer most.

After the year 2000, the prospect is worse. According to the study of the Dutch economist Hans Linneman, whereas there were about 300 million people in 1975 with two-thirds minimum protein requirements, by the year 2010 this will have gone to one billion. Asia which has 57% of the world's population is expected to become more food deficient. There have to be radical changes in the production and distribution and consumption of food if this grim prospect is to be at all alleviated.

The Food Impasse

The food impasse is to be understood in terms of four components: supply, demand, distribution and waste.

Supply: In the past decade, supply per capita has increased in the developed countries which were already well fed. The per capita supply remained about constant in the developing countries where a significant proportion of the population is hungry. In these 10 years, perhaps half a billion people have been added to the number who have inadequate diets. This is because of the rapid population growth. So while the proportion of the world's people suffering from inadequate food remained about the same, there are many millions more hungry people today than there were 10 years ago.

Demand: In the developing countries, there has been no great increase in the capacity of individuals to buy food. The growth in demand has therefore come chiefly as a consequence of population growth. In the developed countries, on the other hand, there has been an increase in the demand for food, largely as a consequence of increased affluence. Meat consumption per head in the USA and USSR doubled between 1960 and 1972 despite price increases. It also rose sharply in Japan in this period. The very high meat consumption in Argentina and, to a lesser extent, in Australia has fallen away somewhat with rising meat prices in relation to income. In the decade of the sixties, the per capita consumption of food in the developed countries increased from 116% of what is required to 123%, while that of developing countries increased from 91% of what is required to 95%. Not only did the gap increase but so did wasteful consumption in developed countries which rose from 10% to 23%.

In poor countries, the average person consumes slightly over half a kilogram of grain a day. The average American consumes the equivalent of five times as much. He eats about one quarter of a kilogram directly as cereal products. The remainder is consumed indirectly as meat and dairy products derived mostly from grain feed. Consumers in poor countries have a great desire for animal protein, but few can afford it. For example, average per capita expenditure on food in India has been estimated at US $36 per year, about 10 cents a day, out of a total annual income of $63. Under such constraints, proteins are consumed mainly as natural ingredients of the chief hunger satisfiers — cereals and pulses.

Distribution: Maldistribution is a major factor in the world food crisis. If all the food available in the world were divided equally among all the people in the world, would everyone's nutritive requirements be satisfied? There is no altogether straightforward answer since nutritionists are not sure what are the real needs of people in general or of particular groups. There is more agreement on calorie requirements than on protein requirements which since 1971 have been estimated to be considerably less than was previously believed. According to recent estimates of the Food and Agriculture Organization, the world consumption of calories in 1970 was 101% of per capita requirements; that of protein was 173%. That is to say, if the food available were equally divided among all the inhabitants of the earth, we would all have enough calories, perhaps even more than enough, and we would all have an excess of proteins. Despite a number of perhaps questionable assumptions behind such estimates, one fact is certain: most of today's hunger can be traced to problems of distribution. This fact is further emphasized in the following table:

Percent of calories and proteins requirements in different regions of the world that were satisfied in 1970

	Calories	Proteins
World	101%	173%
High income countries	121	229
USSR and Eastern Europe	124	239
Developing countries	96	147
Asia and Far East	93	141
Africa	93	141
Latin America	106	172
Near East	97	147

The high income countries consumed much more than their needs and much more than developing countries. In developing countries, the proteins available would have sufficed if equally distributed, but calories were in short supply.

It is important to appreciate that at present only about 4% of total world food production crosses national boundaries, so any attempt to make a major impact on distribution between nations would need a prior major increase in world transport facilities.

One of the major inequities of maldistribution is what is known as "the protein drain". There is now what Georg Borgstrom has called a "protein empire" with Europe, Japan and, more recently, the USSR the major constituents. In the form of grain, oilseed and oilmeal, which of course include much more than protein, Europe produces each year more protein to feed cattle, pigs and poultry than either Africa or India consumes annually as human food. Each of the UK, Italy and the Federal Republic of Germany receives far more grain than India, while India is the top ranking exporter of peanut protein! Fisheries provide one-fifth of the world's animal protein but more than half the ocean catch each year moves to the feeding troughs of the well-to-do world. Most of the Peruvian anchovette fishery (normally about one-tenth of total world fish production) goes to the rich world as fish meal to be fed to livestock and pets. If it were transformed into a high quality product suitable for human consumption and distributed within Latin America, it would probably completely make up the present protein shortage among the poor there. In a world where money, not need, determines the international flow of goods, poor nations all too often export food that is needed at home.

Maldistribution between nations is only part of the story. In virtually all countries, some people are well fed while others go hungry. This is evident from the table above. Millions in the USA do not have an adequate diet. The poorest people in countries like Mexico and Brazil have not shared in what income improvement there has been. They continue to subsist on marginal food supplies.

Waste: Loss of food through waste is enormous. An estimated half of the world's food may be destroyed each year by insects, rats and other pests either in the field or during storage and shipment. Some experts believe that a reduction in these losses may be the fastest way to increase substantially the food available. During the last locust plague in Africa, in one month in 1959 in Ethiopia alone the insects devoured a year's supply of grain for one million people.

What appears to be needed is some combination of increasing supply, reducing demand, altering distribution and cutting waste. That may sound simple. In practice, the necessary changes seem almost impossible to achieve. Many now think that the chances are so slight that there will be a great increase in deaths due to starvation well before the end of the century, quite possibly before 1980.

Constraints on Food Production

The main sources of food now and for the foreseeable future are agriculture and fisheries. The development of synthetic foods and of "single cell proteins", that is, yeasts and microorganisms grown on petroleum or methane, is, as yet, in an early stage. Fisheries are important as a source of animal protein. While the amount of food from the sea increased remarkably between 1950 and 1970, since then yields have been declining at least in part as a result of overfishing. At most, the present fish yield might eventually be doubled, though this now seems unlikely. A possible new source of sea food is plankton and squid, but this does not look feasible in the foreseeable future.

There are physical constraints on the quantities of food that can be produced through agriculture. Production is dependent upon five resources: land, fertilizers, water, energy and capital. All are becoming scarce.

Land. About half the land potentially suitable for agriculture is under cultivation today. It is the best half. Most of the remainder would require immense capital inputs, such as for irrigation, before it would be ready to produce food. The FAO has projected a possible increase of 20% in agricultural land in the developing world by the end of the century. This would involve a doubling or even trebling of irrigation. Much of the potentially cultivable land is in the tropics, and experience has shown that the farming of tropical soils is often not economical. Furthermore, the extension of cultivated land inevitably involves an environmental cost, especially in the tropics, where there is often an ultimate loss in soil productivity. We need to ask whether we want an earth on which every square metre that could grow a crop is cleared, terraced and irrigated, leaving little or no wilderness and forest. The cost of developing new land is so great that more hope is to be placed in increasing productivity of existing cultivated areas. And there we face other critical limits.

Water.   The lack of fresh water is the principal constraint on expanded food production in the rest of this century. It is already the main constraint operating in the Green Revolution. The global demand for fresh water will increase by 250% by the end of the century. To satisfy this demand will require immense capital investment in dams, irrigation systems and necessary conservation procedures.

Fertilizers.   Since 1973, there has been a world shortage of fertilizers. Prices of many fertilizers doubled or even trebled between 1973 and 1974. The quadrupling of the price of phosphate rocks from Morocco, the world's leading source of critically important phosphatic fertilizers, affects the cost of food production almost everywhere. Many developing countries which are highly dependent upon fertilizers are unable to buy the huge amounts which they now need. If India were to apply fertilizers as intensely as the Netherlands, its needs would amount to nearly half the present world output. The prospect for the next few years at least is that the prices of both nitrogenous and phosphatic fertilizers will continue to rise, with the poor, as usual, being priced out of the market. What can be done? Developed countries could restructure their farming systems to reduce substantially their fertilizer requirements while retaining the productivity of the land. The developing countries are dependent upon fertilizers from developed countries for at least half their needs. This dependence could be reduced by the investment of capital in fertilizer plants in these countries. Furthermore, where feasible, organic fertilizers such as dung and green manure crops could reduce dependence on chemical fertilizers.

Energy.   The energy needs of modern agriculture, food processing and food transportation are enormous. In the USA, about 10 times as many calories of energy are used to cultivate and fertilize the land, grow the crop, transport it and retail it as our bodies derive from it. About 90% of this energy goes into transporting and processing the food. But the energy costs of even growing and harvesting the crop by modern agricultural methods are huge compared with those of "primitive" agriculture. For every calorie of energy put into growing a corn crop, the yield is only 2.8 calories. In the USA the equivalent of 160 gallons of gasoline is used to raise one hectare of corn. By comparison, in rice paddies in China, one calorie input gives 50 calories of crop yield. The Tsembaga tribe in the Highlands of New Guinea gets 25 calories for every calorie input. The cost of moving from "primitive" to modern agriculture is a huge "energy subsidy". For animal products, the energy costs are many times greater. This is because it takes about 10 kilograms of grain to produce one kilogram of beef, five kilograms to produce one of pork and three kilograms to produce one of poultry. The grains and other plant products now fed to cattle, pigs and poultry in the developed countries could go a long way to alleviating hunger around the world. The Green Revolution depends upon high energy use technology. The question now arises as to whether with rising fuel prices developing countries will be able to afford this huge energy cost. To reduce energy inputs, agriculture might substitute some of the manpower currently being displaced by machines, use organic rather than chemical fertilizers, and incorporate other practices characteristic of "primitive" agriculture such as multiple crops in single fields to reduce pest infestations. The food needed in the developing world is mainly plant products. The developed world could produce more of these if it would confine meat production to pastoral lands unsuited to crops. This would also conserve energy. But the rich countries invest a lot of their agricultural effort in products such as meat "to tickle the palates of the rich rather than to fill the bellies of the poor".

We cannot continue indefinitely to increase the "energy subsidy" of food production. It has been estimated that to feed 13 thousand million people (the projected size of the world population by 2080) at Western European standards would require as much energy as the entire world now uses for all purposes. This estimate, moreover, includes only the energy for food production; it does not include the energy needed for transport and processing. Nor was the probable ecological impact of such a programme assessed, and this would be enormous.

The Green Revolution

The mid-sixties saw the launching of a remarkable effort to expand food production in food-deficient countries. It was centred around the development of high-yielding dwarf wheats and rices. With adequate fertilizers, these new strains could produce double the yield of indigenous strains. As a result, India doubled its wheat crop in six years. There were also remarkable increases in yields in Mexico, the Philippines, Pakistan, Turkey and other countries. Mexico and the Philippines even became exporters of grain. However, by the mid-seventies both these countries were importing again. For the whole of the developing world, the amount of food available per person increased only a little. This was because the rate of food production only just exceeded the rate of population growth. In the early years of the Green Revolution, many of those involved, including Norman Borlaug, the originator of the miracle seeds, cautioned that it was not a solution to the food problem. The solution depended rather upon putting the brakes on population growth. The Green Revolution was simply buying time, perhaps 15 to 20 years, to get population growth under control. Half of the time is now passed. Time will not be bought so cheaply again.

The Green Revolution has its hazards. It is dependent upon ample supplies of water, fertilizers and energy. These cost money and are getting short. An article on the Green Revolution entitled "More food means more hunger" in the UN *Development Forum* in 1975 described the effects of some large-scale efforts of agro-business in some developing countries which made a few people rich, left the original workers on the land worse off, and directed the produce to the relatively well off while the poor could not afford to buy the food. In recent years, successful agricultural efforts in developing countries have been increasingly linked to agricultural reform and a focus on the small farmer, as for example the programme of the World Bank in India.

The Task Ahead

There is obviously no simple answer to the question — how many people can the world feed? What we do know is that we are not feeding adequately the 4,000 million with us now, that we have no clear idea how we can cope with double this number 35 years hence, and, thirdly, that there is a limit to the productive capacity of the earth: overstress that capacity and productivity declines or ceases.

Zero hunger throughout the world could be achieved only by massive redistribution of food obtained through a drastic reduction of food consumption in developed countries, a massive increase in agriculture in developing countries and reduced population growth. Lester Brown has pointed out that a 5% reduction in meat consumption in the USA would "free" six million tons of grain a year, enough to feed 30 million people. Another important contribution could come from cutting down on grain feeding of beef.

In many countries the long-term needs for food will have to be satisfied by food grown within those countries. Until that utopian solution is approached, there is going to be an ever-present need for emergency food supplies. Nothing short of a world emergency food programme will suffice. The main component of this programme would be an international "food bank", controlled by an international agency and established in suitable regions. The purpose of the reserve would be to act as a buffer against food shortages during droughts and other emergencies. Despite hopes generated by the Green Revolution, weather is still the major factor in determining yields. When people say that weather, not mankind, is responsible for food shortages, they are evading the issue that "bad" weather is a characteristic feature of the earth. Crops are grown in many places where rainfall is unreliable and climate is changing, and where man may be contributing to this through atmospheric pollution. We must face up to the realities of "bad" weather and plan accordingly.

The concept of a food bank is not new. Joseph of Egypt advised the pharoahs that they should build reserves of grain during the fat years so as not to be caught short during the lean ones. At the World Food Conference in Rome in 1974, the concept received only limited support, partly because it runs counter to the present system of marketing food in the world by the large producers. It would also involve huge capital investments which would have to come mainly from the rich nations, including the oil-producing countries. Until the nations agree to some sort of emergency programme, it seems inevitable that increasingly severe mass starvation and famine will periodically strike different parts of the developing world with increasing intensity.

11 · Resources: Limits or No Limits?

A sustainable global society would be one that is so organized that it would not run out of essential resources. The finiteness of the earth imposes three constraints: there is a limit to the amount of renewable resources such as food and timber that can be produced, there is a limit to the amount of non-renewable resources that can be produced and consumed, and there is a limit to the pollution absorption capacity of the planet. It is these three that are the "limits to growth".

Defining Resource Limits

The publication in 1972 of *The Limits to Growth*, the first report of the Club of Rome, raised the spectre of a world running out of essential resources within the next 50 years or less. Since then, there has been widespread debate in the Western world on the urgency of this concern and on whether or not mankind can somehow stretch the limits indefinitely. All the studies in this period tend to conclude that we shall face no absolutely critical shortages within the next 30 years (apart from energy), but after that the future is quite uncertain. One fact is clear: the earth is finite; it has a finite quantity of fossil fuels, iron ore and all the other minerals used by industry. As these are used, they are used up, except as some are recycled back into industry. Any level of use, if sustained long enough, ultimately exhausts conventional non-renewable resources. This depletion can be postponed to some extent through the application of new and sophisticated technology. That is only feasible in a society that is rich enough and sufficiently well organized to generate scientific advances and to anticipate and deal with their side-effects.

According to the 1976 UN Report, "The Future of the World Economy", otherwise known as the Leontief Report, "The world is expected to consume during the last 30 years of the 20th century three to four times as many minerals as have been consumed through the whole previous history of civilization." The report anticipates that in such conditions lead and zinc would run out by the end of the century.

According to a report of the US Senate, the American people consumed in the decade 1959-69 more of the world's resources than had been consumed by all the people of the world throughout history. If everyone in the world were to consume resources at the American rate, the total known reserves of petroleum would be used up in six years and the annual consumption of timber, copper, sulphur, iron and water would exceed available known reserves of these resources. Our time is different from any other period in history because of the rates at which we use resources. The developed countries use most of the world's resources as a consequence of modern technology and industrialization.

The average person in the developed world today is surrounded by tons of steel, copper, aluminium, lead, tin, zinc and plastics, and is every day gobbling up 25 kilos of raw steel and many kilos of other minerals. Since these things are not available in sufficient quantities in his homeland, he ranges abroad in search of them much like a hunter, more often than not in the poorer countries.

If the standard of living of the developing world is to rise, massive additional quantities of resources will be needed to provide homes, factories, transport and other necessities. About one-third of the world's people now have electricity in their homes. Where is the energy to come from to provide electricity for even double the present number which still leaves about a third or more of the people without electricity? No one knows. The need for the world's resources is greatest in the developing countries where so many people still lack the basic necessities. But the demand for these resources is far greater in the rich world where the luxuries of today become the necessities of tomorrow.

The Choices before Us

When a resource becomes increasingly scarce, we have a number of options:

— try to increase the size of the stock;
— reduce the rate of consumption;
— recycle what is used;
— invent new technologies for extraction from low grade ores;
— discover an alternative resource.

Before examining these alternatives, we should look at the relationship between the size of the stock of any resource and the rate of consumption.[1]

---

[1] The distinction between the static and exponential life spans of a resource is one that is often confused. Economist Professor W. Beckerman, for example, in his spirited defence of economic growth often fails to make the distinction or he uses the static life span when he should be using the exponential life span. This leads to serious errors of judgment.

For example: a generous estimate of the coal reserves of the USA is 1.49×10^{12} metric tons. Coal has been described as "the only fuel in which the USA is totally self-sufficient". This would be a true statement if the 1972 rates of consumption were maintained indefinitely. The stocks would last for an infinitely long time. But if the annual rate of increase in consumption were to go up by 1% per year, the coal would all be gone in 342 years. With a 7% increase in the rate of consumption per year it would all be gone in 80 years! If the US coal reserves are to last through the nation's second 200 years, the rate of increase in coal consumption cannot exceed 2% per year. Or to take another example, at present rates of consumption, the world's coal reserves might last for 5,000 years. If the rate of consumption were to rise by 4% per year, they would all be gone in 135 years.

Supposing we have in the earth a reserve of a particular mineral that at present rates of consumption could last for 100 years. Suppose we plan to try to double the size of the stock by new discoveries so it might last 200 years or increase it by five times (500 years) or even 10 times (1,000 years). Suppose that we now increase the rate of consumption of each hypothetical reserve by 3% per annum. The 100 year stock will last only 47 years. The doubled stock would last 67 years, i.e. a mere 20 years longer. Doubling the stock from 500 to 1,000 also adds only 20 years to its life if consumption increased by 3% per annum. As the rate of consumption rises, increasing the size of the stock has progressively less effect on the length of time the stock will last. For example, at an increase in the depletion rate of 0.5% per annum, increasing the initial stock from 1,000 to 10,000 increases the survival time by 430 years; with an increase in the depletion rate of 8% per annum, the increase in survival time of the 10 times larger stock is merely 30 years.

Consider now the effect of varying the rate of consumption of a stock that at the present rate would last 10,000 years. Any growth at all in the rate of consumption has a really dramatic impact. For example, an average annual increase of only 1% reduces the life of the stock from 10,000 years to 464 years. With an increase in the rate of consumption of 4% per year, the life of the stock falls to a mere 153 years. A reduction of 3% per year in consumption has the same effect on the life of the stock as holding the rate of consumption constant (at 4%) and increasing the stock to 10 times the original level. The implication of these trade-offs is obvious. The higher the rate of growth in consumption, the less sensitive is the life span of a resource to errors and revisions in the estimate of the "true" stock. In terms of increasing the life span of a non-renewable resource, the pay off of quite a modest reduction in the rate of increase in its use is equivalent to a massive upward revision in the size of the stock.

In the race towards complete exhaustion, the pace of decline is seemingly slow at first but becomes an avalanche at the finish. The tortoise turns into a hare in the dash to the tape. All this means that "warning signs" of impending exhaustion are late to appear. The implication is clear. With respect to the process of depletion of non-renewable resources, what has happened in the past provides little if any guidance to what will happen in the future. Indeed, sole reliance on past trends could be disastrous. Secondly, just as the pay off is greater in terms of increasing the life span of a resource when efforts are directed towards reducing the rate of growth in its consumption rather than towards increasing the size of its stock, the same is true in terms of heeding earlier warning signs — a longer "breathing period" in which corrective action can be taken.

The most important conclusion to be drawn from these considerations is that in terms of prolonging the life of a resource and increasing the breathing space between the first warning signs and eventual exhaustion, efforts to reduce the rate of growth in consumption have results that are just as effective, and in many cases much more effective, than those produced by efforts to expand the size of the stock.

Increasing the size of the stock: Search and exploration tend to become more expensive as the stock declines. Oil is no longer drilled for in deserts but in the North Sea or in Alaska. With exponential rates of consumption, newly discovered stocks have to be huge to be worthwhile. For example, the world uses the equivalent of two Alaskan oil fields in a single year!

Reserves of nodular materials distributed over the ocean floor are estimated to be sufficient to sustain a mining rate of 400 million tons a year for a virtually unlimited period of time. If only 100 million tons of nodules were to be recovered every year — a target which appears to be within reach in the next 10 to 20 years — this would increase the annual current Western world production of copper, nickel, manganese and cobalt by roughly one-fourth, three times, six times and twelve times, respectively. The critical issues will probably be *a)* the amount of energy needed to extract the minerals, and *b)* whether exponential rates of consumption are applied to the new stocks.

Recycling the stock: This is one obvious way of avoiding waste. However, it involves high energy input and energy is not recyclable. Furthermore, recycling is never 100% complete. But even suppose it were; if total consumption is growing exponentially, the original stock will continue to be depleted, albeit at a slower rate than if no recycling at all were taking place. The critical point would eventually be reached (even with 100% recycling) when the total stock would be made up of recycled material; consumption could continue but further growth in consumption could not. So as long as we still have increasing rates of consumption, recycling does not solve our problem.

Invention of new technologies and extraction from low grade ores: We cannot predict with certainty what constraint-releasing technologies may appear in the future. As a general rule, the lower the grade, the more expensive and the more energy using is the extraction of minerals. Costs are often prohibitive. Aluminium can be extracted from clay. The rocks of the earth contain many minerals in very low concentrations. Theoretically the whole of the earth could be mined to get hold of them. But where are we to get the energy and where will we put the dross? Even if the energy were available, to what extent would this use contribute to thermal pollution and the possibility of reaching the heat ceiling of the planet? No one knows at present.

Discovery of alternative resources: When all the fossil fuel is gone perhaps plastics may be replaced with something else, and aluminium may be replaced with something else when the high grade ores are depleted. Perhaps not. There is no guarantee that technology will provide alternative resources in time and in requisite amounts. It is foolhardy to act as though technology will always come up with answers in time. The opponents of the argument for limits to growth say that it puts insufficient weight on the possibility of new technology saving the situation. It is, of course, true that science and technology have found substitutes for traditional materials that have become scarce. Wood is replaced by coal, coal is replaced by oil, and we are now trying to invent alternatives to oil. But it would be recklessly optimistic to infer from these past events that fears of a future dearth of materials are without foundation. Technological optimists are fond of recalling predictions of the past that did not eventuate — London would be clogged up with horse manure, paper would run out, and so on. But as Professor E. J. Misham has said "There is as much room for optimism in contemplating such precedents as there would be in reminding a sick man of 90 that he also thought he would never recover when he was 20." It is the unprecedented scale of current exploitation of the earth's limited resources that makes the qualitative difference between yesterday and today.

Reducing the rate of consumption of the resource: The present economic systems of both capitalist and socialist countries aim to maximize the through-put of goods and materials. If we wanted a sustainable state, we would aim to minimize it. In a resource-hungry world, there is no logically defensible argument for increasing rates of consumption except where this is necessary to fulfil basic human needs. There is nothing good about inbuilt obsolescence and the conversion of luxuries into necessities. We have already seen that reduced rates of consumption are by far the most effective device for sustaining supplies of a needed resource. Hence the argument for zero growth in the production and consumption of material goods. Reduced consumption and reduced waste are steps in this direction. Some industries, in an effort to be sustainable, have already reached the no-growth phase, for example the Norwegian timber industry. We should study the special needs and problems in no-growth industries and the relation of this to a total no-growth in material consumption economy in the rich world. This is not a totally new economic situation to face. Some countries now have almost a no-growth economy, e.g. New Zealand. Others had it earlier, e.g. France after World War I and up to 1930. And in both cases unemployment was minimal.

Toward an Ethic of Resource Use

There is a wide consensus of opinion that we have already entered the transitional period during which critical decisions must be taken and implemented concerning a major redirection of our technology, particularly as it relates to resource consumption. Although the length of this transition period in a particular economy will obviously depend on its present state of development, there are many who believe passionately that the main change of direction must take place within the time frame 1985 to 2000.

Since we do not know the precise limits of our physical resources, should we generally act *as though* the present known reserves are the only ones? We argue for such an approach on the grounds that it will minimize the risk of resource shortage for future generations.

This does not mean a halt in technological innovations. It does mean that we should not continue to waste resources on the assumption that future technological developments will satisfy our descendants' needs. It also means that we should first develop constraint-releasing technology, and test it to be reasonably sure that it is free from serious side effects. Only after such a breakthrough can society expand with confidence in that direction.

It may be argued that the breakthrough will not occur until sufficient incentive is provided for research and development in these areas. Basically this occurs because of our lack of emphasis on the future effects of current activities. The planning period for industrial societies should be extended forward to encompass this difficulty. A long planning period also reduces risk because it gives us more time to devise solutions to future problems. The scope of this concern falls outside the region of private enterprise and even in some cases of national government.

This risk argument provides an ethical basis for a new approach to technological innovation. This approach must include the following:

— monitoring of technological development for continuing evaluation by politicians and the public at large; this should be done on national levels and at the international level when appropriate (e.g. the supersonic transport);

— assessment of the environmental and social impact of new technology before it is introduced on a large scale;

— a conservation ethic that would achieve a more efficient and equitable use of non-renewable resources;

— a public which is well informed on these issues to provide the necessary political pressure for funding and developing a technology which reflects the values of the community.

Development of Resources — Organic Growth or Cancerous Growth?

The Limits to Growth argued the necessity of altering the direction in which the world was going. It argued for zero population growth in the world, for the reduction of economic growth in the production of consumer goods in the developed world and for an eventual transition to a stable or sustainable economy. It recognized the need for increased production of consumer goods in the developing countries until such time as this too might level off.

The second report of the Club of Rome, made in 1974 and entitled *Mankind at the Turning Point*, developed this latter point in more detail. The emphasis here was on the necessity of narrowing the existing gaps in use and availability of resources between the rich and the poor countries, if world shattering crises were to be avoided. It stressed that this could be accomplished only if the earth's finiteness was explicitly recognized and only within the concept of global unity. By global unity was meant the emerging world system of inter-dependent parts. It may be difficult to detect much unity in the present conglomeration of entities, each growing in a different direction and stumbling over the others in the process. While there is inadequate coordination between the parts, they *are* nevertheless inter-dependent. The image of global unity is that of a living body. The growth and development of one part depends upon the growth and development of others. When one part of the body has a cancerous growth, the well-being of the whole body is threatened. But in a healthy growing body the inter-relations of the parts act as a check on uncontrolled growth anywhere in the body. This insures organic growth as contrasted with uncontrolled or cancerous growth. One part does not develop at the expense of another. Growth is determined by the needs of the various parts in relation to the healthy functioning of the whole organism. Healthy organic growth in a living body takes place according to a master plan encoded in the genes in every cell of the body.

Such a master plan is missing in the processes of growth and development of the world as a system. The options facing mankind in the 20th century are to continue along the present path of cancerous uncoordinated growth or to start on the path of organic healthy growth.

Organic growth does not mean cessation in economic growth. It does mean that economic growth in developed countries will be different from that in developing countries. There will have to be less growth in the production and consumption of consumer goods in developed countries to counterbalance more in the poor countries. This does not mean that the rich countries will be foregoing necessities of life. It would mean that they would not make the luxuries of today the necessities of tomorrow. They would change the nature of growth — from a wasteful and artificially stimulated consumption use of limited resources to one that is more efficient and more conducive to increasing the real quality of life of the community. A main thrust of consumer innovation in our time appears aimed at producing a push-button world in which our whims are to be instantly gratified, while our psychic needs are continuously thwarted. Given the extreme poverty of the great mass of developing countries, a rise in their material consumption will be necessary; enough food and adequate housing are minimal needs that many do not have.

The Dutch economist, Professor Jan Tinbergen, has recommended an annual increase in income per capita of 5 per cent for developing countries, implying a doubling of income per capita in 14 years. This, combined with a reduction in growth of GNP in developing countries to say 2 per cent per annum, would, he believes, produce a stabler world and less inequality. Few politicians and governments are aware of this necessity. Many, if not most, economists would repudiate it. Conventional economic theory tells us that it is not possible for the developing countries to step up their rate of economic growth without a continuous expansion of world trade which largely depends on the economic growth of the rich countries. It may be conventional wisdom but the fact of the matter is that it has not worked out that way at all. "It is true", said Professor Saturo Okita, a leading Japanese economist, at the annual meeting of the Club of Rome in Berlin, October 1974, "that when the economies of rich countries experience recession, economies of developing countries are seriously affected." However, he added that there must be a new world economic order under which the economies of the developing countries *can* grow faster *in spite* of the slowing down of the economic growth of rich countries. He cited as possible measures: transfer of technology, resources and industry from rich to poor countries; the promotion of imports to the rich countries from developing countries; transfer of labour intensive industries from rich to poor countries and the importation of the manufactured goods from these transferred industries by developed countries. At the same time, rich countries will have to explore ways of sustaining full employment in spite of lower rates of industrial growth and increasing importation of manufactured goods from developing countries. Areas to look to for furthering employment are improvement of the environment, recycling of materials and reuse of wastes and research to improve efficiency. Okita insists that there are policies for rich countries to explore to put their own houses in order which at the same time are conducive to a higher rate of economic growth for poor countries and a more just use of the world's resources.

Special Problems of Developing Countries

Many developing countries have been and remain sources of raw materials for former colonial powers and other industrialized countries. Easily accessible resources and low labour costs have made this profitable for the industrialized countries. A consequence of this has been the creation of new national elites in the developing countries which emulate Western affluence without concern for the majority of their people who are poor. These elites show little or no concern for:

— depletion and waste of the nation's resources;

— increased social inequality within the country;

— the damaging effects of imitation of Western consumer attitudes which are irrelevant to the real needs of the people;

— the lack of a technology addressed to the needs and economic possibilities of the masses.

Because of this the developing world may have to turn inwards in order to develop its own quality of life and a technology suitable to its own cultural, human and natural environment.

It is morally imperative that the industrialized countries stand ready to share in the advancement of indigenous solutions as requested and to minimize their technological frivolity and over-production resulting from Western consumer attitudes. Besides being a pragmatic response to a real situation, such an attitude of technological restraint reflects the basic Christian attitude of the stewardship of material creation.

The benefits of economic growth and the development of resources must first go to the poorest of the poor now said to number 600 million people. But existing socio-economic structures in many developing countries tend to serve the interests of the privileged minority who control economic and political power. As a result, the rich become richer and the poor poorer. A high rate of growth tends to strengthen the structures that resist change and the just use of resources.

In addition, international economic processes enter a developing country through non-egalitarian domestic structures and thus become allies and adjuncts of the status quo. In the colonial period there was exploitation by domination of the powerful nations; today it is domination by invitation.

Some specific elements in resource use conducive to greater social justice in the developing world are:

— Resources should be applied to the production of basic needs and withdrawn from less essential production. For instance, low cost housing rather than luxury apartments and five-star hotels; public transportation rather than automobiles for private use; coarse and medium cloth rather than fine textiles, expensive silks, synthetic materials, etc.; small irrigation projects rather than huge multi-purpose projects; training for basic rural health services more than for modern medical skills which lead to a concentration of medical facilities in urban areas. All these shifts in production can be introduced immediately.

— A change in production priorities implies a restriction of consumers' choice in the better-off sections. Such regulation of consumption is an essential part of social justice. Only a small proportion of increments in national production should go to the relatively prosperous sections of society.

— In practical terms, people must have income to buy goods. Hence they must have gainful employment. Big projects and industrialization on the basis of technology acquired from advanced nations have failed to absorb the available human resources. Therefore, a simpler labour-using technology is necessary. Capital-intensive technology also imposes heavy foreign exchange burdens. Thus even on the optimization principle of conventional economics, this kind of technology is of doubtful efficacy for developing countries.

— As under-employment and unemployment are overcome, people are drawn into the production process. This increases the possibilities of people's participation which is so important for successful developmental efforts. The use of simpler technology creates preconditions for decentralized production and can overcome the rural exodus which is forcing increasing numbers of people to migrate to cities and industrial centres. Anarchic urbanization is a dehumanizing force which needs to be arrested, in the interest of social justice.

There are great differences between developing countries in the resources they possess or have access to. Some have plenty, others are deficient. This problem raises the concept of an International Resource Bank with special drawing rights for developing countries. Such a "bank" could also be involved in those world resources which are not, as yet, under the control of any single nation such as the sea bottom, Antarctica and the open seas. Ultimately the maldistribution of necessary resources raises the question as to national ownership of resources. We must face this now with respect to those resources not yet under national control. But we need to question seriously the convention that countries that happen by geographical chance to be endowed with great resource wealth are by right the owners of this wealth. Is it not the common possession of all humanity?

12 · Environmental Deterioration

There are two components of environmental deterioration. One is the global depletion of essential resources for the maintenance of the sort of world we live in. The second is the destruction or deterioration of the quality of the life-support systems on land and in the seas and waters of the earth. We may think of each person as having an impact on the environment in these two ways. The impact of a Western industrialized man is very much greater than that of a Third World farmer. We could, in general terms, then try to conceive of the total impact of man on the environment as dependent upon three quantities:

— population size,

— consumption of resources per head,

— environmental deterioration of life-support systems per head.

If we could measure all three, then we would have a global indicator of man's total impact on the planet year by year.

The urgency of our present situation has been created by the compounding of the population explosion with ever increasing industrial expansion and its increasing appetite for limited resources, and with the newer and more dangerous ways we have learned to contaminate the environment. We confine our attention in this section to environmental deterioration of life-support systems.

Some of the changes are direct and obvious and have been known for a long time such as soil erosion and deterioration of soil fertility following irrigation. Another set of changes are less obvious and are due to pollution. Both are part of the destruction or deterioration of eco-systems. Pollution in the strict sense is deterioration brought about by poisons, smog, oil spills, persistent chemicals such as DDT, radio-active wastes and the more subtle qualitative changes resulting from heating up the environment both in the air and in water.

Our activities threaten what ecologists call "the life-support systems" of the planet. Natural communities of plants and animals tend to be "self-sustaining" in the sense that they recycle the necessities of life such as nutrients. When human activity intervenes, it more often than not breaks the cycle with consequent erosion, loss of nutrients and poisoning of life. A singularity of our time is the extent to which the deterioration of the environment has become a global phenomenon. Industrial activity around the earth is affecting the composition of the atmosphere of the whole earth and possibly the climate also. Insecticides such as DDT put on fields or forests in the USA can end up on the other side of the earth. Industrial smoke from Britain and Germany causes acid rain in Scandinavia. Probably every human being now alive has some radioactive Strontium in his or her bones from atomic bomb blasts and probably every human being has DDT in his or her blood and other parts of the body.

In the 1950's there were relatively few signs of environmental stress. It was not until the late 60's that the so-called environmental crisis became a matter of widespread concern. By 1970 the press throughout the world was daily reporting new evidence of environmental deterioration. However, it did not all start in the 1960's; there had been a long slow simmering which seemed to reach a critical boiling point around about that time. We were able then to see more clearly just what we were doing to our environment. This coming to the boil is associated with the modern phenomenon of exponential escalation of population and industrialization and agriculture.

Pollution — Local and Global

Every year about 10 thousand different man-made chemicals pour into the oceans from continents all around the globe. In 1950 the world production outside the Communist countries of organic chemicals was 7 million tons. By 1970 it had gone to 63 million tons. By 1985 it will reach 250 million tons. At present about 20 million tons of these organic chemicals enter the environment annually. Every day our cities pump more than a dozen chemicals into the atmosphere, some of which get dispersed far from the place of origin. Every large city heats up the environment with consequent changes in air movements and weather patterns. And when all that is added up all over the world, we suddenly become aware that we are changing our environment in a way and a rate that never happened before. In our former innocence we thought it all got mopped up somewhere, maybe in the depths of the ocean or in the upper atmosphere. Some of it does. We now know that the earth has a limited pollution absorptive capacity. It can absorb so much and it can break down so much, but exceed those limits and poisons accumulate. The pollution absorptive capacity of the earth must be regarded as a prime economic resource that is limited. Even the highly poisonous carbon monoxide is eventually broken down by bacteria, but not at the rate at which it is pumped into the main streets of huge modern cities. Even DDT is eventually broken down — there are some bacteria that do just that — but not at the rate at which we have been pouring it into the environment. Nitrogen compounds are needed by plants as food and can be circulated in a nitrogen cycle in nature, but not when they are poured into waterways from all sides from agriculture, from industry and even from motor cars racing down highways. They literally clog up the system. Phosphates are also good; they are needed by plants, but not to the extent of causing great algal blooms that mop up all the oxygen in the water and then leave a stagnant and stinking mass.

No one knows just how much all our polluting adds up to. The US scientific commission on environmental protection estimated (it must have been some sort of informed guess) that global pollution was increasing at a rate of five per cent per year. This means that global pollution is doubling every 14 years. If correct, then the eco-systems of the earth will have been stressed to half their limit only 14 years before they collapse!

A great deal is known about local polluting effects of industry. It is fairly easy to diagnose local pathologies, a lake "dying" with too much nitrogen, oil spills on beaches and pine trees dying of smog east of Los Angeles. The worst examples come from highly industrialized areas: smog in Los Angeles, water pollution in the Rhine, cadmium poisoning in Japan. When the effects of pollution are acute, we get a fish kill or sick people. What is not easy to diagnose are the chronic effects of pollution. We did not know what DDT was doing until egg shells of some birds became thinner. We do not know the possible carcinogenic effects of certain chemicals in the environment because cancers may take 20 years to develop. The same is the case with low-level radiation; to do the necessary experiment would involve 8 billion mice! The time from entry of the pollutant into the environment and awareness of its effects may span decades. The first occurrence of mercury poisoning in Minamata Bay in Japan was noticed 15 years after the release of mercury into the bay. It was diagnosed three years later.

Much less is known about pollution on a global scale. We know what goes into the seas and the atmosphere but we know relatively little about the effects. Only a large-scale monitoring system, now being started, will give us the information we need to know what really is happening to the global environment. There is as yet no indicator needle which swings on a dial to tell us when danger point is near.

Major causes for concern at present are the increasing carbon dioxide content of the atmosphere produced by burning fossil fuel, the heat produced by industrial and urban actvity and the effect of aerosols on the ozone layer of the upper atmosphere.

In many developed countries about 10,000 watts of energy is used per person. Someone living in a non-industrialized society, by comparison, uses only a few hundred watts. With present population and industrial growth rates, it is very likely that within the next fifty to one hundred years the heat from these regions of high energy use per capita will cause changes in global climate that could have most disturbing, if not disastrous, effects on agriculture and other human activities far distant from the source. The matter is of such consequence that the development of huge urban-industrial complexes in the future should be a subject for global consideration and not simply a national issue.

The Atmosphere and the Oceans

The atmosphere and the seas belong to everybody and to nobody in particular; they are the only major resources of the planet we have not partitioned under national ownership. But they are also the two resources which on deterioration affect us all. We have now a wonderful opportunity to act to preserve the quality of the atmosphere and the seas as citizens of the world on a trans-national basis. At present, neither the atmosphere nor the seas are effectively controlled from deteriorating influences. It is unlikely that they will be until certain functions currently belonging to sovereign states are internationalized. The scientific community has taken the first step by establishing workshop and inquiry teams on an international basis (e.g. the Scientific Committee on the Protection of the Environment — SCOPE) and the United Nations has brought together governmental representatives in conferences on the Human Environment and the Law of the Sea. But what the scientists find necessary to be done may not be done unless governments are willing to recognize international management of common resources, notably the atmosphere and the seas. Without recognition of the global nature of the problem, the peoples of the world are unlikely to persuade their governments of the necessity of international management.

— The atmosphere: Among the by-products of spreading industrialization and agricultural activity are heat, gases such as carbon dioxide and aerosols and pollutant particulate matter, all of which affect the atmosphere. It is likely that each has an effect on climate and that within the next fifty to one hundred years these effects will become evident and possibly prove disastrous in their consequences. It is not possible at this stage to attribute changing climate in different parts of the world directly to human activity. This is because the climate of the earth is not, and probably never has been, stable. We are, for example, at present living in an ice-age within which the continental ice-sheets have waxed and waned in polar and middle latitudes and large fluctuations of rainfall have occurred in the tropics and sub-tropics. The "warmer" or interglacial climates of the present ice-age have been 8 to 12,000 years in length, while the "colder" or glacial climates have been about ten times as long. Our present "warmer" period has persisted for about 10,000 years. When and how the next glacial period will begin is not known. Our first evidence might be the failure of snow to melt one summer. It is sobering to realize that the climate of the last twenty years has been unlike that of the previous several decades. Some of the changes are that the northern regions of the northern hemisphere have been cooling down and the northern fringes of the northern hemisphere monsoon regions have been getting drier. Indeed, the period 1930 to 1960 may have had the most "abnormal" climate of the past 500 years. But while climate is changing anyway due to causes unknown, it is difficult to determine the contribution made by human activity until that becomes quite large. What can be said with assurance is that densely populated urban centres in industrialized countries have had quite substantial climatic effects extending over areas of the order of 10,000 square kilometres each and that continuation of exponential growth in energy use would *eventually* lead to intolerable global climatic change from the effects of heat dissipation alone. With almost as much certainty we can say that the build up of carbon dioxide in the past 75 years has been due mainly to the combustion of fossil fuels and that one effect of that build up would have been (in the absence of other changing factors) a modest increase in average global surface temperature. Finally, we can say that the magnitude of other human interventions in processes that influence climate (such as the destruction of the ozone layer — according to UNEP aerosols alone have reduced this layer by 1% to date), alteration of coverage of Arctic sea ice, modification of the atmospheric-particulate load over large regions already are or soon will be great enough to raise the possibility of significant disruption of climate in ways whose details cannot be predicted with any confidence.

— The oceans: The oceans cover two-thirds of the planet. The worst pollution is on coastlines and estuaries close to cities. For example, about 500 tons of lead enters the coastal waters off Los Angeles each year from a daily consumption of 24 tons. One per cent of the lead accumulates in coastal sediments. The two most polluted seas on the planet are the Baltic and the Mediterranean. They are enclosed and near heavy industrial areas.

More oil is spilt on the high seas today than was transported across them 50 years ago. No one knows the effect this may have on the life of the oceans. When fishery catches fall, as has been happening in the Baltic and in other oceans recently, it is often difficult to know whether this is due to over-fishing, pollution or both. Pollution of the oceans will become worse as more oil rigs are erected and when the ocean floor is mined for minerals. We have to develop methods which as yet hardly exist for monitoring, not only the accumulation of poisons, but the "health" of the seas as such. About the latter we know little.

Is Pollution Control the Answer?

The answer to environmental deterioration was seen by industry and governments in so-called "pollution control". We needed, they said, a massive mopping up operation. There was hardly a government anywhere in the developed world that has established a department to deal with this.

But is pollution control the answer to the problem of environmental deterioration? We can raise chimney stacks to put wastes higher into the air so that they come down as acid rain on someone else far away. We can divert industrial wastes with their mercury and lead and cadmium from their outlets into streams into the sewers or drains that go into the sea. Or, as someone has said, if you want to get rid of garbage, gift wrap it and leave it in the back of your unlocked car. It will end up somewhere else.

Pollution control is, for three reasons, only a partial solution to the problem of global pollution.

1. Most pollution control is a shifting of impact. Replace coal with nuclear power, you get rid of gas wastes but replace them with longer lasting nuclear wastes and thermal pollution. The conversion from buses to street cars and trains removes pollution from the streets to the power plants that drive the street cars and trains.

2. Pollution control is not keeping pace with industrial expansion. In the developed countries, industry has been growing at a rate of 7% per year, that is to say, it doubles every 10 years. If pollution were successfully cut back to 50% of the average this year, current rates of growth would restore the original level of pollution within 4-8 years.

3. To control pollution is to see only the tip of the iceberg. It is to treat symptoms and ignore causes. The huge unseen part of the iceberg is the social, political and economic roots of the problem.

Pollution control has been widely acclaimed as the answer to our problems. It is accepted, if not in practice then in theory, by governments and industry. It is easy to accept because it involves no change in values and therefore no change in the basic social, political and economic structures of communities. Industry can fit into the strategy without changing basic direction. It puts the price of goods up and that can be put onto the consumer. "The polluter pays" really means "the consumer pays". Economists can applaud it because it involves no change in economic strategy. But it never gets at the basic cause, the disease itself.

To change the direction of growth and to reduce the extent of production of some sorts of things is a threat to many enterprises. To do that involves a change in values and that is not easy. To free the air of our cities means removing the internal combustion engine, which means replacing motor cars and eventually buses with electric trains and trams. That means curbing the production of the sort of motor vehicles we live with today.

Any radical solution to the problems of environmental deterioration must involve a recognition of the causes and attempt to deal with them. The basic cause is the wrong sort of economic growth which places emphasis on consumption instead of on a balance between production of consumable goods and production of services such as public transport, health care, education and the arts. The wasteful and polluting industrial development characteristic of the developed countries is a bad model for developing countries. Manufacturing corporations should be prevented from installing plants in developing countries that do not conform to environmental requirements of the countries of origin.

Outer Limits and the Poor

The concept of limits imposed by the environment is now beginning to have an impact on economic thinking. Up to now economic activity has been considered essentially an "open" process: the amount of goods and services an economic system could produce was limited only by human capacity to generate and accumulate capital, and to increase productivity by continuously improving the technologies used. Natural resources — available in unlimited amounts, at least at world level — were considered only as a cost. The concept of "externalities" made it possible to ignore in the economic cycle most of the effects on the environment.

Although these ideas were often challenged in the past, they remained basically unchanged in economic practice. Only now, when an exponential increase in economic activity and the introduction of direct or indirect economic planning at national level requires economists to think in terms of much more extended time horizons than before, is the concept of possible environmental limits starting to affect economic practice as well as theory.

However, the impact of environmental limits or constraints on economic practice varies greatly according to its nature.

To consider the differences, we can broadly divide the effects into two types: short-term local effects and global or regional long-term effects. This division, obviously, is not rigid — local impacts, for instance, can add up to global long-term effects — but it is accurate enough for our purpose.

The local effects of economic activity — such as the environmental impact of factories, energy-generating plants, big dam and irrigation projects — can be more or less effectively assessed, and preventive or corrective measures can be taken. In addition, as these projects are usually decided in a national context, the community affected has the legal means to exert pressure on the authorities involved so that its interests are taken into account.

In the case of global long-term environmental impacts — such as pollution of the atmosphere and the seas, use of pesticides and fertilizers, depletion of natural resources and heat generation — the situation is different for two main reasons:

1. The limits imposed by these long-term effects — "outer limits", as they are frequently called — are very difficult to assess, as there is insufficient information about such things as the absorption capacity of the biosphere, synergistic effects and the total amount of natural resources eventually available to mankind. In every case, the problem depends on so many variables that it is not possible to define an absolute limit; at most, we can refer to a certain degree of risk whose evaluation is, to a great extent, subjective, as can be seen by a glance at the current literature where completely opposite conclusions are reached by different authors using the same data.

2. Although the global long-term impact on the environment affects the whole of humanity, the negative effect of the measures to prevent or correct it will be felt mainly by the poorest part of the population of the world, first, because most of those measures, as conceived today, imply restrictions in the use of resources and in economic development in general (if these can be adopted by developed countries without endangering their high standard of living, they impose a further sacrifice on the already deprived masses of the Third World), and second, because these preventive measures require action at international level, and the economic and technological superiority of the advanced countries gives them the power to transfer the risks, to a certain extent at least, to the developing countries. Recent proposals — which are beginning to be implemented — to transfer polluting industries to the Third World countries are a case in point. Finally, the Third World does not have the means to exert pressure so that its needs and aspirations can be taken into account in the international arena.

Absolute and Acceptable Risk

These considerations do not obviate the fact that there are real environmental dangers, and that an environmental policy at world level is needed. The problem is: in what context should that policy be framed?

Since the beginning of the "crisis of the environment" two approaches to environmental strategy have emerged. One of them — not the most important numerically, but one that has appeal in certain centres of power — considers man as only one more element of a natural ecosystem and would go so far as to recommend abandoning all forms of help for the poorest part of humanity, on the principle that the "survival of the fittest" is the way nature controls population and the distribution of resources. In a less extreme form it is argued that, unless there is the absolute certainty that the dangers can be avoided, any activity that can possibly endanger the global environment should be abandoned, whatever the social costs. This position is based on two main tenets. The first is that it treats the science of the environment solely as a natural science; as such, it has no values, and man does not differ in behaviour from any other living being. The second is that it considers risks in an absolute sense: if there is a risk that in any way endangers the future of mankind, it should be avoided at any cost, even if it implies the deliberate sacrifice of a considerable part of humanity.

The other position, that is the basis of some of the most important of the documentation which has been produced up to now,[1] takes a different stand.

In the first place, it poses the environmental problem in the broad setting of human civilization; people are social beings, the product of culture and, as such, their attitude, when confronted with a common danger, is influenced by consciously accepted values which transcend the mere irrational drive to survive of other living beings. As a consequence, the notion of absolute risk is replaced by the concept of "acceptable risk"; in other words, the risk that should be confronted to survive at the same time maintaining the central values of civilization. The determination, in this context, of what is an acceptable risk is not simply a technical or biological problem; it is, above all, a moral issue.

However, the recognition that a policy on the environment should not hamper the possibilities of development of the poor countries is not enough to enable us to devise and implement specific policies. For this purpose a more concrete long-term frame of reference is required. Although long-term forecasting is always difficult, there are a few facts that we can certainly predict, and which are enough to constitute a broad basis for a rational and socially just environmental policy. The most important is that the population of the world will be about 7,000 million at the beginning of the next century, and will probably stabilize at around 12,000 million by the middle of it. Each of these future human beings has the absolute right to a life worth living. For that time horizon, and for the whole of humanity, we can then define the minimum acceptable risk as the risk involved in providing all future human beings with the basic needs required for a full and productive life in their own culture.

---

[1] For example the *Stockholm Declaration on the Human Environment*, Stockholm, June 1972; the Founex Report, *Environment and Development*, Paris, Mouton, 1972; *The Cocoyoc Declaration*, Cocoyoc, Mexico, UNEP/UNCTAD, 1974.

What Is "Acceptable"?

The satisfaction at an adequate level of the basic needs of the whole future population of the world is, admittedly, a very broad objective, but it constitutes an adequate frame of reference within which to devise specific long-term environmental strategies. At any rate, only objectives that highlight the sheer magnitude of problems facing mankind can mobilize the imagination and creativity needed to confront them. It is time to admit, at last, that planetary problems cannot be solved by parochial measures.

What types of strategies are needed? For analytical purposes we can conceive the biosphere as a system composed of two interrelated subsystems: the human society and the physical and biological environment which surrounds it.

Most of the forecasts (or better, projections) that predict a catastrophe in the not-too-distant future assume — explicitly or implicitly — that the human subsystem is almost invariable. As we can do very little to influence the behaviour of the biosphere on a planetary scale, it is no wonder that the catastrophe appears unavoidable. However, if we admit that human society has great potential capacity to change, the degrees of freedom of the whole system greatly increase, and with them the possible alternative paths to cope with the limitations posed by the environment.

A good example of how changes in social organization can affect the environment is given by income distribution.

The "Bariloche Model"[2] has calculated the GNP per capita needed to satisfy basic needs under two assumptions: *a)* with an egalitarian distribution of income; and *b)* with the present income structure. The calculations show that, in the developing countries, the GNP per capita required to satisfy the basic needs with the present income structure is between three and five times the one needed with an egalitarian distribution.

In the case of Latin America, for example, the standard run shows that basic needs could be satisfied before the year 2000 with a GNP per capita of US $ 809 (1960). Assuming current income distribution, the satisfaction of basic needs could be attained fifty years later with an income per capita of about US $4050.

What Can Individuals Do?

Every single person contributes to environmental deterioration. Every single person can do something about reducing his or her impact both by changing personal ways and by influencing public opinion through

---

[2] *Catastrophe or New Society*, Ottawa, IDRC, 1976 (IDRC-064c) (the complete report on the Model has been published in French: Amilcar O. HERRERA *et al.*, *Un Monde pour Tous*, Paris, Presses Universitaires de France, 1977; there are also editions in German and Japanese).

group activity. By changing the climate of opinion, we lead the way for governments to act.

But first we must be correctly informed. On very few of the problems discussed in this chapter are the issues clear cut. Their understanding involves an acquaintance with some scientific data, with political and economic systems and with human nature. Since we are all responsible for the deteriorating world, we all have a responsibility to keep ourselves informed and to develop judgments on important issues. We can do this by reading popular science journals and by selecting for reading those newspapers and weekly magazines that are most informative.

But we then need to discuss together what we learned. Discussion can lead to local action and then to political action. We shall soon find ourselves caught up in issues of national and international significance.

In the end we shall find that no solution to global environmental deterioration is possible without a new international economic and political order in which national sovereignties give way to trans-national management. That is an ultimate political goal.

13 · Population Growth and the Sustainable Society

The world's population in mid-1978 was well over 4,000 million according to the Population Reference Bureau. It was growing at a rate of 1.8% per year which gives a doubling time of 38 years. There are of course great variations in growth rates in different countries. Developed countries are increasing their numbers at a rate which implies a doubling every 63 years. Developing countries have an average doubling time of 29 years.[1] The United Nations gives three forecasts for the world's population in 2075; the high estimate is 16,000 million, the low is 9,000 million, the median 12,000 million. So we appear to be committed to a world that within the next century will be over twice as crowded as at present and possibly three times as crowded. These numbers do not reveal the large differences in rates of growth of different nations. We are not able to feed, clothe and house the 4,000 million people on earth now. No one really knows where another 4,000 million will live or how they can be fed. The main burden of this rapid increase will continue to fall on the poor who are already oppressed by dehumanizing living conditions and social injustice. The revolutionary impact of public health programmes on the population increase has not been matched by a broad strategy for social change, self-reliance and economic development. Hundreds of millions of poor still do not have access to means of family planning and the children they cannot properly care for are being maimed in body and mind by malnutrition.

The population problem is global in scope. The affluent societies bear a large share of responsibility for it. Despite dramatic declines in birth rates in developed countries, patterns of wasteful production and consumption at home and of domination and exploitation abroad continue to

---

[1] Near the beginning of the decade the rate of world population growth reached an all time high. It then began to slacken. This was due to a number of causes: the success of China's population policy, a significant fall in birth rates in most developed countries, lowered birth rates in some developing countries especially some of the smaller Asian countries.

threaten the common environment and to intensify the problems of the poor societies. The situation demands that the rich societies respond in terms of a broad strategy of justice throughout the world and of redevelopment at home.

The Carrying Capacity of the Earth

A critical question related to population is the carrying capacity of the earth.

While we may not know the carrying capacity of the earth or any part of it, nor how this may change up or down in the future, there are some things we do know.

1. Few people seriously doubt that we are fast approaching, if we have not already reached, a critical point. We may have already exceeded the number of people the earth can sustain indefinitely. Humanity reached its present numbers in a succession of waves that rose first from the Agricultural Revolution, then the Industrial Revolution, and more recently the Bio-medical Revolution. Some scholars believe we have now to anticipate a fourth revolution: the steady-state revolution in which somehow the steep upward curve of population until the 70's will have to be reduced and eventually levelled out. They think sooner or later this is inevitable on a finite planet.

This means that each generation would replace itself and no more. Some developed countries now have birth rates that would result in zero population growth after about 60 years. But even where birth rates are low, numbers will continue to increase for many decades at least.

2. There is a time lag of from 60 to 70 years after birth rates drop to equal death rates before the population stops increasing. Population growth does not cease as soon as all parents have only two offspring. Tomorrow's mothers are already here. They constitute a high proportion of the total population compared to that in a non-growing population. Precisely because population growth is slow to control, countries find it urgent to act now, even in the face of uncertainty as to what may be the optimum population for any region. The momentum of growth is such that no matter what we do now, the world population is destined to at least double in the future. However, what we do now can affect the number of people there will be some generations hence.

3. There is nothing in the science of demography to suggest that as the carrying capacity of the earth is reached there will be a natural transition from growth to no-growth populations. Indeed, the opposite would seem to be more probable. Left to themselves, populations tend to overshoot limits with subsequent catastrophic declines through starvation or disease.

Nor is it enough to place our faith, as some do, in the so-called "demographic transition" — in the tendency of population growth to level off as a response to affluence.

Deleterious Effects of Over-Population

Existing population growth rates are leading to problems of over-population, with consequent serious declines in the already low levels of quality of life in many regions, in both developed and developing countries. Over-population has a number of deleterious effects:

— It reduces the possibility that all the world's people can be adequately fed and housed. In the developing countries, the increases in food resulting from the Green Revolution have done little more than maintain existing levels of food per person because of the continuous population increment.

— It increases the pressure on most other resources, many of which are difficult to obtain.

— It accentuates the problem of urbanization. Increased population means more people migrating to already overcrowded cities.

— It negates the effects of economic development in developing countries, and it exaggerates still further the disproportionate consumption of the world's resources by developed countries.

Controlling Birth Rates

Unprecedented high population growth rates (on a wide geographic scale) in the last few decades, urban crowding and pressures in rural settlements have led an increasing number of countries to adopt population policies and to sanction family planning programmes for reasons of family health or basic human rights. The United Nations Conference on Human Rights at Teheran recognized the fundamental rights of parents to determine the size and spacing of their families. These rights need to be exercised in the light of the parents' obligation to the larger society. This is an important addendum.

Concern for the quality of life, which has material, intellectual, spiritual and social dimensions, must be the main base for a responsible approach to parenthood. The concern is for truly human development which satisfies basic needs and facilitates the creative use of the individual's faculties within a just and harmonious community. This development must be consistent with social and economic justice and with the rights of future generations. The way quality of life is conceived is inevitably influenced by the values of diverse cultures; but it also has universal aspects which underlie these diversities.

The majority of churches no longer regard procreation as the only, or even the chief, end of sexual intercourse, but recognize the role of the sexual relationship in strengthening the bond of love between people. They have come to hold the view that couples must be free to limit procreation, provided the methods are mutually acceptable, and not injurious to either spouse nor to the new life. These churches generally do not accept abortion as a method of family planning, but they have tended to broaden the range of acceptable therapeutic reasons for abortion. For example, the consultation of the World Council of Churches on "Genetics and the Quality of Life" recommended that the choice of whether or not to undergo abortion following foetal diagnosis of genetic disease should be made by the individuals concerned guided by their understanding of the facts and by their conscience. "Decision making on these subjects is best governed by the principle of responsible parenthood, that is, by placing the decision in the hands of the prospective parents to be exercised by them after careful consideration of a number of factors."

The decision on how many children a couple is to have is also primarily up to them. Institutions including governments have a role to play in providing information on which a decision may be made and in persuading couples of the merits of family planning and population control.

Every child should be a wanted child. To this end, all means of birth control which are medically acceptable should be freely available. There should be no restriction on the establishment of family planning centres nor on the advertising of where birth control means can be obtained.

With all this, the achievement of a stationary population will be much more a case of changing social values than of providing contraceptives and family planning facilities. The information and family planning services provided by public and private agencies are not likely to get very far unless they are closely linked with substantial efforts to bring about the social, economic and psychological changes essential to reinforce the motivation of the community and the family to regulate the number and spacing of children. Examples of such action for change conducive to an increase in distributive justice and to respect for human rights include: efforts to achieve a more just status for women, so that mothers may be genuine partners in family and community decisions; measures to increase productivity and thus raise the level of living and aspirations; programmes to reduce infant and child mortality — the fear of which leads many parents to have large families; expanded employment opportunities including opportunities for women; improved educational opportunities linked to suitable prospects of employment; and effective old age security so that parents need not be totally dependent on their children.

Conditions which deny women their full and rightful place in the family and society need to be overcome. Any plan to improve the quality of life must give careful attention to this underprivileged majority of humankind.

Women — those who bear the children and suffer the consequences of too frequent pregnancies, who are mainly engaged in child care, feeding and pre-school training (and in many developing countries in the production of the family food supply) — have a central stake in family decisions regarding the number and spacing of children. The churches, whose teachings have both contributed to the traditional subordination of women and helped in their partial liberation, have a duty to give more consistent attention to the definition and achievement of social justice for women.

Population Control: Ethical Issues

The urgency of population pressures and the proven inadequacy of voluntary family planning has led some governments to formulate policies of population control which go beyond the provision of birth control facilities. These governments are convinced they have a responsibility to implement population policies which are in line with the hopes of their peoples for a higher quality of life and protect future generations. They believe they have a right, indeed a duty, to bring home to their people the implications of population trends. The critical issues are whether the policies and actions proposed are congruent with a truly human development of society and with the dignity, worth and prior claims of the family. Responsible parenthood implies taking into account the rights of the child to the prospect of health, love, education, and a fully human existence, and also the rights of society and of future generations. Mere survival is not enough. Life more abundant means enlarged opportunities and more favourable conditions for spiritual growth. Both affluence and grinding poverty are its enemies. Community can foster it, but overcrowding increasingly dehumanizes and stands in its way. From this perspective, the need for national and global population policies is both urgent and complex.

Government intervention in the area of procreation does not raise problems that are significantly different in kind from such other interventions as the legal regulation of marriage and the existing pro-natalist policies of some governments. Governments have as much right to interfere in procreation-related behaviour as they do in other areas of behaviour affecting the general welfare. The critical issue is the way in which this right is exercised.

The ethical acceptability of population policies may be judged according to, *inter alia*,

a) how the policy affects distributive justice, e.g. measures that penalize most heavily children of large families are unjust.

b) how the policy affects the individual's freedom to determine his/her own life and economic and social status. The individual's wishes concerning family size may conflict with society's needs. Society's restrictions then reduce the individual's freedom. To reduce this tension, society has an obligation to provide information that will encourage and assist individuals to limit births voluntarily for their own welfare and the common good. If this fails some degree of intervention may be justified, but not every form of intervention can be justified, even as a last resort. Governments have an obligation to use those methods that most respect freedom of choice.

If a government considers that some intervention is required, that government must:

(i) demonstrate that continued unrestricted liberty poses a direct threat to human welfare; that the common good is threatened;

(ii) demonstrate that the proposed restrictions on freedom promise in the long run to maximize options;

(iii) see that the restrictions on free choice fall upon all equally;

(iv) choose the programme that entails least intervention.

The churches in turn should examine carefully all government methods or proposals for population control. The above principles are commended to this end. In light of them, it should be possible to rate proposed methods in order of desirability, from non-coercive positive-incentive programmes at one end of the scale, to so-called "last resort" coercive proposals, such as compulsory sterilization and abortion, at the other.

The following are a few examples, some of which may be acceptable and others completely unacceptable.

1. Positive incentive programmes. These are ethically the most desirable. Some, however, have the drawback that they are designed primarily to appeal to or to penalize the poor. They include:

   a) Comprehensive programmes in sex education, education in physiology, studies in population and personal relationships pointing to the advantages of small families.

   b) Direct payments by governments or industries to persons practising contraception or to couples who do not bear children for specified periods; free contraceptives and free advice on their use; payments or gifts upon vasectomy and tubectomy. Of course the question can be asked whether impoverished people are not bribed into this which becomes a form of coercion.

   c) Tax and welfare benefits: reversal of tax benefits to favour the unmarried and parents of fewer than N children; pensions for poor parents with fewer than N children as social security for their old age (South India Tea Estate); provision by the state of N years of free schooling for each family, to be allocated by the family as desired among the children; payments into a savings account on each annual visit by a woman to a medical clinic provided she is not pregnant (Malaysian proposal).

d) Provision of housing for couples with few or no children (Singapore).

e) Free medical treatment for mother and baby when the mother agrees to tubectomy (Ambur, South India).

f) Rewards to canvassers and field workers for every person they persuade to be sterilized or to have an intra-uterine device inserted (this is practised in Taiwan and Pakistan).

2. Negative incentive programmes. These are ethically more objectionable than positive incentive programmes. All the examples have the serious fault of penalizing the poor more heavily than the rich, and especially the most innocent parties, the children.

a) Withdrawal of maternity benefits after two children or unless certain limiting conditions have been set such as child spacing and the practice of family planning (Pakistan).

b) Withdrawal of child allowance after the Nth child.

c) Tax on births after the Nth child.

d) Increased medical charges for the Nth child (Singapore).

e) Limitation of governmentally provided medical services, housing, scholarships, loans and subsidies to families with more than N children, e.g. in the Uttar Pradesh State government in India any government employee who gives birth to a fourth child is not eligible for maternity leave and must pay all hospital and delivery costs.

f) Restricting education and subsidy benefits to the first two children (under consideration in Egypt).

3. Coercive programmes. With the exception of the first example listed below, most coercive programmes have major ethical deficiencies. Some are totally unacceptable and governments should avoid the temptation to impose them.

— Increase in minimum age of marriage through legislation.

— Sterilization or abortion following the Nth child required by law; abortion for all illegitimate pregnancies.

— Marketable licences to have children.

Problems of a Stable Population

A world in which the number of people has levelled off and is maintained that way would be a very different world from the one we live in. We would have solved some problems and would face many new ones. There would be a high proportion of aged people in the population. The median age would increase by about 10 years, about one-fifth of the population would be under 15, and roughly the same number over 65. However, the labour force or "productive group" would constitute a higher proportion of the total than in a growing population.

We cannot have low mortality and low fertility without an ageing population. However, many of the supposedly undesirable features of this are socially induced. Youth have their place. So do the aged. We have tended to put all our emphasis on the virtues of the one to the exclusion of the other. To grow old should not mean to grow out of society, but rather to grow into another aspect of society. There can be countless interests for the aged. Finding ways to incorporate them into the mainstream of life, rather than pushing them out of it, could be beneficial to both young and old. A new arrangement of the nuclear family would bring them into the circle of the young more than happens at present in our community and which is not uncommon elsewhere.

Education of the young could be of higher quality because there would be fewer of them. And it would not be confined to youth but be for life. It need never cease. Adult education would be a major feature of the stable society. School buildings would be used throughout the summer and in the evenings. Interests need not stultify with age. Their direction can change. It is absurd to suppose that there is nothing worthwhile to do when we stop working from nine to five. We do not live in order to work. We could work in order not just to make a living but to live. In our society we train people to believe that economic man is paramount and that work should be the basis of the individual's life. Another feature of the stable population would be that women would have more time to do other things than raise families and look after the home. There would be more opportunity to practise equality of the sexes.

The prospects of a population with a somewhat higher average age should not be viewed with alarm. We can plan now to avoid the difficulties and to make the most of its advantages.

Population Policy, Social Justice and Development

The poorest of the poor — those people with an annual income of $50 or less — now number about 600 million. The size and misery of this group continue to increase as population increases. In any development strategy, first priority should be given to their needs. Unless the resources of society are used in a way that improves their lot, there is no genuine development. Concern about population thus forces us to rethink developmental strategy. It is not enough to think about the poor countries. We have to think about the poorest of the poor in a poor country — indeed in every country. That is what "development with a human face" implies.

The economic growth of some poor countries over the last two decades has at times been impressive. But this growth cannot be equated with true development, because, by and large, the size of the marginalized groups has increased and the poverty gap has widened. If this trend continues, the world is headed for catastrophe. Increases in GNP can be statistically gratifying but intrinsically deceptive. Goods can increase while more people are left in greater misery. Economic growth is important only if it benefits the needy.

Anxiety about population problems should foster an understanding of development wherein social justice acquires primacy. Given an unjust social framework, increases in the GNP strengthen the strong and emasculate the weak. Inequality and dehumanization inevitably increase. There is ample evidence from all parts of the world that this has been happening. We need new social, economic and political institutions based upon new social values, which hold people to be more important than things and quality of life than quantitative accretions.

Fears generated by the population explosion seem to have pushed policy towards a quantitative rather than a qualitative approach: towards reducing birth rates without improving social and economic conditions. It is assumed that a slower rate of population growth will promote a higher rate of national saving and make more goods available for the needs of people, that population control will contribute to development and human welfare. But where is the institutional framework to ensure this? In recent years both savings and GNP have increased, but so has the number of people suffering from deprivation. Efforts to reduce birth rates must be undergirded by efforts to build a more just and egalitarian social framework.

Recent studies relating to Taiwan, Mexico, Turkey, Egypt and the India-Pakistan-Bangladesh sub-continent suggest that programmes of social justice in particular localities may lead to a decline in birth rates, while birth rates remain high where growth is not linked with a concern for justice. Such indications, if confirmed by subsequent research, could bring a significant shift in the approach to population problems. Instead of a stress on economic growth and reduction in birth rates as the main preconditions and agents of social well-being, improvement in the lot of the common man may be seen as essential for an effective population policy.

The imbalance between population and resources, which is the crux of the population crisis, is caused more by developed than developing nations. By their much higher per capita use of resources, developed countries are aggravating the existing disequilibrium. Further, as we begin to see the ravages of environmental pollution, ecological imbalance and depletion of non-renewable resources, we become aware of a new aspect of the population crisis, linked with patterns of production, consumption and resource utilization in affluent countries. The developed nations need to stress reducing not only population growth rates but also the wasteful use and, in the long run, the per capita use of the world's resources, with an attack on the environmental and ecological problems which pose a threat to all humanity.

Concern for population problems in developing countries should lead to a re-examination of the fundamental nature of their economic objectives. Many have more people than readily available resources can adequately support; hence the need for population planning. Most of them are avidly pursuing economic goals patterned on those of affluent nations. Even before coming to grips with the existing population problem, they are committing their economies to a style of production, consumption and over-use of resources which is giving rise to a new form of the population problem already facing developed nations. The demographic concern should lead developing nations to search for a different economic system.

Just as distributive injustice within a developing economy contributes to the misery of the masses and gives a visible face to the population problem, so lack of international economic justice contributes to the impoverishment of the Third World. Thus international economic justice must be seen as an essential remedial measure for the global population problem.

This question is linked with the quest for new economic structures. It is not realistic to assume that industrial nations will, in the near future, voluntarily change their pattern of resource use, abandon their pursuit of ever-rising material standards and give up their dominant position in the world's economy. And if they were to cut their per capita use of resources immediately, this would be disastrous for many developing nations whose present economic systems are tied to the export of such resources. That is the paradox of the situation. Without an adequate institutional framework, both international and national, attempts to implement international justice could impose back-breaking burdens on developing nations. We must not sentimentalize about social justice within and among nations, but recognize that it calls for many institutional changes. Such changes cannot be brought about as long as we cling to outmoded concepts of development, growth and progress.

14 · The Technological Revolution and the Oceans *

The Technological Exploitation of the Common Heritage

"*Four kinds of technological advance have totally changed the perceptions of national interest in the oceans: the ability to drill for oil and gas on the continental shelf at ever greater distances and depths; the military triad of submarine, ballistic missile and atomic warheads; the industrialization of fishing techniques; and the ability to mine the hard minerals of the deep ocean floor and subsoil. Nearly every point at issue in the United Nations Conference on the Law of the Sea III deals with the ramifications of these technological developments.*

"*Almost as important as the magnitude of change in oceanic technology has been its speed. When the Second World War ended only one offshore oil well was in production in 80 feet of water in the Gulf of Mexico. Thirty years later there were to be more than 2,000 wells off the coasts of 60 countries and at water depths of up to 800 feet. In 1977 more than 20 percent of all petroleum produced in the world was from offshore fields. In 1945, only the US had the atomic bomb, and there was no other delivery system for it than a propeller-driven airplane. Today the oceans are teeming with submarines armed with nuclear missiles and capable of cruising beneath the polar ice cap. Man's deepest descent into the oceans by 1945 was 1,200 feet. By 1960 a descent of 35,800 feet had been made. Off the coast of West Africa in 1977 the American research vessel Glomar Challenger drilled 200 feet into the abyssal subsoil at an ocean floor depth of 13,000 feet, then returned two weeks later to re-enter the same drill hole, which was just eight inches in diameter. Although ocean exploration had not captured the public fascination to the same degree as the moon landing, a growing number of scientists and industrialists were aware that the ocean frontier might be far more important.*

---

* The author of this chapter is Prof. ALFRED H. KEIL, Professor of Engineering, Massachusetts Institute of Technology.

"On November 1, 1967, Maltese Ambassador Arvid Pardo made his now famous speech calling for the wealth of the seas to be placed under international jurisdiction as the 'common heritage of mankind' and the income from their exploitation to be used for the economic development of the poor countries. Pardo envisioned that living and mineral resources found beyond 12 miles from land could provide an international authority with an income of $6 billion a year by 1975.

" It hasn't exactly worked out that way. Since 1945, about one-quarter of all ocean space has been effectively nationalized by the coastal states through the extension of economic rights to a distance of 200 nautical miles. And what a quarter it is! More than 90 percent of the world fish catch is within this 200-mile extension and an estimated 80 percent of all ocean hydrocarbon resources are found in it. The 'common heritage' — i.e., the oceans and sea-bed beyond 200 miles — remains huge of course, but the cruel truth is that nearly all its wealth has been lost to what has fairly been called 'the world's greatest land grab'. The major outcome of the United Nations Conference on the Law of the Sea III will be to legitimize rather than reverse this immense confiscation." *("Sea Law: The Unpleasant Options" by Nicholas Raymond, Ocean World, January 1978, pp. 6-7.)*

Three-quarters of the surface of our planet is covered by the oceans. The name "planet ocean" would seem therefore more appropriate than "planet earth". Life on our planet started in the oceans, and man's inter-action with the seas has grown ever more intense since the most remote times of his existence. Thousands of years ago the planet's waters already provided food (fish) and mineral resources (salt), and the oceans served as migratory highways on which populations, plants and animals spread over the globe. Marine transportation was the key to the discovery of continents, the development of colonial empires, and, during the past century, the development of all industrial and most developing nations with their dependence on international trade in raw materials, goods and food products. Demand for the fishery resources grew over the centuries and created the high sea fishing fleets which are now large industrial enter-prises. Demand for the resources in the sea bed created the present off-shore oil and gas industry which produces now more than 20 percent of the total world supply; and visions of the mineral resources on and under the ocean bottom have led to plans for large-scale sea floor mining. Each of these developments has been coupled with the evolution of new technical capabilities and new industries and enterprises, more often than not involving drastic breaks with past practices and thought patterns and vast economic, social and political impacts. With these rapid developments triggered by the industrial revolution, the world's oceans have become of greater and greater importance to mankind. The impact of man's present and future ocean activities on the world's nations as well as the oceans themselves has, therefore, become a matter of concern for all nations. In order to appreciate the multitude of present and foreseeable opportunities and problems relating to man's use of the ocean, the major ocean uses must be understood and are therefore summarized.

The Ocean's Living Resources

The living resources most intensely sought are fish, shellfish and selected mammals. Although the development of modern fishing fleets after World War II and the use of modern technology for locating schools of fish and for catching and processing them have resulted in enormous growth of the annual fish catch, fishing is still a process of hunting and harvesting. Following the end of World War II, total fishery catches doubled every decade, but leveled off in the early 70's and have recently begun to decline. The United Nations reported that the world's fishing fleets during 1975 caught 70-75 million metric tons of fish. About two-thirds of this was used for human consumption, and provided a critical 17% of the direct animal protein consumed by the world's population. The remaining 83% of the world's protein needs were met with dairy products, poultry and livestock.

Most of the world's fish catch is harvested in the major fishing grounds of the North Sea and the North Atlantic around Iceland, the continental shelf of the northeast coast of the United States and Canada, the North Pacific region stretching from Japan, past Alaska to the northern United States, and the regions along the west coast of South America and the southern part of the African continent. Major modern fishing fleets of the world are now those of Japan, the USSR, Korea, Norway, and Spain.

Many of the fishing grounds throughout the world, because they have been overexploited, are now delivering close to their sustainable yields. Indeed, some areas are so overfished that species once abundant within them are in danger of extinction. Nationally imposed strict controls and international agreements are being used to ensure the long-term survival of the ocean's renewable fishery resources so that this food from the seas will be available for future generations.

As societies have concentrated fishing efforts on a few, popular species of edible fish, they have ignored and rejected large available stocks of other fish living in the world's waters. This, however, is changing. Many of these un- or under-utilized species are being explored and could promise dramatic increases in food supplies if retrieved from the seas. For instance, Japanese and Soviet experts, investigating the distribution, abundance and processing of the Antarctic crustacean krill, estimate an annual sustainable yield of 100 million tons. This projection for this one species alone exceeds the present total annual world fish catch.

The squid population in continental shelf waters could yield 8 million tons per year instead of the present 1 million; and potential annual sustainable yields are estimated at 50 times that value! The annual sustainable yield from systematic fishing of lantern fish presently not sought at all could exceed 100 million tons per year. Overall sustainable yields of the world oceans of three to five times the present yield have been projected with proper international resource management, but only on condition, of course, that the necessary investments and energy resources are available for operating expanded fishing fleets, and that people learn to appreciate and eat the new species.

The harvesting of marine plants provides another food potential. In addition, mariculture of fish, shellfish, and marine plants may play a major role in supplying the world with marine food products.

The Ocean's Mineral Resources

Immense ocean mineral resources including those dissolved in the water masses of the ocean are often reported. Use of dissolved mineral resources by industry is currently difficult and costly except where these minerals are recovered as a byproduct of desalination. The first major industrial effort for recovering dissolved resources may be made in the processing of a typical deep-sea brine found in some deep trenches in the Red Sea.

The resources that lend themselves more readily for mining are the deposits on and under the continental shelves and the ocean bottoms. Sand and gravel for the construction industry, sulfur and sulfides, phosphates and tin ore are major minerals presently mined on the continental shelves. The manganese nodules on the ocean bottom have attracted particular attention as a mineral resource. Recent extensive explorations have identified the location of major manganese nodule deposits, and yielded estimates between ten billion and a hundred billion tons of nodules located in deep ocean basins, particularly in the mid-Pacific. These deposits are rich in manganese, copper, cobalt and nickel, all metals of great importance for industries, and must be considered as competition to the present land-based deposits of related ores. A few corporations in some of the highly industrialized nations have made large investments to develop mining and processing techniques. Pilot mining projects are being carried out by individual industries or by international consortia to test and improve mining methods.

Energy from the Ocean

At present the energy resources of the ocean exist in the oil and gas fields on the continental shelves, slopes and ocean bottoms; but inherent energy extracted from the ocean's waves, tides, major currents, osmotic pressure gradients and the temperature differential in the ocean water should be considered, though utilization of these energy forms on a large scale is remote. In relation to fusion technology, the heavy water contained in the ocean must be considered an energy source as well. Offshore oil and gas have become of increasing importance for the energy-hungry world — in 1977 more than 20% of all crude oil produced in the world came from offshore fields. Utilization of these resources in the US started in 1947 with the development of offshore exploration and drilling off the coast of Louisiana and California, and grew rapidly off the gulf coast of the US where a total of 15,200 wells had been drilled by early 1975. In the 1950's, offshore exploration and production began in the Persian Gulf, Cook Inlet in Alaska, Venezuela and Indonesia, followed in the 1960's off Nigeria, Gabon and Angola, and later in Bass Strait off Australia; and in more recent years in the North Sea. This production grew from 7.3 million barrels per day in 1970 to 9.3 million in 1974. Offshore exploration is growing rapidly in all parts of the world. Most of the present production of offshore oil and gas occurs on the continental shelves of coastal states, typically in water depths up to 200 meters and within 200 miles of the coast. Under international law, recovery of these oil resources falls within the control of coastal states. In the case of the North Sea, the neighboring countries divided the sea floor into national regimes for offshore oil and gas production.

Marine Transportation

In a world which depends increasingly on international trade in raw materials, oil, natural gas, chemical products, food products and manufactured goods, marine transportation now carries practically all (i.e., more than 95%) of the cargo flow among continents. The phenomenal growth of marine transportation can be appreciated if one considers the growth of the tonnage of the world's fleet from 80.3×10^6 tons in 1948 to 290×10^6 tons in 1973; or the increase in the number of ships from 20,300 to 59,606 over the same period.

The major single commodity carried by the world maritime trade is crude oil, which amounted to 1,300 million metric tons in 1970, about 40% of that year's total maritime cargo. Projected growth for 1980 amounts to 2,000 million metric tons. Crude oil is mainly carried by tankers which have grown in size from 25,000 tons for the supertankers of the late 40's to over 300,000 tons for today's supertankers. Liquid natural gas (LNG) and liquid petroleum gas (LPG) are becoming of growing importance for maritime trade in energy products, and pose special safety problems. Special large LNG carriers have been developed as well as special loading and unloading facilities.

The dry bulk cargo commodities carried by marine transportation consist of iron ore, coal, grain, bauxite, phosphates, etc. Total volume in 1970 was 523 million metric tons, and is expected to increase to

1,300 million metric tons per year in 1980. This type of cargo is carried mainly by bulk carriers which have grown substantially larger to reduce transportation cost per ton-mile.

The remaining "general cargo" commodities consist primarily of manufactured and semi-manufactured goods and are carried on container ships, special purpose ships, and freighters. In 1970 "general cargo" amounted to 600 million metric tons which is expected to grow to nearly 800 million by 1980.

The drastic increase in cargo volume triggered two major revolutions in marine transportation during the past two decades. One is based on the throughflow concept which was coupled with containerization and the introduction of container ships, and roll on/roll off freighters; and the other on the development of "superships" for the transport of bulk cargo such as crude oil and ores. With the introduction of container ships and the resulting growth in container shipment, drastic modifications of existing ports and the establishment of special container ports became a necessity. The introduction of large deep draft ships for carrying bulk cargo led (1) to the development of deepwater ports with water depths of more than 60 feet at their piers, and (2) to the development of "offshore ports", which are loading or unloading facilities for tankers and where crude oil is transferred from oil fields via offshore storage facilities into the tankers, or at the point of destination where the crude oil is transferred from the tanker via pipelines to shore-based storage and processing facilities. Deep water ports were soon coupled to industrial complexes in developments like Europort Rotterdam and the deep water port-industrial complex in Genoa. Examples of new centers replacing traditional ports are the new Europort South which is developing on the Mediterranean coast between Marseille and the Rhone; and the port-industrial complexes in Jurong/Singapore, Hong Kong and Japan.

Mankind and the Ocean Environment

The oldest and still most important impact of the oceans on mankind results from their influence on the climate and particularly on the weather of the earth's land masses. In addition to the moderating influence which the oceans have on the temperature of the atmosphere over the land masses, they provide much of the humidity in the atmosphere over the oceans which then produces the major rainfalls on the continents. The oceans thus affect the agricultural productivity of the land masses.

Man's activities in turn have increasingly affected the oceans. Throughout the world, populations usually have clustered close to coastlines. The resulting high population densities and industrial developments have affected the quality of coastal waters. Pollution has resulted from the outfall of sewage into coastal waters, the discharge of industrial fallout into harbors and rivers, and the dumping of dredgings containing the integrated pollution of many decades. The impact of such pollution must be appraised for the effect it has on marine life and the ecosystem in general. At the same time pollution must be seen in light of esthetic and health problems which it generates for mankind's use of coastal waters and beaches.

During the past thirty to forty years, pollution resulting from transportation of crude oil and processed oil by means of freighters has increased substantially. This pollution is created by the practice of oil carriers cleaning tanks after they have delivered the crude oil and while they are on the way back to the oil fields. The resulting crude oil/water mixture resulting from "washing down" the tanks has been frequently discharged overboard while underway. The ballast water which is carried in the tanks is discharged overboard when the tanker gets ready to be loaded with crude oil near the oil fields. Pollution also results from accidents, particularly if a tanker is rammed or runs aground. Oil spills from the Torrey Canyon, the Argo Merchant and the Amoco Cadiz exemplify this kind of pollution problem. Substantial efforts to reduce oil pollution have been made during the past decade by the International Maritime Consultive Organization (IMCO) by establishing international standards for ship design as well as ship operations, including the tank-cleaning practices. In addition, equipment and methods have been developed both to contain oil spills and to retrieve the spills from the ocean.

Extensive studies to assess the hazards from such oil spills to marine life showed that the effect of a crude oil spill on the marine ecosystem is much less serious than of the spill of an equal amount of processed oil products.

Possible pollution dangers from the development of non-living marine resources are different for offshore oil and gas and offshore mining. Practically no pollution or hazard for marine ecology occurs during the geophysical exploration for offshore oil and gas. For the next step, exploratory drilling, which determines what kind and what level of offshore oil and gas resources are present, the offshore industries have developed safety measures to prevent blowouts and spills, so that the probabilities of such pollution occurring are remote. Successful exploratory drilling is followed by production of the offshore oil and gas resources requiring storage of the developed offshore products *in situ*, such as the Ecofisk storage tank for the Norwegian oil fields in the North Sea; and transport of the crude oil either by ship or by pipeline to shore. The actual pollution hazard caused by offshore oil and gas exploration and production falls in the same category as the marine transportation of crude oil discussed earlier.

Pollution from offshore mining as of sand and gravel, tin ore, etc. or of manganese nodules disturbs the ecosystem to a degree, and mining in coastal waters could represent a potential hazard in those areas where fish breed and congregate. On the other hand, impact from offshore, and particularly deep sea mining should be small because sand, gravel, etc. are inert ingredients. The impact of all these activities varies from case to case, and each should be evaluated separately when the resulting pollution or development affects the survival of renewable resources.

Increasing Ocean Use: Conflicts and Problems

Today's driving forces for increased ocean use are based on national interests in living resources, energy and mineral resources of the oceans and increasing international maritime trade. The national interests in ocean resources distinguish between living (renewable) and non-living (non-renewable) resources which have to be managed differently; and between resources within ocean regimes under national control and those resources which might fall under international control. National actions to prevent the depletion and possible destruction of living (i.e. renewable) resources, to manage marine-based resources, and to control pollution in the ocean environment have generated serious conflicts which must be resolved.

Particularly intense debates have developed over the ownership of deep ocean resources and the process through which the benefits from recovery of these resources should be shared. In resolving this debate and controversy, it is important to put into perspective the relationship of ocean science and technology to the development of ocean industries. There is no recovery of marine mineral resources without an ocean mining industry, just as there is no recovery of fish from the oceans without fishing industries. Both the living and mineral resources of the oceans remain "potential resources" until they are extracted and brought to market. In the meantime, it is important that potential ocean-based resources be identified, explored and assessed, and that technical means be developed to extract them. A few examples will illustrate the costs of achieving actual capabilities through research and development, and the actual investment necessary to develop a prototype activity by which one can prove the actual feasibility of such mining and production efforts. The capital investment required for acquiring one modern offshore drilling platform is about $100 million; for a modern liquid natural gas tanker about $150 million; and for an offshore nuclear power plant with a breakwater about $1 to $1.5 billion; and the anticipated investment that will be needed to develop a mining capability to deliver 3 million tons of manganese nodules per year is between $500 and $700 million. The projected forecast of total capital investment for development of new oil and natural gas resources for the period 1970 to 1975 is estimated as $400 billion worldwide (with $185 billion for offshore developments) and $135 billion for the United States alone (with $55 billion for offshore developments).

Historically, the principle of freedom of the seas — the principle of *mare liberum* for the high seas — has been accepted by nations since the seventeenth century. International maritime trade, however, requires also that there be freedom of passage through narrow straits and interoceanic canals as well as access to ports. International agreements have been developed to ensure such passage. The national claim for sovereignty over coastal waters dates back to 1702 when Cornelius Van Bynkershoek argued that national jurisdiction should extend only as far as a nation could easily exert control; since at that time the range of cannons was about three miles, a three-mile terminal line for territorial waters became widely accepted. In this century, some nations extended this limit to twelve miles. The discovery of large offshore oil resources in the Gulf of Mexico off Louisiana and Texas during the early 1940's prompted Harry S. Truman, then President of the United States, to claim in 1945 exclusive US jurisdiction and control of the resources of the seabed and subsoil of the continental shelf off the coast of the US, while safeguarding the international rights of navigation in the waters above the shelf. Shortly thereafter, Ecuador, Peru and Chile claimed sovereignty over an area extending two hundred miles from their shores in order to preserve the fisheries there for their own economic benefit.

In 1958, eighty-six nations met in Geneva in the United Nations' first Law of the Sea Conference to resolve some of the disputes relating to sovereignty and jurisdictional rights of the seas. Agreement was reached that resources of the continental shelf belong to and may be exploited exclusively by the coastal state and its nationals or by such persons and firms as the state permits to operate in this area. The region of sovereignty was proposed as "*a)* the seabed and subsoil of the submarine areas adjacent to the coast but outside the area of the territorial sea, to a depth of two hundred meters or, beyond that limit, to where the depth of the superjacent waters admits of the exploitation of the natural resources of the said area; *b)* to the seabed and subsoil of similar areas adjacent to the coasts of islands". This definition would shortly prove unsatisfactory since newly developed technology permitted exploitation in the deepest parts of the ocean, well beyond any geographical continental shelf formation.

The first Law of the Sea Conference also tried to resolve the issue of the proper breadth of the territorial sea without reaching an agreement, and was unable to reach a satisfactory agreement on the status and management of fisheries. It is important to remember that with respect to the living resources of the ocean (i.e. fisheries), the process of developing agreements on individual fisheries issues has been quite successful from the time when the European Fisheries Convention reached its agreements in 1884. These original agreements were finally superseded by the conventions of the Northeast Atlantic and European fisheries held in 1959 and 1964. The International Convention of the Northwest Atlantic Fisheries (ICNAF) concentrates on fishing off the Grand Banks and is particularly concerned with maintaining the maximum sustained catch. Many other agreements have been concluded as well, for instance, between the US and Canada relating to Atlantic salmon and halibut fishing; and between these countries, the Soviet Union and Japan for the conservation of these fish in the northeastern Pacific Ocean.

A second Law of the Sea Conference was called in the early sixties to address some of the unresolved issues of the first Conference, but it did not succeed. In the late 1960's, the plans for conducting a third Law of the Sea Conference were initiated aiming at developing a legal comprehensive treaty which would be a foundation for a permanent international legal regime for governing the world's oceans. The negotiations proceeded toward establishing a framework for management and control of ocean developments and ocean uses and for working out compromises accommodating national aspirations, national or multinational investments in ocean technology and ventures, and national or international claims for ownership.

The seventh session of the third United Nations Law of the Sea Conference convened on March 28, 1978, in Geneva. It is perhaps the most important current test of the world community's ability to deal with its common problems. The negotiations will be based on the "Informal Composite Negotiations Treaty" (ICNT). The Text is called "Informal" because it provides a "working document" on which further negotiation can be based. It is called "Composite" because it combines in a single document the work product of the three working committees of the Conference to which the major substantive issues have been delegated. Broadly, Committee I deals with the issue of seabed mining — the single most stubborn issue confronting the Conference. Committee II considers a collection of subjects including the exclusive economic zone, the territorial sea and contiguous zone, international straits, island archipelagos, the continental shelf, and the interests of landlocked and economically disadvantaged states. Committee III is concerned with protection of the marine environment and with scientific research. A special plenary committee deals with dispute settlement procedures.

About one hundred and fifty nations are participating in the Conference in an attempt to negotiate a treaty which may finally consist of over three hundred articles and a number of detailed annexes. The difficulties in reaching an agreement at this third Law of the Sea Conference result from the high aspirations to develop an all-encompassing international law (in essence a constitution) for the oceans. This is in contrast to the historical process of developing international agreements on an issue-by-issue basis. In addition, the delegates face the relatively new philosophical dimension of addressing the ocean resources as the "common heritage of mankind" at a time when only a few nations have the technical capability to develop the ocean resources while all expect to share in the anticipated benefits. Agreement has been reached on nearly all issues, but it is doubtful whether progress will be made toward reaching a workable and mutually acceptable agreement on how to approach the development of the deep ocean resources, and how to share the resulting benefit. This issue of "sharing" has led to polarization between three different groups, referred to as GS (Britain, US, Soviet Union, France and Japan); Group of 77 encompassing the large number of developing countries, and LLGDS (landlocked geographically disadvantaged states). If all nations are united in the desire to derive a base for a meaningful balance between mankind's use of the oceans and their protection for mankind's future, they should be able to overcome their national differences and reach an agreement.

Questions for Discussion

1.   What instances of serious environmental deterioration are evident in your own region and how effectively do the churches in your community join in the struggle to overcome them?

2.   What steps are being taken in your community to educate its people about the waste of resources? Is it possible to do anything effective at a local level? What supportive national action is needed? And do you feel the need for supportive international action?

3.   What in your view would be involved in a new and just distribution of world resources? At what points do you think people in your country would be most ready to share their resources with poorer countries? At what points would they be most opposed to doing so?

4.   Sometimes the debate about environmental protection versus economic growth is interpreted in terms of unemployment and employment. Does this happen in your community? If so, how does your community resolve the conflict between the differing demands of humanity and nature?

5.   What is the central point of discussion in your country about population policy today? Over-population? Under-population? Or effective means of population control? How does the discussion of issues in chapter 13 bear upon your concerns?

6.   What is your country contributing to the deterioration of the oceans, and what is it doing to combat it? Discuss ways by which this issue could become more real for people in your community.

IV.

Science and Technology as Power — Its Distribution and Control

15 · Technical Power and People: The Impact of Technology on the Structure of Government *

The structure of government within the nation state, as now organized, is unlikely to survive in its present form. It evolved in response to circumstances very different from those that now exist and, as is evident, it is proving itself incapable of coping adequately with the amount of power that mankind now has at its disposal. It is both too small to exercise really effective human control over the destiny of its own citizens in a tiny and dangerous world; and it is too big and too clumsy an instrument to deal with the rapidly changing and diverse needs and values of people in the communities where they live and work.

This is the inescapable conclusion to which one is driven by even the most superficial examination of the impact of the technological revolution through which we are passing.

This process of political obsolescence has been going on for a long time; and it began to accelerate with the development of weapons systems that extended the range of warfare beyond the heavy artillery and relatively light and slow aircraft which were in use up until the Second World War. With the advent of nuclear weapons and intercontinental missiles, the nation state was forced to surrender its basic claim on the allegiance of its people — namely, that it served as a necessary and effective instrument for defending its citizens against assaults from the outside. Modern weapons led to the move towards the bloc system of defense which represents, even for the senior partners in each bloc, a permanent erosion of their national independence and sovereignty. And it was recognized at about the same time that the ultimate logic of modern weaponry required the establishment of some world organization like the United Nations, with the implication that one day it would develop into an embryonic world government, however long it took to reach that state. Meanwhile the paralysis of the superpowers when they try to use their military arsenals is only too apparent.

---

* The author of this chapter is the Rt. Hon. Anthony Wedgwood Benn, Secretary of State for Industry in the UK. His paper first appeared in the *Bulletin of the Atomic Scientist*, December 1975.

But it is not only the emergence of external forces that has brought into question the credentials of the nation state. Technology has had an equally dramatic impact on the lives of the citizens, in both less developed and highly developed societies. Their experience of modern life, amplified by the mass media, rendered more intelligible by improved education and made progressively more vulnerable and fragile by the interdependence that is inseparable from economic development, has led to demands being pressed from below which the modern state with a centralized power structure may be incapable of meeting quickly enough to avert intolerable strain, and possibly violent upheaval. Thus the second claim of the nation state — that it can effectively protect a society against the risk of internal disorder or disintegration — is also in doubt. Looking around the world, we see that the stresses in many countries are dangerously above the safety level.

Nor is it only in terms of military or civil insecurity that the nation state has found itself on the defensive. Industrial development — especially by the multinational corporations — far exceeds the scale of operation of industry a generation ago, and the power of these new companies, not to mention their rate of growth, now exceeds that of many nation states. Governments of even quite advanced societies can no longer, therefore, claim to be wholly effective in safeguarding the interests of their citizens against possibly harmful decisions taken by these firms.

Moreover instantaneous worldwide communications available on more and more television channels means that the nation state can no longer guarantee to erect on its frontiers effective censorship that filters out unacceptable foreign ideas and preserves the sort of broad identity of views, culture and outlook that could be said to represent its way of life as embodied in the consensus on which its society worked.

The death-throes of the self-contained nation state may last for a very long time, but the process of transformation in the constitutional structure of society is as inevitable for the nation state as it is for any firm which finds technological change destroying its old management structure and requiring it to adapt itself accordingly.

The emergence of international managements controlling military and industrial power has now virtually ousted the shareholder or stockholder as a center of power and has simultaneously stimulated greater demand for popular power.

In this process the role of science in society has come to occupy a central ground of argument between the new bureaucracies that see it as an agent for promoting their own aims and purposes, and people who increasingly see science both as a threat to their survival and, if properly used, as one of the key instruments for solving the problems that press on them most directly. Thus science has been drawn out of the academic atmosphere from which it drew its inspiration and original funding, and into the vortex of political controversy.

Science as instrument for political domination has given birth to the military-industrial complex which is immensely powerful in both the communist and non-communist worlds. Enormous sums of money are made available from general taxation to develop new weapons systems which it is claimed will preserve a favorable power balance for those nations that are ready to pay the bill and spare the necessary qualified manpower.

But meanwhile, from below, more and more voices are being raised to divert these same resources to meet the needs of development and to improve living conditions. It is not just that modern war with its inevitable killing is becoming unacceptable; there is a growing conviction that war-making absorbs money and skill on such a scale that, were they to be turned to constructive purposes, the causes of many conflicts that lead to war might be eliminated.

The same tug of war is evident in civil industrial developments. The bureaucracies which govern large firms (sometimes supported by governments) are forever seeking to maximize their return on capital invested by using science to make more sophisticated products and by employing complex techniques of persuasion to create a demand for them; at the same time, the public is beginning to question the whole process. First, they are concerned with the side effects that may follow from the unchecked economic growth that has up to now been regarded as an unmixed blessing. Second, they are beginning to wonder whether there are not other needs to be met than those which express themselves through market forces. The conflict between private and public transport in major cities is one example, and the whole structure of educational provision with its tremendous concentration on graduate and postgraduate work is another.

National governments are caught between these two formidable forces which are pulling in opposite directions. They know — because it is their business to know — that large and efficient managements will be required if the delicate balance in any world system is to be maintained. To this extent they are necessarily in close and continuing contact with the big organizations concerned.

At the same time, especially in societies where the vote has been granted, national politicians are painfully aware of the pressures coming from their electorates conveying, however imperfectly, the problems and aspirations of ordinary citizens.

National governments are thus the fuse box connecting two conflicting realities. A great deal of current passes through that fuse box, and the heat is intense. If it blows, there could be a total blackout and a total breakdown. President Truman once said: "If you don't like the heat, get out of the kitchen." But somebody has to stay in the kitchen at least until we can find a cooler way to cook.

Until recent years the centralized bureaucracies seemed to be having it all their own way. They generated technology, and controlled the use to which technology was put. The public was so astonished by the new scientific miracles and felt so humble in the presence of the experts in science and technology who masterminded these achievements that they hardly questioned the purposes to which this power was being put. Henry Ford was seen as a man who had put technology at the service of man. Military scientists were seen as key figures through whom security could be achieved and our enemies vanquished. Technical decisions were uncritically accepted as lying outside the capabilities of ordinary people to question, and they stood back while the experts decided. Thus it was that President Kennedy's historic decision to put an American on the moon by 1970, and the Anglo-French Treaty to build the supersonic airliner, were accepted without public debate. Both these ventures were seen as glorious examples of man's freedom deriving from new-found power to control nature.

But once freedom — in this case scientific freedom — had been won, people started to question how that freedom should be used. It may take a highly skilled chemist to develop a contraceptive pill or a brilliant engineer to develop a new system of communication. But the use to which either is put involves the application of a scale of values which it is entirely within the capability of everybody and anybody to use on their own. The problems of the control of technology in a scientifically permissive society can therefore be seen to be no more complex than any other value judgment which democratic societies now accept and that electors and voters are qualified to take.

Indeed, there is now growing evidence that more and more people are quite independently coming to the same conclusion, and this is expressing itself in more forceful demands from below. These demands are not new ones, but what is significant about them is that for the first time the technology capable of satisfying them now exists.

Take first the demand for sufficiency from those who are still experiencing poverty — both the poor in developed societies and the even greater number of poor in societies that have not developed. These people are different from their forefathers in that they know that other people have escaped from poverty and that the technology that made escape possible is available to them. It is one thing to be poor when there is no choice, but it is another to accept what may appear to be an unnecessary poverty. This is the cause of the revolution of rising expectations in both developing and developed societies. As living standards rise, expectations seem to keep well ahead of them and produce the curious phenomenon of levels of personal dissatisfaction rising in parallel with affluence.

The demand for greater equality is also gathering force, similarly fanned by the mass media. This is not merely a demand for greater economic equality, but also for racial and sexual equality which sees in discrimination an entrenchment of unacceptable privilege and a perpetuation of a more fundamental oppression. The use of resources, including scientific resources, to secure greater equality is highly relevant, especially in the educational field.

The worldwide demand for educational reform touches directly on the control of science. More and more people are becoming skeptical of the established objective of education to educate elites, including scientific elites. Even if looked at from a purely practical point of view, it would appear that the main barriers to human advance lie more in our failure to apply well-established techniques than in our tardiness in evolving new ones. For example, millions more lives could be saved by raising the general level of simple health services than by pouring millions of pounds or dollars into perfecting heart transplants or other sophisticated surgical operations. There is even a curious convergence of views between a community which doesn't quite know how to employ the many PhDs emerging from graduate schools, heavy with honors but short of experience, and the students who everywhere are discontented because their studies are so academic and appear to lack "relevance". This feeling is shared on both sides of the Iron Curtain and there are more similarities between modern thinking on this in China and the United States than there are between the old school academic establishments in both these countries and the communities they are supposed to serve. Educational bureaucracies are already finding themselves on the firing line along with the military industrial complex as this pressure begins to build up.

The demand for greater popular power — or participation as it now tends to be called — follows from the demands described above. Where the franchise has not yet been won, it is being demanded; and where it has been achieved, there is a mounting pressure for further democratization of decision-making.

This pressure is not really new at all. It is as old as political philosophy itself, but what is new is that it is being extended far beyond the simple demands of the Founding Fathers of the American Republic or the French Revolution, or the modest advocates of universal adult suffrage. More and more people are coming to suspect that democracy has slipped through their fingers while they were busy watching science proving its apparently limitless capability.

The New Bosses

Now, all of a sudden, people have awakened to the fact that science and technology are just the latest expression of power and that those who control them have become the new bosses, exactly as the feudal landlords who owned the land, or the capitalist pioneers who owned the factories, became the bosses of earlier generations. Ordinary people will not now be satisfied until they have got their hands on this power and have turned it to meet their needs.

This may sound like a very revolutionary doctrine, and so indeed it is. But once we understand what is happening, it is no more frightening than the demand for power that emerged in the past as a popular clamor for political democracy.

What we lack are the institutions capable of realizing that demand in today's world, and making it effective. It must necessarily lead to the strengthening of international and supranational institutions big enough to encompass the totality of man's needs as he gradually learns that brotherhood has moved from a moral aspiration to an essential prerequisite of survival. We are mainly short on imagination bold enough to extend our sense of responsibility to embrace the area of our common interest. This imaginative leap is difficult for the old and the middle aged, but it comes quite naturally to the young. Their view of the Spaceship Earth with its people living closely together will in time replace the distortions of Mercator's flat projection showing every country highly colored within its political frontiers — just as Galileo's view of the universe replaced the flat concept of the Ptolemaic astronomers.

Popular Pressures

Nationally, the demand will express itself in more subtle ways. The pressure for open government which reveals the choices before they are made will intensify. Decisions affecting the use of science and technology, whether by governments, corporations or universities, will become increasingly the subject of critical scrutiny, as has been shown most vividly by the recent economic and environmental debates and decisions on the development of the supersonic transport. People may still argue as to whether the decision was right or wrong, but no one can doubt that it was taken openly and that the decisive pressure came from below in sufficient strength to overturn the wishes of an administration and the aerospace industry, both of which wanted to go ahead.

Similarly, the environmental pressures that have built up over recent years can be seen as having a political significance greater even than the actual cause which the environmentalists espoused. They can be seen as a direct political demand under the classification of technology assessment aimed at securing a proper consideration of the consequences of all decisions before they are reached, so that the side effects can be taken into account at the time of the basic decision. This is a move to better and more democratic decision-making, and if it can be made a permanent feature of political life, it will be far more important even than the improvement of the environment. It may, in fact, serve to check the wildest environmentalists who are now pressing for unrealistic policies which could have unexpected industrial and human side effects.

But the pressure for democratization will not stop there. It is bound to extend to the democratization of industrial power, through workers' control, educational power and the power of the mass media which, by their control of information output, can play a decisive part in shaping society.

We are presently so conscious of the centralizing forces that derive from technological change and of the huge new and powerful bureaucracies that they have created that many people tend to be despondent, to believe that ordinary human influences are quite powerless and the cause of democracy is irretrievably lost as man surrenders to the new power centers. The emergence of countervailing power from the grass roots is less easy to recognize. It is dispersed so widely, its exercise is so uncertain, and the time scale of its successes is so long that many people do not believe it really exists. At the moment it may be only a potential power, but its potentiality is far greater than most people realize. We have not yet learned to organize ourselves to use the power that has fallen into our hands because we are not fully aware of it and because it requires us to think about our system of government in quite a different way.

The study of civics or political institutions, as most of uslearned about them at school or through the mass media, always focuses up on the formal structure of the nation state. We are told how accountability has been secured by freedom of speech and the vote. But even this interpretation stresses what our leaders do and say. Policy and changes of policy are presented to us as coming from the top.

Change from Below

But is that really how our political system works? I greatly doubt it. There is an interpretation of political change under which one can argue that it is change from below that has been and is really significant and can, over a period, be decisive. Certainly, the demand for the vote was a demand that came from the grass roots and was reluctantly conceded by the political leaders of the time. The demand for human rights or racial equality has never been particularly acceptable to those in authority in societies which denied these rights. The groundswell demand for free trade unions or socialized education or socialized medicine in a welfare state was not thought up in the corridors of power. It bubbled up in the community, lapping around the foundations of the establishment until it acquired sufficient momentum to swamp the opposition in Congress or Parliament. By this means, too, the environmentalists captured the White House and Number 10 Downing Street, making it clear that they would no longer tolerate the barbarities of technology. The new movement for women's rights has also gathered force outside the system and is already making progress within it against the entrenchment of male privilege.

It is arguable from this that the historic function of the politician is to capitulate, and that the good politician capitulates only to forces that he has helped to create by education and argument and by his encouragement of those who are trying to extend the area of human responsibility.

Indeed, the task of statesmanship today requires leaders to be more than bureaucratic administrators of vast governmental machines. For anyone who looks around him and, even more, anyone who looks ahead should see one fact staring him in the face. The amount of power that the technological revolution has created far exceeds the capability of even the most inspired, dedicated or brilliant leaders to control unaided.

In June 1940, when the seemingly unconquerable German army stood poised on the French coast ready to attack Britain, Winston Churchill pledged himself to carry on the struggle "until, in God's good time, the new world with all its power and might steps forth to the rescue and liberation of the old". That is exactly the position confronting the statesman of today as he observes the massive and menacing power of technology which encompasses us. He must carry on the struggle until, in God's good time, the people with all their power and might step forth to the rescue and liberation of mankind.

Only a massive dispersal of power conveying responsibility beyond and within the nation state to those upon whose wise exercise of it our survival depends can possibly redress the balance in favor of the people in their battle to gain control of the machine. To pretend otherwise would be an illusion — an illusion we can ill afford to nourish.

16 · Technology Transfer and Dependence *

To understand the present situation of science and technology in a region of the Third World, in this case Latin America, we must bear in mind that the nations of this continent were, for more than three centuries, the colonies of Portugal, as in the case of Brazil, and of Spain. The dependence of Portugal on England, especially after the Treaty of Menthuen in 1703, gave to Brazil the character of a kind of hidden colony of the United Kingdom. The colonial economic system was based on exploitation and exportation of raw materials (e.g. gold from Brazil went directly to England as payment for the Portuguese imports of English manufactured products); and these agricultural activities and mineral exploitations required only the most rudimentary knowledge and techniques.

The independence of Brazil, proclaimed in 1822, did not essentially change this situation of economic dependence — it was considered rather as the development of direct relations between Brazil and Great Britain.

During this period and until the beginning of the 19th century, the agricultural interests of Brazil maintained a complete domination over the state; the sectors of the economy which were asking for a more advanced technology, like rail transport and navigation, remained under foreign domination, the realization of these steps requiring foreign equipment and capital. In this same period an ideology was developed in Brazil which affirmed its "agricultural calling" — the country would not be able to produce industrial goods as developed as those produced in England. And if it tried to do so, and for that purpose adopted protectionist measures, it could be certain that corresponding measures would be taken against its agricultural exportations by the industrialized countries. The dominant class in Brazil based its power on this ideology, established during the

* The author of this chapter is Prof. J. Leite Lopes, a Brazilian scientist and, since 1975, Vice-Director, Centre of Nuclear Research, Centre National de la Recherche Scientifique, Strasbourg, France, and Director of its Division of High Energies. The paper was first presented to a UNESCO Colloquium, Paris, November 28-29, 1977.

phase of exporting primary products; the repercussions of this would be felt both in the further evolution of the economy and also in the development of science and technology in the country.

The schools of higher learning in Brazil, set up for the education of a tiny minority coming from the rural elite and the upper layer of the middle class, aimed at preparing lawyers, who formed the leadership group of the country, and later doctors. It was only in 1810 that King John VI, a refugee in Brazil because of the invasion of Portugal by the armies of Napoleon, created the Royal Military Academy, which in 1874 was transformed into the Polytechnique of Rio de Janeiro, for the preparation of engineers. In 1875 the School of Mines of the City of Ouro Preto was founded, and in 1879 the Polytechnique of Sao Paulo. The first research institutes date from the early years of the 20th century when the government was obliged to create institutes of research in biology and medicine — the Butantan Institute of Sao Paulo and the Oswaldo Cruz Institute of Rio de Janeiro — to fight against the plague and yellow fever and certain diseases of coffee plants.

But at the beginning of the 20th century according to the historian O. G. Velho, "Brazil imported all manufactured goods, everything from locomotives to matches".

The variations in the international demand for primary products gave rise to occasional declines in Brazil's capacity to import industrial products, and these stimulated initiatives in the country to industrialize in order to satisfy the needs of the domestic market. This industrialization process, a substitution for imports, resulted however in developing means of production based on imitating and importing technology developed abroad.

Thus the system of economic dependence of the colonial era was transferred, in another form, to the building of the Brazilian industrial system. The demand for manufactured products similar to those which were imported made necessary a technological dependence on the outside — the scientific knowledge and the techniques essential for the industrialization which was beginning came as part of the capital goods imported and in the specifications for manufacturing purchased abroad.

This process of industrialization was accentuated by the First World War, the world economic crisis of 1929 and finally by the Second World War. And England, which had replaced Portugal as the dominating partner of the Brazilian economy, ceded its place, as we know, to the United States.

After 1930 the schools of chemistry of Sao Paulo and Rio de Janeiro were founded and the faculties of sciences were established for the preparation of teachers and researchers.

The grouping of these faculties with the other schools of higher education to form universities dates from this period, and the number of universities in Brazil increased considerably after 1946.

Nevertheless, the industrial establishments belonging to Brazilian businessmen depended on imported machines and technology, and as a result they were never interested in the problems of technological or scientific research necessary to develop or improve their manufactured products. Linked to foreign enterprises by the rentals for patents and services, the national industries rarely called upon the institutes of technological research, such as the Institute of Technological Research of Sao Paulo and the National Institute of Technology of Rio de Janeiro, which in the beginning confined themselves to the tests of building materials and the checking of instruments for measurement.

Beginning in the sixties when a reasonable number of scientists were coming to occupy teaching and research posts in the Brazilian universities, a new form of dependence was imposed on the Brazilian industrial system. The massive entry of great multinational companies into the country had very important consequences for the economy and also for science and technology in Brazil.

Before this transformation of the Brazilian economy, the scientists of my generation hoped that, through publications, discussion and intervention in the press and in the meetings of the Society for the Progress of Science and of the Academy of Sciences, it would be possible to establish one day a close liaison between the national industries and the institutes of technological research, supported in their turn by the scientific research institutes and the universities.

But from the moment when the national industries disappeared because they were not able to compete with the great multinational firms, and were in fact absorbed by them, this hope vanished.

For it is absolutely clear that the multinational industrial firms have their own laboratories of research and development in their own countries. It is these laboratories and their scientists and engineers who make the discoveries which are finally incorporated into the products exported by the multinationals or manufactured by their subsidiaries in a country like Brazil. The multinationals implanted in developing countries have no need of the researchers, of the research institutes and of the universities of these countries.

A study undertaken by three Brazilian scientists (Biato, Guimaraes and Poppe de Figueiredo, 1971) inquiring into the 500 largest industrial enterprises of Brazil and the 132 institutions having technological activities, reported (p. 76):

"The information concerning the origin of the technology utilized in the installation of industrial enterprises — a necessary preliminary to the examination of the technological activities of these firms — shows clearly the predominance of the expertise of outside origin. 62% of these industries had recourse to exterior sources. In most of the firms, that is about $^2/_3$ of them, this expertise underwent no adaptation in the transfer into the national production system; in 21% of these enterprises, however, the imported technology was adapted to Brazil." The same study affirms:

"It must be underlined that $^3/_4$ of the foreign enterprises which utilized foreign technical services, requested them from their parent firms, and as for the national institutions of research — universities and institutes — their services were rarely used by the foreign companies which we investigated, and as a result they have provided little stimulation to the national technological complex" (p. 99).

These considerations naturally lead us to examine and clarify what is meant by the transfer of technology, a magic expression, a myth so often used in discussions of development and which can lead to a false conception of what actually happens in developing countries.

What the economists and the technocrats understand by this word is nothing other than the installation in these countries of imported factories, ready to manufacture products which have been developed abroad, in the laboratories of the multinational firms which install such factories. The fact that our workers learn to manipulate the machines and to press the necessary buttons to make the cars, television sets, radios, phonographs and parts of computers, has only a relative importance since these machines are invented, developed and constructed abroad, and the plans and designs for making them cannot be altered by the engineers of the underdeveloped countries concerned. The transfer of technology as it is conceived by the technocrats never includes the installation of laboratories of scientific and technological research, associated with the industries installed in the developing countries by the multinational societies. The role of these industries is to import, to assemble, or produce locally the goods and to sell them to the elite of the country in question or to export them. How to improve these products, to modify their techniques of production, etc. is the concern of the laboratories located in the advanced countries, in the headquarters of the multinational firms owning the factories.

In a word, the expression "transfer of technology" does not signify, in the present situation, the transfer of the means of research and of scientific and technological creativity.

I would like to present a specific example which serves to illustrate these considerations — the question of nuclear energy in Brazil.

As noted previously, after the Second World War the Brazilian universities began to undergo a certain development. Especially in Sao Paulo and at Rio de Janeiro, a team of physicists was formed which produced research work in theoretical physics, in cosmic rays and in nuclear physics. A betatron and a Van de Graaf generator were installed in Sao Paulo in the 50's and students were attracted to the work in this field. Brazilian physicists were involved in studies and research abroad and one of them, C. M. G. Lattes, contributed to the discovery of mesons pi in cosmic rays (1947) and in their production, for the first time in a laboratory, through the cyclotron in Berkeley (1948).

The prestige of this work and also the prestige and rapid development of scientific research in the industrialized countries after the Second World War led the Brazilian government to create in 1951, under the pressure from our scientists, the National Research Council. The purpose of this institution was not only to strengthen and to stimulate fundamental scientific research but also to develop and control all activities relative to atomic energy in Brazil.

Between 1951 and 1954 this Council tried to obtain the cooperation of the US government, through the Atomic Energy Commission, to develop nuclear energy in Brazil. For several years minerals containing thorium were exported to the United States. The National Research Council of Brazil asked that in payment for these exports research reactors and nuclear power reactors be installed in Brazil. Since the MacMahon Act in the United States prohibited both the export of nuclear equipment and the communication of information in this field, the Brazilian Research Council tried to obtain the cooperation of France, from which it ordered a factory for processing minerals and producing uranium alloys; and from the Federal Republic of Germany it asked for the installation of a pilot plant for the enrichment of uranium by the ultracentrifuge process, a technique which about this time had begun to be studied and developed in that country. These contracts were, however, not made because of the intervention of the US government which opposed the installation in Brazil of this technology.

In 1956, after the information about this had been published, thanks to the testimony of Admiral Alvaro Alberto, the first President of the National Research Council, before the Chamber of Deputies of Brazil, the National Security Council cancelled all the contracts for the export of thorium minerals to the USA and created the National Commission for Nuclear Energy which was to set in motion a new policy destined to encourage work on nuclear energy. This Commission adopted however a policy which did not favour the kind of development which had been recommended in 1957 by the National Security Council. The First International Conference on the Peaceful Application of Atomic Energy, meeting in Geneva in 1955, when information in this area had been published, provided an opportunity for the Brazilian government to make cooperative agreements with many countries for the carrying out of research in this field, as was being done practically everywhere. However, the proposal made by several of us, for the creation of a National Laboratory on Nuclear Energy which would bring together Brazilian and foreign researchers for the realization of a national programme, was rejected by the Nuclear Energy Commission. For about 20 years after the Conference of Geneva, Brazil made little progress in the field of nuclear energy —

three small research reactors installed in three universities. The research programme was directed only toward the production and application of radio-isotopes. No study project or reactor construction programme by our engineers and physicists was forthcoming. It would have been of interest for Brazil to have secured the cooperation of foreign institutions for the realization in Brazil of research on the utilization of thorium as a fissile element in reactors, a possibility which had been announced during the Conference in Geneva in 1955.

I participated in the discussion of these problems; and I was a member of the Committee on Atomic Energy of the National Research Council which preceded the National Commission for Nuclear Energy. I fought for the creation of a National Laboratory on Nuclear Energy and in 1958 I wrote articles exposing the difficulties. But the resistance against a dynamic programme on nuclear energy, and the research necessary to the later industrialization, was immense. The foreign industries which wished to sell research reactors (the turn-key approach) — and the latest gadgets and measuring instruments — won the battle.

In 1975, as we know, the government of Brazil, faced with the rising price of oil, announced the signing of an accord with the Federal Republic of Germany for the installation of a group of eight nuclear power stations, with a capacity of around 10 million kilowatts. The agreement also included installing of the necessary infrastructure which comprised the production of enriched fuel and the reprocessing of irradiated fuel for the separation of plutonium. I shall not examine the details of this programme, nor the criticism made by the representatives of the US government on the possible military applications of the plutonium obtained by the reprocessing of irradiated fuel. The important point to call attention to is that this decision has been taken apparently by the technocrats of the government without any consultation with the scientific bodies of the country. In fact, the Brazilian Physical Society published a manifesto approved July 14, 1975, in which there is the following declaration:

"There could be a risk of repeating certain experiences encountered in other fields of the Brazilian economy where foreign technology has been imported without bringing any significant benefit to the national technology. The participation of Brazilian scientists and technologists in the formulation of methods and systems to be used in the overall policy for the energy choices of this country, is indispensable for national scientific and technological development."

According to an article published recently on the German-Brazilian Nuclear Treaty by Vargas (1976) it is clear that the transfer of technology will be realized in this field, as in others, without the possibility of the participation of Brazilian scientists and technologists, either in the elaboration of the project or in the process of its creation.

Thus we read:

"The national effort concerning the use of the nuclear reactor technology of the PWR type is determined by the very nature of the agreement, as it relates to both the objectives and strategy of the programme and the transfer of the technology.

"The agreement foresees the transfer of technology relative to all the stages of an integrated nuclear programme, from the fuel cycle up to the progressive manufacture in the country of the reactors themselves, beginning with the acquisition and construction of nuclear power stations of the Biblis type. There are some difficulties characteristic of the complexity of the nuclear system for producing energy:

a) the difficulty of mastering a nuclear plant with only the information received;

b) the difficulty of anticipating in time the technological improvements of the plant;

c) the difficulty of obtaining in the future technological autonomy in the field of advanced or fast reactors."

"To overcome these obstacles", Vargas continues, "it would be necessary to achieve two fundamental intermediate objectives through the assimilation of 'savoir-faire' and 'savoir-pourquoi faire':

1) the immediate development of a capacity for applied engineering;

2) the gradual development of the capacities of the programme as a whole and of the process (savoir-faire).

"Concerning the possibilities for effective acquisition of the technology during the several stages of the programme leading to the installation of the nuclear power station, it is necessary to underline that a superficial examination of the technological sectors involved is sufficient to show that we will not have the opportunity to participate initially in the elaboration of the total technology.

"The conception of the reactor up to the primary circuit of the heat exchanger, that is to say the philosophy of the project as it is often called, is not open to discussion. It is a given. All the economic and technical confrontations of this phase have been confidential, not necessarily secret, but not easily and practically accessible to the recipient."

Thus we see that after twenty years of governmental inaction in this field there is suddenly a repetition of the experience of buying of machines, of technology and of projects, without the experts of the country having a chance of contributing to the study or even to the preliminary discussion of the options in this field, so important for the national technological complex. Is it not a new step towards, a new aggravation of, technological dependence?

I conclude by saying that what we need, perhaps above all, is discussion in depth of these questions, a realistic analysis of these difficulties, because the developing countries must demand that they be able to create and collaborate in the work of development and the application of science and technology for the benefit of their populations, that they have the power to decide on such projects and on the corresponding policies.

It is necessary that science and technology be effectively utilized for the welfare of all the peoples — at the moment they are applied only to a fraction of humanity which lives in the industrialized countries.

The scientific discoveries and innovations must be realized also inside the Third World. And for that we must replace the policies and models of development which serve only an élite. New ones must be adopted for the benefit of all men and women who live in these countries.

17 · The Quest for Appropriate Technology *

"Choice of Techniques" is an important sector of discussion in various analyses of economic development. It has received much attention in India's economic planning over the last two and a half decades. However, since the seventies, and especially since the Draft Outline of the Fifth Five Year Plan, it has become a "live" policy issue, demanding a careful re-examination of the dominant technological trend and ethos in our society. India has in the past relied heavily on technology acquired from developed countries. Such "modern technology" tends to be capital-intensive and requires an elaborate infrastructure of organization, training, resources and research. More significantly, it reflects the social realities of industrial nations and serves as a carrier of their values and systems. In our avid pursuit of rapid industrialization for economic growth, we have, perhaps too hastily, opted for imitative technology, without assessing its suitability in terms of our realities. The fundamental need of a developing country is not technology per se, but an on-going technological revolution. Imitation can sometimes be a helpful first step, if it promotes adaptation and innovation and generates a scientific mind-set conducive to authenticity. If that does not happen, as seems to have been the case in many developing countries, then technology acquired from developed nations leads to economic subservience and aggravates the domination-dependence relationship between the North and the South, so characteristic of the prevailing international economic order.

The Disillusionment with "Modern" Technology

In the Indian context, two factors are responsible for the new technological mood and the related quest for appropriate technology. *First,* is the sense of disillusionment with the technological direction pursued

---

* The author of this chapter is Prof. S. L. Parmar, Dean of the Economics Department, Allahabad University, India. His paper was presented to the WCC sponsored regional Seminar on Science and Society, New Delhi, November 17-20, 1977.

thus far. There is a growing awareness of its inappropriateness. The Technology would be deemed appropriate when it helps to attain desired socio-economic objectives, is rational in terms of a country's factor endowment, has lower social cost over time, and provides the underpinnings of technological self-reliance. *Second:* is the significant shift in planning priorities with primacy to social justice, self-reliance and people's participation as vital adjuncts of economic growth.

This calls for greater concentration on the uplift and well-being of the rural sector; on the large masses struggling for survival below the poverty line. This in turn necessitates a radical change in the technological mix that dominates the Indian scene.

Why the disillusionment with our rather impressive technological achievements? Mainly because these have not succeeded in attaining some of the important goals of economic planning, such as: eradication of unemployment and under-employment; reduction of socio-economic inequalities; curbs on concentration of economic power; promotion of a process of self-reliant development, and establishment of a socialist social order.

It is true that technological factors are only one of a number of reasons for our shortcomings. However, their negative impact needs to be identified. There is ample evidence from the Indian economic experience to support each of the following points:

1. Modern technology tends to be increasingly capital-intensive. It, therefore, gravitates towards the organized industrial/urban sector. Economic dualism has been and continues to be a predominant characteristic of our economy. The large "traditional" sector is dominated and exploited by the small "modern" sector. The process of planned development was supposed to correct such imbalance and establish greater equity between the two sectors. Reliance on modern technology has worked against this. Perhaps in line with the "percolation" or "trickle down" notion of economic growth it was assumed that extension of modern technology would strengthen the organized sector and enable it to pull up the traditional sector. The contrary has happened. Just as economic growth has conferred greater benefits on the relatively privileged minority in society and failed to relieve the deprivation of those below the poverty line, so also have the major gains of modern technology been appropriated by privileged groups in the industrial/ urban sector without making an appreciable dent in unemployment and under-employment or in mobilizing the productive potential of the vast rural populace.

2. The capital and energy intensiveness of modern technology, together with the specialized skills it requires, have led to a limited absorption of our huge humanpower resources. According to one estimate, the

present 3.6% annual rate of industrial growth will take nearly 306 years to provide workplaces for India's labour force.

This should help to explode the myth of a rational allocation of national resources claimed by advocates of "modernization". India is short on capital and advanced skills and long on semi-skilled and unskilled labour. Modern technology injects distortions in factor usage and cannot, therefore, be considered appropriate.

3. The imitative technology that we have supported is a carrier of consumerism and anarchic urbanization. As the majority of our people lack purchasing power to respond to consumerism, it follows that only a small affluent minority is the beneficiary. As a result, a substantial part of our limited investible resources is diverted from production for basic needs to production of luxuries and less essential goods. Here again one sees a misdirection of resources which subverts any process of rational allocation. Efficiency of production should be judged by what is produced and for whom, rather than by the aggregative quantum of output. Production for social needs in accordance with priorities that aim to raise the condition of the poor from "misery" to "sufficiency", this should be the criterion for judging efficient use of resources. From the point of view of reducing economic inequalities, a cherished goal of India's economic policy, it should be recognized that equality is not possible at the level of affluence but at that of non-affluence. In order that the poor may move up, it is imperative that the rich be moved down. Otherwise the production mechanism tends to be harnessed to production for the "surfeit" of the few at the cost of the needs of the majority. A socially desirable minimum for all requires acceptance of a permissible maximum for the privileged few. Consumerism in the West has brought about an "alarming degree of product obsolescence and the 'throw away' philosophy". These are completely out of place for our economy of scarcity and massive poverty.

4. Modern technology leads to a concentration of economic power because it increases socio-economic inequalities, transfers the gains of growth to a relatively affluent minority, favours large-scale production and gigantism, and offers special incentives to owners of capital and means of production, both domestic and foreign (e.g., multinationals). All this contributes to alienation and diminished social participation and control. India's economy provides many instances of such counter-development tendencies.

5. Industrial nations are experiencing disastrous environmental consequences of modern technology. An ever-increasing scale of production threatens to push pollution beyond the limits of sustainability. The

"ceaseless pursuit of affluence" is rapidly exhausting non-renewable resources and has already caused a serious maldistribution in resource-use between rich and poor societies and rich and poor groups within a nation. Under the rather callous notion that developing countries have a comparative advantage in absorbing pollution, many industrial nations have shifted their production units to these areas and are despoiling both natural resources and the environment. Thus far India has not paid adequate attention to environmental and ecological problems. But in any assessment of modern technology these deleterious features should be taken into account.

6. In economic calculations it is customary to consider unit costs of production rather than social costs. A similar narrow yardstick is applied to judge efficiency. If total output increases and cost per unit goes down, it is rather too facilely concluded that resource utilization and production techniques are efficient. Large-scale production through modern technology is generally advocated on such grounds. The crucial question, however, should be of social costs. If a production process fails to relieve unemployment, the social loss in terms of the human wreckage is almost incalculable. In addition to the heavy social cost of pollution and misdirection of limited resources, we have to reckon with the negative aspects of unplanned urbanization and the social breakdown it causes. Co-existence of the prosperity of the few alongside the misery of the many is a potent force for dehumanization. The affluent are dehumanized as they build walls of material security around themselves and almost become oblivious to the widespread misery surrounding them. The deprived are dehumanized by the compulsions of their sub-human existence. We have failed to bring into our socio-economic calculus these heavy social costs that the so-called "modernization process" has imposed.

The Need for People-Oriented Technology

Since modern technology appears to be ecologically unsatisfactory, since it magnifies inequalities and reduces social participation and control, it needs to be replaced by a more appropriate technology that is in harmony with nature, serves to meet basic human needs and strengthens self-reliance.

In terms of the emphasis now being placed in India's economic planning on social justice, self-reliance and people's participation, we need to evolve technologies that are labour-using, capital- and energy-saving, small-scale and amenable to decentralization. These conditions can be largely met if technology is built primarily on natural, human and renewable local resources, if it can be linked to traditional skills, crafts and techniques, and if it is geared to production that will meet the basic needs of the poor. We should be realistic enough to recognize that even in a so-called poor country like India there is a small affluent group which is not poor. Obviously the focus of development should not be on them. Instead of looking at poverty in terms of economic aggregates and averages, it is necessary to view it in terms of people who are socially and economically deprived. Their well-being should be the primary goal of development. The appropriateness of technology would then be judged according to its effect on the poor.

A technology oriented to the concerns expressed above will promote self-reliance. The central element of self-reliance is to frame social priorities in terms of the needs of the people and to utilize available resources and mobilize potential resources to meet these needs. We could think of Gandhiji's khadi movement as a simple model of self-reliance and "development from below". Clothing is a basic need which the poor could provide for by using their spare time, simple skills and locally grown raw materials. Their actual and potential productive capacity was effectively mobilized, and the products of their labour liberated them from dependence on foreign cloth as well as from the debts incurred to purchase it. Gandhiji did not intend that the most elementary technology should continue indefinitely. That is evident from his own experiments to improve the "charkha" (spinning wheel) and his encouragement to others to invent more efficient models. The Ambar Charkha is technically much advanced over the simple spinning wheel. Thus technological progress is an important aspect of self-reliance. The economy should not remain congealed at the level of rudimentary technical skills, but keep moving to improved techniques and higher levels of production. Emphasis must, however, be on need-based, non-exploitative production and optimal utilization of available resources.

Self-reliance need not mean an absence of inter-dependence within and between nations. To the extent that foreign resources of materials, expertise and technology could be aligned to socially-determined priorities in production and resource-usage, these would be welcome. In general, such has not been the Indian experience with respect to foreign assistance, investment, transfer of technology and the pattern of specialization and trade. That is why the introduction and success of appropriate technology calls for a radical social restructuring, including that of the externally linked sector of the economy. A society that fails to use what it possesses in abundance (humanpower and simple skills as in India) is unlikely to use responsibly what it produces and receives. Appropriate technology must, therefore, play an important conservation and utilization role as a preparation to add to the flow of essential goods and services. For example, energy generation through advanced technology has its place, but the prior step should be the use of potential energy resources that exist and can be activated through simpler technology, such as humanpower, human and animal waste, windpower, solarpower, etc. Similarly fertilizer production may require modern technology but we must undergird it with development of organic manure through simple processes of recycling wastes. Parallel examples can be found from other sectors of economic activity. Agricultural output can be raised by new techniques of production, but it is equally important to develop methods of storage, packing, etc., to reduce the enormous post-harvest wastage. One can see the close linkage between appropriate technology and self-reliant development.

What kind of production process would ensure social justice and people's participation? One which immediately draws people into production, i.e., employs them, and produces goods and services that will meet basic needs. Transfer of incomes and goods through increased employment and diversion of resources into essential production become the mechanism of distributive justice in a poverty-dominated society. Instead of waiting for the fruits of growth to "trickle down" to the needy, we must begin by producing by and for such sections of the population. They must receive immediately a share of the social product. Tangible benefits in the short-period act as a spur to effort and serve as an incentive to contribute effectively to production. This, in turn, becomes a significant measure to promote people's participation in economic effort. Often we lament the scarcity of capital and the low saving potential in our society, forgetting that labour is the generator of capital and savings. Appropriate technology should be seen as a potential force for capital formation. It promotes distributive justice which leads to people's participation. The "spirit of the people" has sometimes been described as a nation's potential capital. We must increasingly place reliance on technological modes and processes that utilize people's productive capacity and motivate them to join the mainstream of national production.

To change technological direction in India is not an easy matter. Some important issues require consideration:

1. How do we arrest the production processes that are now firmly entrenched in our economy? Large-scale enterprises, an expanding organized sector, a supportive network of plants and institutions, and a burdensome urban complex are our inherited structure. Those who control the related establishments, whether in the private or the public sector, exercise considerable influence on socio-economic policies. Their political pull is also not negligible. Trade unions represent another pocket of power in this milieu. They will resist attempts to decelerate, much more to arrest, the existing trends. The interests of the organized and traditional sectors, at least in the short-period, are likely to be in conflict. Since appropriate technology tends to give relatively greater weight to the latter, its promotion will face strong resistance. Undoubtedly there is need to work out the socio-economic feasibility of appropriate technology vis-à-vis modern technology. But

it seems evident that efforts to move in new directions require political decision and action.

2. Economic dualism will remain a fact of life in India in the foreseeable future. Can its present inequitable character be changed into a mutually sustaining dualism? Is it possible to harmonize the operation and interests of the two sectors in a way that poverty, unemployment and social injustice are overcome? The organized sector is bound up with "modern technology"; progress of the traditional sector requires "appropriate technology". There is an ever-present danger that the more powerful organized sector will impose its technological methods and values on the rest of the economy as has been the tendency thus far. This is an important existential issue which has not received adequate attention as yet.

3. Re-thinking the choice of technology is part of the larger issue of re-thinking the conventional understanding of development. Quantitative growth with its predilection for higher GNP has failed to deal with the problems of poverty. There is now a shift from a narrow quantitative approach to a qualitative approach. Fundamental questions are being raised: What is being produced and for whom? Which group gains from growth? Why has growth increased inequality and failed to benefit the poor? Why has it hardened the institutional forces that in the first instance were responsible for poverty and injustice? Should policies of social justice and self-reliance not be seen as essential pre-conditions rather than consequences of growth? And so on. The focus is now on "human development", which involves mobilization of the deprived sectors and an increase in their socio-political power so that they can wrest a more equitable share of national output. Disillusionment with imitative notions of development based upon the experiences of rich nations have prompted the quest for self-reliance and authentic development relevant to our conditions. The linear view of development with its "catching-up" philosophy stands suspect.

Simplicity, limitation of wants, small-scale production, decentralization, breaking the tyranny of the market mechanism and the profit motive, socially-oriented production, etc., these are the supportive elements of appropriate technology. In short, the quest for appropriate technology is part of the quest for "Another Development". This is still an unexplored area and requires the urgent attention of social thinkers, scientists, planners and decision makers.

4. Scientists and technologists in India face a special challenge. They should not accept the social framework as a given datum but question its goals and ideological presuppositions. If science is to be in the

service of humanity, it must have a social orientation and be concerned with the values and structures of society. More than in any other developing country, science in India has made remarkable contributions to the development of appropriate technology, but these methods have not yet become a central part of our technological policies and practices. Scientists must play a more active role both in pushing the new technology from the periphery to the centre of things and also in helping to harmonize, if that is possible, "modern" and "appropriate" technologies.

Questions for Discussion

1. Discuss the term "appropriate technology" in the context of your community and its economic and social development. How would you describe "inappropriate technology"? Does this term apply only to new, large and complex technologies like nuclear energy or do some older technologies also begin to look inappropriate in the contemporary context?

2. What means are used in your community to guard against the misuse of new and untested technological developments? How well do these work to protect the community? What steps will be necessary in the future to safeguard community welfare?

3. What is the contribution of popular participation in the evaluation and use of technology today? Can you think of instances where popular participation helped? And where it failed? What is the relation between popular participation in technological decision-making and the ongoing work of government bodies set apart for this purpose?

4. What forms of ownership and control of technology seem most helpful in favoring responsible technological development? What is the experience of your community or country in guarding against placing too much power in the hands of a minority of experts or so-called technocrats?

5. What do you think is the best way to secure world-wide sharing and control of the power which science and technology bring? What further controls would your country accept on the way it uses or exports technologies which if employed universally would result in extensive social and political problems?

V.

Economic Issues in the Struggle for a Just, Participatory and Sustainable Society

18 · Growth, Technology and the Future of the World Economy *

Aside from major cataclysms such as an atomic war, the three factors that can be expected to dominate the overall development of the world economy in the future, as they did in the past, are population trends, technological change and the availability of basic natural resources.

The recently completed UN Report on "The Future of the World Economy" [1] presents a set of alternative projections — each derived from a different scenario — of economic growth from 1970 through 1980 and 1990 to the year 2000.

Based on a detailed quantitative description of structural, essentially technological, interdependence among all the various branches of production and consumption within each of the fifteen geographic regions into which the world economy was subdivided for this purpose, each one of these projections is comprehensive and internally consistent, i.e., balanced both from the point of view of each individual region and the world economy as a whole. The world-wide output of every type of good and service is balanced with the corresponding sum total of regional inputs, and the world-wide exports of each kind of internationally traded good are balanced with the sum total of its regional imports. Moreover, for each region and, consequently, for the world economy as a whole, the projected increase in every type of output is matched not only with the required current flow of raw materials, semi-fabricated goods, energy, labour and all other current inputs, but also with requisite increases in fixed investment, that is, additions to the stocks of machinery, buildings and all other types of physical investment.

* The author of this chapter is Prof. Wassily Leontief, Head of the Department of Economics, New York University. The paper was first presented to a meeting of the World Federation of Metal Workers, Munich, October 27, 1977.

[1] WASSILY LEONTIEF, ANNE P. CARTER, PETER PETRI, *et al.*: *The Future of the World Economy: A United Nations Study.* Oxford University Press, New York, 1977.

I dwell on these methodological details only to show that in contrast to world-wide projections based on extrapolation of statistical relationships between a few aggregative variables, the so-called input-output approach employed in this study permits incorporation — both in each of the alternative scenarios and in each of the long-run projections derived from them — of a great amount of sectoral and regional detail. This increases the reliability of the results and, what is especially important, facilitates their substantive criticism.

Resource Shortages and the Cost of Environmental Protection

One of the principal conclusions of the UN study is that neither a critical shortage of basic natural resources nor the costs of environmental protection should be expected to pose a serious threat to the maintenance of a high, overall rate of economic growth up to the year 2000 and beyond.*

Even under relatively conservative assumptions, the average per capita income — that is, the amount of commodities and services that can be consumed or allocated to investment — will probably be nearly twice as high in the year 2000 as it was in 1970. This estimate is based on the assumption that in the advanced industrialized countries abatement activities will be stepped up to prevent — despite continued economic growth — the emission of the principal types of pollutants from exceeding the level specified (but, incidentally, not yet attained) by the rather stringent US Antipollution Act of 1970. The proportion of total real investment devoted to abatement activities will, for some time, continue to rise. However, even in highly industrialized countries it will, according to our calculations, hardly exceed 4% of the total capital stock. In North America, after reaching 3.4% by 1980, this proportion can be expected to decline to 2.5% by the year 2000. (As new technologies developed under strict anti-pollution regulations are gradually adopted, the distinction between abatement expenditures and other production costs becomes, of course, more and more blurred.) Pollution is generated mainly in the course of extracting and processing minerals and in the production and consumption of agricultural and manufactured goods. As the per capita income becomes very high, the demand for material goods seems to approach a level of saturation (only the demand for arms seems to be insatiable!), and additional spending is directed more and more toward the outputs of non-polluting service industries.

The inevitable exhaustion of relatively easily accessible reserves of mineral resources will necessarily lead to a progressive rise in extraction

---

* *Editor's note:* At an *Ecumenical Consultation on Political Economy and Ethics,* Zürich, June 5-10, 1978, Prof. ANNE CARTER, the second author of the UN Report, questioned whether this statement is supportable on the basis of the UN study.

costs accompanied by the expanding use of more and more expensive substitutes. All this does not mean, however, that the physical limits of economic development and growth are about to be reached. A recently completed detailed study of energy production and consumption in the United States, for instance, seems to indicate that a combination of structural adjustments — not involving the introduction of entirely new, not yet developed technologies — would permit the level of the present per capita income to be doubled without a significant increase in the overall amount of energy consumed and without drastic changes in the present life style.

The Gap between the Developed and Less Developed Countries

While allaying some of the widespread apprehensions, the same long run projections lead, on the other hand, to conclusions of a rather pessimistic kind: As long as the volume and direction of international capital flows and of international developmental aid continue to be dominated by the same economic forces and the same political considerations that have governed them up till now, the gap between the developed and the so-called less developed countries will not diminish; in some instances, it might even increase. Only for the few, until recently, poor areas that happen to possess oil or other valuable natural resources is the outlook bright. The rest of the Third World, containing over 60% of the world's total population, but producing and consuming only 15% of the global output of goods and services, will continue to fall behind. According to the official UN statistics, in the year 1970 the average per capita income in these areas amounted to only $1/12$ of the average per capita income of the developed, industrialized countries. Should the structural and institutional relationships that now govern the economic growth in all parts of the world continue to operate in the same way in the future, that ratio might fall to $1/18$ by the year 2000.

In the face of this disquieting conclusion, it was only natural to ask what it would take to reverse this trend — that is, to accelerate the rate of growth of the less developed parts of Asia, Latin America and Africa — so that the present income ratio of $1/12$ would be reduced by the year 2000 to, say, $1/7$, that is, be nearly cut in half.

In an endeavor to provide a more or less objective, factual basis for answering this question, the UN Report presents a set of alternative projections that show, in some detail, what changes in the economic relationships between the developed and the less developed countries could make the attainment of such a goal possible.

This second set of projections is based on the same assumptions concerning the available reserves of natural resources and the same assessment of future rates of population growth, and it contains provisions for the maintenance of the same environmental standards that were incorporated in the first. The narrowing, if not closing, of the gap between the less developed and the developed countries could not be accomplished, according to these computations, without dramatic changes in the magnitude and direction of international commodity flows.

Measured in terms of national incomes and the present levels of external economic transactions of the less developed countries, the shifts referred to above would, indeed, be very large. Compared with the total output of goods and services in the developed countries or even the total volume of trade carried on year after year between them, they appear, on the other hand, to be relatively modest — a fraction of a percentage point here, a few percentage points there.

To make the difference between the two sets of developmental scenarios more tangible, let me fill in some of the missing details by presenting the following, entirely imaginary picture. The dramatic rise in the price of oil has brought about a great increase in payments that the less developed oil exporting countries receive now, and will continue to receive for many year to come, from the advanced industrialized oil importing countries. While a substantial part of that potential payment surplus is being spent on current imports, permitting the oil exporting countries to raise rapidly the level of their domestic investment and consumption, a large part of it is being lent back to the industrialized countries. This permits the latter to maintain a higher level of domestic investment and consumption than they would be able to afford in case the costly oil imports had to be paid for by increased exports.

Now, if the trade surplus, earned by the oil exporting countries (that is now being returned in the form of capital investment and loans to the developed industrialized countries), had, instead, been lent to or invested in the poor, less developed countries, these, in their turn, could have spent it on additional imports from the (oil importing) industrialized countries. The level of these additional imports happens to match closely that of the external trade deficits that — according to projections referred to above — the poor, less developed countries should be able to maintain while slowly catching up with the developed countries.

There are, of course, two things wrong with this picture. It implies that the advanced industrialized countries would, in fact, be willing and able to pay for the expensive imported oil in cash, i.e., by increased exports rather than by buying it on credit. Moreover, to the extent to which the aid granted to the less developed countries would have to be given in the form of low interest loans or direct grants, the burden of development assistance would, under the arrangement described above, fall largely on the oil exporting countries. While the rising oil revenues have benefited them enormously, one must not forget that even according to the most optimistic projections, the level of per capita income in these countries will, even in the year 2000, be half of that of Western Europe and only one-third of that in North America.

Military Spending

A major yet untapped potential source of economic assistance to the less developed areas and, one might add, to the backward regions and the underprivileged groups in the developed countries as well, is the $400,000,000,000 worth of labour, capital and valuable natural resources employed year-in and year-out in support of military establishments throughout the world.

In the world-wide economic projections to which I referred above, military expenditures are assumed to grow at the same rate as other government expenditures. This is a conservative assumption since arms limitation agreements that have been negotiated up to now prescribe only specific, already known types of weapons and thus encourage rather than discourage increased spending on the development of powerful but more expensive new weapons and on stepped up production of conventional arms of unrestricted types.

The opposition to proposals to limit the overall level of military spending stems not only from a sceptical appraisal of practical possibilities to reach and to enforce these kinds of agreements; it comes also from the powerful, although not necessarily overt resistance on the part of those whose investments or whose employment would be jeopardized by a reduction in the demand for military goods. This brings me to the second set of questions which I would like to raise in this paper, namely, the adequacy, or rather the inadequacy, of economic institutions inherited from the past, in meeting the challenges and grasping the opportunities that the advanced, industrialized societies — the so-called free world — will be facing in the coming years.

The Government's Role

I have spoken of the practical difficulties involved in shifting resources absorbed now by military production into activities devoted to the satisfaction of civilian demand. The same problems arise when domestic industry is threatened by foreign competition. Workers employed in the old, well established shoe plants in New England are now losing their jobs because cheaper shoes are imported from Italy, Taiwan and Korea.

International division of labour made possible through steady expansion of international trade certainly contributes greatly to more efficient utilization of economic resources, particularly labour, and consequently to better satisfaction of human needs in all parts of the world. But it does so at a price. To those who have to pay the price, it exceeds by far their small share in the potential benefits that such "structural adjustment" might bring to the national and to the world economy as a whole. A family whose breadwinner loses his job in a shoe factory or munitions plant and has to look for new employment can find little consolation in the fact that this contributes indirectly to increasing, in the long run, the average per capita national income, say, by fifty cents. It is not surprising that workers turn to the government for protection of their jobs. Joining hands with the managers and stockholders, they often succeed in preventing or, at least, in retarding "structural adjustments" of this kind. It has to be admitted that, in the long run, this means a slowdown in economic development and growth.

Thus, modern society is facing a dilemma that only further extension of governmental responsibilities for management of the national and even international economy can solve. Proponents of unrestricted free enterprise ignore the fact that, whenever their advice is followed, government intervention is not avoided; it simply takes a different form — that of violent suppression of social unrest resulting from ruthless operation of the proverbial "invisible hand" of private competition or, one might add, of private monopoly. The question faced by the advanced capitalist countries is not whether government's role in the operation of the economic system should be expanded or contracted, but rather, how, while expanding, it could be rendered more effective.

According to prevalent academic doctrine, a proper combination of fiscal and monetary policies should be capable of securing steady economic growth with reasonably full utilization of productive capacities, high levels of employment and stable prices. After many years of trial in many countries and under a great variety of circumstances, practical experience with the application of this approach has proved disappointing. Neither the Keynesian nor the so-called Monetarist prescription seems to work.

National Economic Planning and the Profit Motive

In the meantime, new problems — energy, environment, chronic unemployment — are added to the old, and governments relying less and less on simplistic, general solutions endeavor to meet them one by one. The advantage of such a piecemeal approach is that policy makers can acquire in that way first-hand practical understanding of the operations of every part of the complex machine of the modern, industrial economy: an understanding that those who center their attention on aggregative variables usually lack. Its cardinal weakness is that, in the absence of overall coordination, action taken to alleviate one problem is liable to aggravate another. In the United States, at least, we often witness what amounts to cut-throat competition between the different departments of the central government — not to speak of self-defeating rivalry among local governments. This frustrating experience necessarily leads to a demand for systematic overall coordination, which is another word for planning.

Coordination on a national scale is national planning. This certainly is the most difficult, most ambitious task a society can undertake. Its technical aspects involve capabilities to gather and analyze masses of detailed data, to draw up feasible scenarios and devise means for their practical implementation — capabilities that even the most advanced countries began to acquire only in recent years.

Even more problematic are the political implications of democratic economic planning. A well prepared, realistic, internally consistent, that is feasible, scenario is bound to display — for everyone to see — not only the sought for, desirable effect of every major policy decision, but also its undesirable repercussions that more often than not will have to be borne by groups other than those who can count on benefiting from it. This obviously will not facilitate reaching a political agreement. The unavoidable battles about real issues between conflicting interests will, at least, be fought on firm ground. A close examination of major policy proposals that become objects of heated public disputes at the present time would show that many, if not most, were built hastily on shaky ground and would not work out in practice as originally intended.

Among the major economic issues with which advanced capitalist countries continue to fumble are income and employment policies. The general direction of evolution in that field seems to be pretty clear. It reflects a gradual realization of the fact that neither of these problems can be solved separately. Nor can they even be understood separately from the problems of prices and investment, from questions of international trade and international migration, or from any of the other major economic problems of the day.

Even when the general political conditions are favorable to national economic planning, as they were, for instance, in France after the end of the last world war, when the first so-called indicative five-year plan was inaugurated, it is liable to fail due to lack of the required technical capabilities. Even now, thirty years later, no western capitalist country, except possibly Norway, seems to possess a statistical organization that can provide the steady flow of comprehensive and detailed information needed for the construction of alternative scenarios — each of them concrete, detailed and, above all, feasible — among which the policy makers could choose one with confidence that it would work.

The United States, a country in which the concept of National Economic Planning is viewed in many influential circles with great suspicion, if not outright fear, has developed, nevertheless, in recent years greater technical capabilities for handling large scale planning problems than any other large capitalist or even the socialist countries. Not only major private enterprises, but many departments of the Federal government as well as some State and local governments make use of large scale planning models. Even Congressional committees concerned with energy, environment, natural resources or transportation base some of their deliberations on formal quantitative models and scenarios prepared by their staffs. Statistical and other data gathering activities of the government are systematized and expanded, often in close cooperation with private business and only occasionally with some resistance on its part. This is particularly important since, at least in the United States, it is the lack of basic factual information — not of computing facilities and certainly not of theoretical treatises on planning methodology — that sets limits on the practical applicability of the planning approach. The gap between what is theoretically thinkable and what is actually possible, however, is being gradually narrowed.

The indifferent performance of the centrally planned socialist economies has often been invoked as evidence that national planning cannot work. The planning methods actually used in these countries have been, until recently, rather primitive. But still more important is the fact that having dispensed with the use of the profit motive — the driving force that in capitalist countries turns the wheels of the entire economic machine — the socialist countries have not yet succeeded in discovering or creating another equally viable and resilient source of propelling power. Hence, they find themselves in the position of a vessel equipped with sophisticated steering gear, but a weak and not very reliable engine. Even if kept on the right course, it can move only slowly. Those who have had the experience of steering a boat on choppy seas, moreover, know that when going slowly it cannot obey the rudder as well as when it advances at a good speed.

As long as no substitute for the profit motive has been found, national economic planning can be expected to be effective only to the extent that it succeeds in harnessing the profit motive without unduly weakening or even paralyzing it.

Organized Labour's Role in a "Mixed" Economy

With the government taking on greater responsibilities for the conduct of national and international economic affairs, organized labour, in order to safeguard its interests, will have to take a more active and more direct part in the formulation and implementation of all aspects of national economic policies. Its concerns must extend far beyond conclusions of bilateral agreements with the employers (negotiated on a single company, an industry-wide or even economy-wide basis) lest what is gained on the one hand in money wages be lost, on the other, through inflation or, say, an unanticipated energy crisis. It is very doubtful that inflationary pressures can be brought under control and that a full and productive utilization of the labour force can be secured by any measure that falls short of comprehensive national economic planning. In democratic countries, the exercise of explicit political choice among alternative scenarios and implementation of appropriate economic policies must, as I said above, necessarily involve hard, long and highly technical negotiations between all interested parties. To be viable, a "social contract" — to use the new, fashionable term — must comprise much more than a wage freeze combined with price control: an emergency device that, while it might forestall a sudden crisis, is bound to generate, in the long run, serious structural maladjustment.

To marshal telling arguments in political debates over economic policies is one thing; to possess systematic knowledge of technical economic and financial problems confronting each industry and every part of the country within the framework of the national, and if called for, the entire world economy is quite another. Such knowledge is now in the possession of private business. To be able to participate effectively — not only nominally — in the formulation and implementation of national economic policies, trade union leadership will have to acquire it too. Some of this kind of factual information can be acquired only from or through government. The gradually spreading inclusion of workers' representatives in the management councils of private firms — even while having only marginal influence on company policies — offers the trade union organization an excellent opportunity to acquire first-hand understanding of the operating characteristics of the various sectors of the economy.

Income Policies in the Age of Automation

If asked to single out one force that has contributed more than any other to the phenomenal economic growth of the last two hundred years, one would say technological change. It was, however, the newly invented power loom that deprived thousands of English weavers of their jobs about one hundred and sixty years ago. Today the American Telephone and Telegraph Company is installing automatic switching equipment that will permit it to handle the anticipated increase in the volume of long-distance calls and reduce the number of long-distance operators.

The fact that machines do displace labour cannot be questioned, but many economic theorists (Karl Marx was not one of them!) hastened to point out at the time of the Luddite Rebellions that this did not mean that the total demand for labour and total employment must, because of that, diminish. An equal or even a larger number of new jobs, so they said, will necessarily be created in the machine building and its subsidiary industries. But is this, in fact, so?

The answer to that question is of crucial importance for the understanding of the economic, social and political problems faced by labour in times of accelerated technological advance, and that answer is "No"; new machines, new technology introduced because it cuts production costs can, indeed, reduce the total demand for labour, i.e., the total number of jobs available in all sectors of the economy taken together at any given price of labour, that is any given wage rate.

To use a somewhat crass and even shocking analogy, new machines can reduce the total demand for human labour for the same reason and essentially through the same process that, a generation ago, led to the replacement of draft horses by trucks, tractors and automobiles. To argue that workers displaced by machines should necessarily be able to find employment in building these machines does not make more sense than to expect that horses displaced by mechanical vehicles could have been directly or indirectly employed in various branches of the expanding automotive industry.

Moreover, — and this is particularly important in the context of the present discussion — the transition from a horse driven to a motorized economy was accomplished quite smoothly despite the fact that the demand for oats, harnesses and new stables was drastically cut. The flows of "purchasing power" simply changed their direction under the prodding of impersonal market forces, and so did the commodity flows. The output of goods and services required for the sustenance of horses declined, while the output of steel and gasoline, not to speak of automobiles, went up. The economic system adapted itself to the new technology quite smoothly, and if the operation of blind market forces imposed some hardships on oat growers and harness makers, in a perfectly organized system capable of anticipating the impending shift and preparing for it, the transition could have been managed without the slightest hitch. If horses could have been organized and were able to vote, this, indeed, would have been quite a different story.

One way of meeting the threat of potential technological unemployment is the creation of new and maintenance of the old jobs through increased investment, i.e., economic growth. But this possibility has definite limits. How fast would the economy, and with it the volume of investment, have to grow in order to keep the number of long-distance telephone operators from decreasing in face of the fact that each of them will soon be able to handle ten million instead of one thousand telephone calls? The rate of investment required to accomplish this end might turn out to be so high that very little would be left for current consumption. In the pursuit of full employment through a greater and greater volume of productive investment, the society ultimately would find itself in the position of the proverbial miser who deprives himself of the bare necessities of life while depositing more and more into an already swelling savings account, and this despite his steadily increasing annual income. This is exactly what might happen in the long run under the relentless pressure of technological advance, if the forces of unrestricted cut-throat competition were permitted — let us hope they will not be — to govern the operation of the labour markets and conditions of employment.

Opponents of the trade union movement argue that if wage rates had not been maintained on what they call an artificially high level, the introduction of labour saving equipment would have been retarded and the number of available jobs increased. There can hardly be any doubt that without trade union action the level of (real) wages would be lower and the conditions of work harsher. It is, however, doubtful whether the introduction of labour saving equipment would have been retarded very much by the availability of "cheaper" labour: By how much would the wages of telephone operators have to be cut in order to prevent the installation of modern, automatic switching equipment? In the event that the wage rate fell, say, by ten percent and the total employment had increased as a result of this by five, there still would be a net 5 percent loss in total labour income.

There is, of course, a problem — in case the total labour income is effectively maintained by union action — of sharing it directly or indirectly between those who are employed and those who are not. Spreading the work through reducing the number of working hours per week and of working days per year provides an answer to this question. Increasing leisure — while every one is assured of a steady job — can contribute greatly to the general welfare in a developed society. It has done so in the past and it certainly can do so in the future.

Distribution of Income and Technological Advance

If technological advance continues, as let us hope it will, permitting substitution of more and more capital for labour not only in mining, manufacturing, agriculture and transportation, but in the service sectors as well, the traditional union action of the type I mentioned above is bound to become less and less effective: Even the most powerful monopoly cannot maintain its income — not to speak of increasing it — if the demand for its product — the supply of which it controls — tends to fall.

Thus, in the long run, the ability of large masses of the population to benefit from technological advance will increasingly depend on the direct transfer of property income derived from ownership of capital and natural resources. In a utopian society in which everyone would combine — as some of the prosperous farmers in the United States and other countries actually do — the function of a labourer with that of the owner of capital and land, technical advance involving substitution of machinery for labour would present no problem: The share of the family income entered on the labour account would gradually diminish, but that accruing to its capital and rent account would increase. Moreover, the total income — derived from these two different sources — would grow.

In a complex modern society, whether capitalist or socialist, the distribution of income between groups performing different economic functions and, consequently, occupying different social positions will continue to be a major problem. So will the maintenance of sufficiently strong and steady incentives for purposeful, effective economic performance on the part of every member of the society whatever his role and responsibilities might be.

It has to be admitted that conditions favourable to the attainment of one of these twin goals — efficiency and distribution judged to be equitable — are liable, to some extent, to make more difficult the attainment of the other. A satisfactory solution of both problems will necessarily be in the nature of a compromise.

What is true of the domestic economic order applies, of course, to international economic relationships as well. No country, however self-sufficient and strong, will be able to solve its national economic and social problems without regard to the economic and social problems facing other countries. The oil crisis brought this realization home with a jolt. It is, however, the rising, practically irresistible, tide of international migration that poses a new, unprecedented challenge to the trade union leadership in the developed countries. In the long run, only an accelerated rate of economy growth in the less developed areas will enable it to meet that challenge. If international economic planning is ever to become a reality, the international labour movement must play a leading role in it.

19 · The Environment and Social Production — A Soviet View *

In the late 1960s, at the acme of brilliant achievements in science and technology, when man had harnessed atomic energy, learned to create new materials, deciphered the genetic code and sent men into space and rockets to the planets of the solar system, the world's attention turned to the problem of the environment. And what is more, many people were surprised to learn that they were faced with a problem of calamitous proportions.

Disquieting information began to pour in from all directions that the most important natural resources — the oxygen of the air, the purity of fresh water and the water of the world ocean, the earth's temperature regime and the diverse animal kingdom — were threatened, that modern production had come up to the boundary beyond which the basic conditions of man's life on earth began to break down, and in some places already crossed this boundary.

In his time Frederick Engels wrote: "Let us not, however, flatter ourselves overmuch on account of our human victories over nature. For each such victory nature takes its revenge on us. Each victory, it is true, in the first place brings about the results we expected, but in the second and third places it has quite different, unforeseen effects which only too often cancel the first." [1]

This observation has not lost its significance. On the contrary, the development of industry, the growth of cities and the creation of increasingly powerful means of transportation have brought about a considerable increase in the load on the environment.

* This chapter is taken from the book *Society and the Environment: A Soviet View*, prepared by Progress Publishers, Moscow, 1977. Prof. Pavel Oldak is Doctor of Economic Sciences, Novosibirsk State University, and Senior Scientific Worker of the Institute for the Economics and Organization of Industrial Production under the Siberian Department of the USSR: Academy of Sciences.

[1] F. ENGELS: *Dialectics of Nature*, Moscow, 1974, p. 180.

It will only be possible to assess the full significance of these processes at some time in the future. But it is already evident today that man has begun to interfere in the profound processes of development of life on earth, thereby worsening the conditions of his very own existence.

Researchers have come up against a number of serious methodological problems in attempting to assess ecological prospects for the future. First and foremost it became clear that they had to examine much longer periods than those for which the processes of man's impact on nature were investigated until quite recently. This involved switching from long-term forecasts (10 or 20 years) to super-long-term forecasts (30, 50, 100 or 150 years), for it is only by examining long-time intervals that we can produce a complete description of the processes of interdependence between society's development and the environment.

The future is like a sharp sword. Recognize opportunely the problems of the future and you will grasp the hilt of the sword in good time. Miss the opportune moment and you are faced with the need to grasp the honed blade of the sword with your bare hands, that is to correct the unfavourable development of events hastily and at the cost of great losses, and not to use one's opportunities to the full.

But to understand the future it is not sufficient to investigate just the "technical links" — the interdependence between natural and economic parameters inside a particular socioeconomic system. It is essential to analyse this system itself.

The Link between Social Production and the Environment

With the present-day scale of transformative activity, nature can no longer support independently the normal conditions for the development of life on earth, and the burden of solving this problem is shifting increasingly on to human society. Having reached up to the heavens, man must henceforth bear them on his shoulders like the mythical Atlantes.

Radical change in the correlation of forces between man and nature is one of the greatest landmarks in the history of human society. The coming of a new era requires a new stage of development not only in scientific research, but also in social thought. It is essential to recognize the strict dependence of the development of society on the maintenance of the equilibrium of the entire ecological system of life on earth. Modern man should match the great power which he has acquired with great intelligence. Man is a creator, but not an irresponsible creator. He is predestined to realize the most vivid dreams, but only if he does not destroy the medium of his own habitation "on his way to the stars".

Today we find a rigid two-way dependence between the system of social production and the environment. It is expressed in the fact that stable development of production and the all-round development of the personality (the span of life, physical health, complete satisfaction of man's vital needs and fulfilment of his creative potential) can only be realized if the purity of the environment is preserved; the latter is, in turn, only possible if there is a transition to forms of transformative activity which take account of the requirements of neutralizing wastes from production and consumption.

Analysis of this dependence shows that natural (ecological) processes and man's economic activity cease to develop as detached systems; they close up and grow into a single "production-environment" metasystem, or bioeconomic system. Accordingly the problem of controlling social production begins to develop into the tremendously complex scientific problem of controlling a bioeconomic system.

We still know very little about the nature of the bioeconomic system and the requirements which should be borne in mind to ensure stable and harmonious development of its subsystems (social production and the environment). The material accumulated has generally speaking received insufficient theoretical interpretation and generalization. Nevertheless it may be said that a new branch of research — the theory of control of bioeconomic systems — is developing at the junction between ecology and economy. This new science could be called *bioeconomics*. Bioeconomics is based on the results of research in both natural and social sciences. At the same time it has its own objective — the study of the interrelation between the rate of economic growth, the level of technology and the quality of the environment.

Analysing the bioeconomic system constitutes one of the major problems of the modern era. The vital need to formulate the laws governing the maintenance and development of this system has given a powerful stimulus to the development of a number of spheres of knowledge. It was this very need which pushed ecology — a science which until recently was the preserve of a small circle of experts — into the front rank of the disciplines which determine the modern stage of cognition of the world. The range of problems touched on by philosophical research is broadening. Increasing attention is now being given to developing a new attitude to nature as one of the most important aspects of modern world outlook. The task of conserving the environment has determined a new field of technological research — the development and application of closed technological cycles and the complex use of raw materials, which in turn presupposes fuller utilization and neutralization of production and consumption wastes.

But the environmental problem is having perhaps its most profound impact on the development of economic science. The transition from a conception of social production as an isolated system to analysis of the interrelation between production and the environment serves as a definite borderline for the development of economic ideas. We are gaining a broader idea of the boundaries of social production, the aims of economic development, the essence of the notions of national wealth and national income, the demands made on long-term planning, the problems which the system of economic regulation should resolve, and the criteria for assessing the effectiveness of the decisions taken.

Until quite recently social production was thought of as an open system which takes the initial raw materials and releases the wastes into a medium external to itself. An open system is based on the principle of one-time use of the natural starting material and in this sense constitutes a peculiar form of "open end" economy. In fact production uses only a part of extracted primary materials. The rest is converted into waste.

Progress will always take the form of destruction of the old and affirmation of the new. But the larger the scale of social production, the fewer the opportunities for having an "open end" economy and the more urgent the demand for a switch to a different, higher form of economic interaction with nature.

This may be represented figuratively in the following way. In the past we took some "building blocks" of natural resources and created economic wealth from them, converting half or more of these "blocks" into waste. In due course the outmoded economic wealth also became waste; production, however, continued to seek new "blocks" of natural resources.

This sort of management of our planet will be impossible in the future. We need a consistent transition to what might be called a closed system of production.

The essence of this system is that it is based on the repeated use of these very same "blocks". The latter presupposes two extremely important conditions. Firstly, primary natural resources should not be extracted each time for separate types of end product, but at one time for all possible types of economic wealth. Secondly, the products created should be of such a form that after use for their own direct purpose they may be converted relatively easily to the initial elements of a new production process.

A closed system may be considered as consisting of two subsystems, one which *uses* the elements of the environment (that is, converts nature's products into economic wealth) and one which *restores* the used elements of the environment (by this we mean, on the one hand, the conversion of the wastes of economic activity into raw materials for new production cycles, and on the other, the restoration of the disturbed ecological equilibrium). The switch to the closed system — a continuous cycle of matter in the production process, where the processing of waste will constitute the last link of one cycle and the initial link of the next — is one of the most important demands of the modern stage of economic development.

The Social Aspect of Analysing Bioeconomic Systems

Analysis of the internal link between the development of social production and the state of the environment brings into even bolder relief the problem of affirming the advanced social forms.

As we know, the process of environmental pollution is farthest advanced in the industrialized capitalist countries — a state of affairs which cannot be regarded as accidental. The capitalist mode of production, which is based on private ownership and aimed at achieving maximum profit, inevitably leads to a situation where the development of production is bought at the cost of environmental damage. In the past we criticized capitalism as a system which exploits the working people, and engenders unemployment, crises and imperialist wars, whereas today we also emphasize a new important aspect — the destruction of national and planetary systems of life support. The capitalist system of production is at variance with the interests of preserving the environment, a fact which is becoming clear to increasingly broader sections of society.

The production of fundamental wealth in bourgeois society is marked by the creation of more and more consumer goods for the continuous accumulation and renewal of property and the stimulation of artificial demands. Today the false orientation of this kind of production is plain for all to see. It has engulfed the consumer in a world of material things and turned property and the renewal of property into a prestige factor, a means of demonstrating and affirming one's position in society. The consumer society with its property cult is hostile to nature. Modern industry in its present form gnaws into nature in an increasingly rapacious way, undermining the basis of man's life on earth.

The purity of the environment is a natural blessing for mankind. And the countries where the accelerated growth of production proceeds at the expense of this purity are nothing like as prosperous as it might appear. Tokyo smog is so thick, for instance, that its inhabitants ask themselves more and more often whether the advantages of owning one's own car outweigh the disadvantages of breathing polluted air.

Thus, in the initial stages of analysing bioeconomic systems, one realizes the historical limits of a production system which proceeds without national economic programs, is oriented only towards extraction of profit and cultivates the social standards of the consumer society. It is not difficult to see that the limiting factors of the capitalist system — the principles of private capitalist production and the bourgeois conception of the value of fundamental wealth — appear from a new point of view.

At the same time it would be incorrect to always link environmental pollution rigidly with capitalism. There is more to the problem than that. It has its roots in both social and technological factors. By the latter we mean the lag between the technology of modern production and those requirements which are dependent on the rapidly increasing load on the environment. This lag is due to a number of reasons, among them the inertia of production (the long period for which developed technological systems are in use) and the inadequacy of scientific research. One can single out, in particular, the narrow spectrum of ecological research, the small amount of work done on the technology of closed-cycle production and the failure to develop the criteria for assessing the effectiveness of production development with due regard for the restoration of the environment.

The limited nature of resources is also a significant factor. If one takes account of expenditure on research, the development of new technology, the re-equipping of production and the rehabilitation (albeit partial) of destroyed ecological systems, conservation of the environment is becoming almost the largest and most expensive program. It will only be feasible to set aside sufficient resources for it, if there is a significant advance in the field of international detente and the curtailment of military programs.

In the context of technology, the problem of environmental protection is of a general nature and concerns the two socioeconomic formations of the modern era.

The Notion of the Metapotential of an Economic System

Man has striven for millennia to conquer nature. But when he had achieved his greatest victories, there appeared the urgent need to "protect nature".

Essentially man needs to find the correct fusion of the interests of the present and the future. We must not ignore the interests of the present, or sacrifice the interests of the future. We must not, for the sake of pure love for nature, prevent its economic utilization. But neither must we squander the capital of nature, forcing society in the near future to spend colossal amounts of money and effort on restoring the general system of life support. "For us and our grandchildren" — this is the demand which is being made more and more urgently on social production.

Rational combination of the interests of the present and the future presupposes that in future labour expenditures should be accounted for in economic decisions being taken.

This is a fundamentally new task. It is well known that, since the birth of scientific ideas on the nature of economic processes almost three centuries ago, economic analysis has revealed and compared the expenditure of materialized and live, i.e., past and present, labour.

Today we see that economic decisions should be considered from the standpoint not only of expenditure on the production of goods and services, but also of the labour that will be needed to make good the damage caused to the general life support system by the production and consumption of the corresponding goods.

This is certain to produce a considerable change in the composition of a number of the most important economic categories, and specifically a certain broadening of the concept of national wealth.

Until quite recently national wealth was interpreted as a category describing the sum total of production for a given year. Some economists associate the concept of national wealth with the size of accumulated material values — the material results of production; others with the size of the flow of reproducible wealth — goods and services. It is obvious that in both cases attention is concentrated on the present. At the same time today, as we have pointed out, we find an increasingly close link between the present and the future. Consequently, analysis of the results of production is coming to embrace the growth potential of the economic system when normal conditions for the development of life are maintained. In other words, attention is moving from the level at which the economic system satisfies the needs of the present to the level which determines the opportunities for development and satisfaction of the needs of the future. The concept of wealth as a product should, it seems, be combined with the concept of wealth as a potential for economic growth.

By virtue of the fact that the opportunities for development are dependent upon a number of quantitatively heterogeneous elements, let us employ the concept of metapotential (MP). By MP we mean a generalized description of the power (potential) of detached national systems, and consequently the extent of their impact on the future situation. We can distinguish four aspects which describe the MP of a national system: 1) economic potential, 2) scientific and technological potential, 3) human potential, 4) ecological potential.

Economic potential reflects the level of output of the end national product. Scientific and technological potential — education, science, management — describes the accumulated reserves of growth. Human potential — the size of the population, its physical and mental health, and the level of creative activity — characterizes the social conditions for using the available development opportunities. Ecological potential — the degree to which the purity of the environment is maintained — reflects the boundaries of possible expansion of production without the apportionment of great resources for the rehabilitation of the damaged environment.

The concept of MP enables one to see clearly that an index such as the gross national product (GNP) does not describe in full the effectiveness of the development of a particular national economic system over a given period. GNP describes the growth of only part of the MP. If the GNP has grown in one particular country, this can only mean a growth in the MP of the system if the other elements of the MP have not suffered a decrease. If, however, a growth in the GNP goes hand in hand with pollution of the environment and deterioration of the population's health, which is the case in the industrialized capitalist countries, then it is not known whether the MP of the system has increased or decreased.

Until very recently GNP was regarded as the most generalizing index of economic development. A high rate of growth of GNP was considered as reliable evidence of progress, almost a synonym of the economic achievements of society. The experience of the 1960s, however, prompts one to think seriously about this. In Japan, the USA and a number of capitalist countries of Western Europe demands are being made that the GNP no longer be considered the supreme aim of economic development, that this growth be decreased and a portion of the resources be redirected into conservation of the environment.

Several bourgeois economists in the West are now advancing the concept of zero growth, which is based on the idea of holding back the rate of economic development. Despite the fact that this concept proceeds from an analysis of real contradictions, its overall conclusion cannot be acknowledged as being correct. It is unacceptable first of all in the social respect. A zero growth rate would really mean the maintenance of the existing division of countries into "rich" and "poor", and consequently the consolidation of the developed capitalist countries' advantageous position. The peoples of the developing countries can obviously not agree to such a state of affairs. The demand for a zero growth rate is also unrealistic in the purely theoretical respect: it is impossible to halt economic development, for it is born not only of the need to satisfy man's requirements for material wealth, but also of his striving to apprehend the world and manifest creative abilities.

A distinction should in our view be made between the growth and development of an economic system. Growth describes the increase in the system's productive potential, the raising of its "weight category", if one may express it in this way. Development, on the other hand, reflects the ability to realize specific programs. It depends not only on the "weight category", but also on qualitative parameters such as accumulated knowledge, the state of the human factor and the environment.

One of the most important factors in the development of an economic system is the level of technology; the extent to which the production systems in use are closed serves as an index of this. It is obvious that under modern conditions stable growth rates are closely linked with progress in the field of production technology. The higher the level of technology, the greater the growth that can be guaranteed without destruction of the environment. Contrast between the demands for production growth and the preservation of the quality of the environment is only present in medium-term programs. Here in the interests of an economic manœuvre it is possible to ensure an increase in the growth rate by limiting expenditure on the preservation of environmental quality. But both social criteria and the purely economic demands made on the quality of the biosphere's resources place extremely narrow limits on such a manœuvre. And if we move to long-term programs, then it turns out that the achievement of stable growth rates is inseparably linked with the improvement of technology to ensure that certain limiting parameters of environmental quality are maintained. And it is the MP which describes the ability of a system to realize long-term development programs.

With the help of specialized research it will be possible to show what the correlation between the main elements of MP should be for the economic system to realize the most extensive development program for the given initial conditions (manpower resources, natural resources and accumulated production funds). This will characterize the normative structure of the MP. By comparing the normative structure with the actual one it will be possible to determine the priorities for the growth of different elements of MP.

Determination of the structure of MP and selection of preferable growth rates raises the question of measuring the MP elements. The complexity of the problem lies in the fact that to compare the elements of MP which belong to the qualitatively heterogeneous links of the bio-economic system we need a new, broader unit of measurement than the one that has been used so far.

As we know, economic science has from its earliest days right up to the present operated with the standard of measurement which was developed within the framework of commodity exchange, namely the category of value. Value has been the universal standard for ascertaining the relative worth of the results of economic activity, for it has served as a single yardstick for measuring qualitatively different kinds of labour. Value has also been recognized in the socialist economy as a general economic unit of measurement.

But as soon as we go beyond the realm of purely economic activity, value ceases to be a general quantitative measure of worth. Naturally the accumulation of knowledge, the maintenance of public health, and the preservation of the environment's equilibrium can be expressed in units of expenditure on achieving the appropriate aims. Such measurement is of great significance when considering the extent of restructuring the MP an economic system can allow itself inside the chosen interval of time and for a given initial position. But it is possible to have a number of different variants of MP corresponding to a certain given size of expenditure. Which of them is to be regarded as the most preferable? To answer this question we need to have an idea of the normative structure of the MP and the framework of reference which allows the degree of approximation to the normative structure to be determined.

Here we have come right up to the determination of the principles of a new measurement system: the elements of MP should be compared not just in terms of the size of expenditure, but in terms of the correlation of the contribution to the achievement of an integrated result, to the fulfilment of those "ultimate ends" which the economic system undertakes for the period in question. A solution to this task, which merits special attention, may be achieved, we believe, by building a "tree of aims" and assessing the relative importance of each of its elements.

Change in the Assessments of the Effectiveness of Economic Decisions

Up until now economic assessments were restricted to the comparison of direct input and output. Technical solutions were thus considered effective if the product obtained or the service rendered enabled requirements (or, as was more often the case, demands prompted by the very production of new wealth) to be met more satisfactorily. Economic decisions were considered effective if the selling price of the product (service) exceeded by a certain margin the cost of production. It was tacitly supposed that the completion of the production process — the creation of the product or service — was a summary of the final results of the work done.

While man's impact on his environment was limited and nature herself made good the damage caused by production, this sort of calculation was quite sufficient. Now that there has been a sharp increase in production's secondary, tertiary and even more distant effects on nature, to limit ourselves to a comparison of direct input and output is to obtain not simply an incomplete picture of the real state of affairs, but frequently a false picture.

The time has come, it seems, to broaden the systems of economic assessments. This applies first and foremost to the notion of economic efficiency. Today it can no longer be measured by the ratio of the effect obtained (the value of the product or the amount of profit) to the expenditure that produced it (production costs or advances). Expenditure on overcoming the consequences of environmental pollution is now acquiring increasing importance together with expenditure on the creation of the product. These could be defined as *reproduction* costs.

Until now these costs have not been taken into account in evaluating the efficiency of a specific line of production. But if individual enterprises are spared the necessity of bearing reproduction costs, this means that society as a whole sustains them or that it pays in some other ways for refusing to make good the expenditure on maintenance of the normal process of reproduction.

And so we arrive at the conclusion that it is essential to take account of the entire social costs of production, i.e., the amount of directly productive and reproductive expenditure.

The primary tasks will be to assess the complete social costs of production of the entire end product inside the specific economic region. This calculation is of great significance in revealing the relative efficiency of production in various regions of the country and primarily in comparing developed and developing regions. The fact of the matter is that in developed regions the production load per unit of the biosphere's resources is very high; by virtue of this the index of the costs needed to maintain a normal reproduction process will be extremely great. Conversely, in regions of primary development the production load per unit of the biosphere's resources will be small (it is often lower than the level which ensures natural self-renewal of resources). This means that the reproduction cost index will be small or even nil.

Calculation of the total social costs of production and of each given industrial enterprise is of great importance. Comparison between the effect obtained (the value of the product or the amount of profit) and the amount of the total social costs of production gives an index which describes the integrated efficiency of production.

Socialist economics cannot be oriented simply towards the solution of the tasks arising out of the current needs of society. The solution of future tasks is also extremely important. These include the development of education and science, the restructuring of production and improvement of its technical equipment, the levelling out of social differences and the raising of the standard of living. From this it follows that a stable growth rate must be maintained in the long term.

"Guidelines for the Development of the National Economy of the USSR for 1976-1980", which was approved by the 25th Congress of the CPSU, defines the elaboration and implementation of measures on the protection of the environment and the rational use and reproduction of natural resources as one of the tasks of the tenth five-year plan.

In order to resolve these tasks in sufficiently short periods and with a minimum of expenditure, it is essential to rely on a carefully coordinated work program embracing such spheres as science, production and management.

20 · Plea for a Post-Modern Society *

There are many trends, events and phenomena today which form part of a stream which may be described as "post-modern": the present disintegration of the economic system and its values; the emergence of new values such as quality of life and self-fulfillment; the call for regional and decentralized power; the growing anti-urban and anti-scientific attitudes; a new understanding of development opposed to the Western growth models. All of these have a post-modern character over against the still dominant modern reality.

What do we understand by "modern" and "modernization"? Since the nineteenth century, "modernization" has been the central impulse of Western development, and Western evolutionary philosophy has propagated the concept of modernity. Commitment to modernity underlies our Western theories of development. They map out the entire course of human history according to the criteria of modernity. They place various societies in a clear hierarchy according to their "degree of modernization", and define the stages which must be traversed by any society to attain the "modernity" of Western industrial societies.

The hegemony of the West over the non-West since the nineteenth century has been a hegemony of modern models of thought and action, of industrialization, rationalization and bureaucratization. The Western model of modernity consists of the permanent growth and diffusion of a set of institutions and structures. Peter Berger speaks of "the primary carriers of modernization" such as the modern state — particularly the bureaucracy and technological production. Marx and Schumpeter understood industrial capitalism as a mechanism that guarantees the permanent expansion of purposive rational action, as the first method of production in world history to institutionalize growth.

---

* This chapter is a shortened version of a paper presented by Prof. THEODOR LEUENBERGER, of the University of St. Gallen, to the WCC Consultation on *Political Economy and Ethics*, Paulus-Akademie, Zürich, June 5-10, 1978.

Rationality, Growth, Bureaucracy and Power

Max Weber introduced the concept of *rationality* in order to define modern capitalist economic activity and the forms of modern bureaucracy. The progressive "rationalization" of society, linked with scientific and technical growth, is a new form of domination — the domination of an abstract rationality according to which everything is evaluated in terms of precise quantifiable criteria. The world of technological production is dominated by the superstition that only that which is "real" can be quantified. The concentration on quantifying analyses has caused the present assymmetry in our development, and the backwardness in our moral and political consciousness. Economic theories have left out what refers to human thinking and to internal changes, and only given attention to those parameters which allow quantifiable results.

Another feature of technological production is *maximization*. For both technological and economic reasons, the logic of production always tends towards a maximization of results: bigger and better, stronger and faster. Expansion is the *sine qua non* of modern systems — technological, economic and bureaucratic. These three expansionist systems are intimately related. Their expansion and proliferation have little to do with necessity, but a lot to do with providing new avenues of power-promotion or make-work for the ever growing white-collar bureaucracy. As Keynes predicted, the essence of modern bureaucratic structures is that they view as a dead operation a stable balanced system which does not lead to expansion or more output. Today there is expansion for the sake of growth and power rather than because of functional necessity and the demand for greater productivity. The concentration of economic power within the industrial system is an example of this. The growth of big industrial firms is motivated by the desire to concentrate power, to dominate other firms through financial participation, rather than to increase productivity. The power-status of the decision-makers in these organizations is linked with the size of their organization: the larger the company, the greater the internal and external power of its direction. And all this in the name of rationality.

A third feature of the modern system is *orderliness*. Everything must be manageable. Bureaucracy is not only orderly but orderly in a imperialistic mode. The bureaucratic demiurge views the universe as a chaos waiting to be brought into the redeeming order of efficient administration. Bureaucracy presupposes general *organizability*. Everything should be assigned to a specific agency where it will be planned, organized and rationalized. All activities should be part of a clearly organized structure, and this structure must be centralized. *Centralism* — the emergence of growing economic, political and bureaucratic power-centres — is a further characteristic of modern society. Modernization means a shift from somewhat autonomous groups, traditions and values to more centralized power.

All autonomous groups are absorbed; local autonomy is abolished. Thus modern society has developed monolithic state structures based on monolithic models of thought and action, which attempt to monopolize and regulate as much as possible.

I agree in part with Robert Heilbronner who suggests that the emerging economic and technological structure will be characterized by large bureaucratic corporations which control the institutions and privileges central to a business civilization. The role of a central state power will be to avoid any disaster that threatens the stability of the economic and technological systems.[1] Heilbronner describes the coming era as one of planned capitalism — "the era of transition between the still business-dominated system of our age and the state-dominated system of the future". It will see the growth of a political-bureaucratic "super-structure", covering and controlling the economic mechanism. The present anarchic situation of industrial production itself provokes much of the bureaucratic trend which is an effort to guarantee orderly working conditions and to repair the damage caused by miscalculations of the system.

The history of modern Western society may be described as the replacement of lay solutions by rationalized expert solutions. Our everyday life is governed and controlled by highly specialized political, bureaucratic and economic institutions. This economic-technological system has developed a momentum of its own. More and more areas are beyond the comprehension of the individual and are inaccessible to public control and participation. Everywhere there are paths along which economic-technological power moves unchecked. It is the power not only of state bureaucracy, which is proliferating at all levels and in all spheres, but also of the association between big science and big business that has grown up in the West virtually outside the structure of public control. These concentrations of power have overstepped the bounds of the classical democratic institutions. Traditional national politics can scarcely cope with them any more. The big transnational industrial corporations, together with the banking system, constitute the central power structure. Often they take over non-economic functions especially in the political and military sectors. In the Third World, the power structures formed by big industrial corporations may act as the agents of modernization. They possess both capital and high industrial technology — one of the most powerful combinations possible. We are experiencing today the emergence of a highly potent cosmopolitical techno-culture, a transnational system of the giant business corporations, a concentration of economic-financial power so complex that resistance becomes more and more difficult and more and more abstract.

---

[1] Compare ROBERT HEILBRONNER: *Business Civilization in Decline* (New York, 1976).

Is China a Model for the Post-Modern Society?

According to Heilbronner, we cannot escape for long the necessity of strongly centralized administrations to put restraints on our expansionist systems. The only alternative he can envisage is a social order that will blend "religious" orientation and a "military" discipline.[1] In his view, China comes closest to this new civilization form. He discerns in the monastic Chinese model certain paradigmatic elements of the future — "a careful control over industrialization, an economic policy calculated to restrain rather than to stimulate individual consumptive appetites, and, above all, an organizing religiosity expressed through the credos and observations of a socialist 'church' ". Heilbronner believes the present societies will gradually approximate "tightly disciplined, ascetic religious orders".

Will China provide a model for a post-modern society? In certain respects! Especially in their attempt to decentralize with soft types of co-ordination and to develop goals related to social justice and participation rather than to growth, the Chinese have departed from the Western formula. They are attempting to dominate the powerful tendency of science and technology to develop a momentum of their own. They sense that in scientific-technical development lies the danger of a new power elite with exclusive access to a body of knowledge.

The Chinese developmental model represents a radical questioning of this tendency of big technology and big business to create their own momentum. It represents so far a refusal to abdicate in favour of an exclusive expert rationality and its monopoly of competence. Everything will depend upon how and for how long China manages to stay free of the dominion of technology as a self-generating constraint. Is it possible to create technological alternatives that will not evolve into the power structure of the technological society? Here the concept of a middle technology is decisive. This views technology not as unchangeable but as an element to be adapted to particular situations. This strategy does not begin with the question, "How much capital and advanced technology do we need?" but with "How much capital and technology can we afford without surrendering to the autonomous momentum of large-scale industrialization?"

Technological Breakthrough vs. the Equilibrium Economy

We in the West have thus far failed to control and regulate our system. Technological rationality constantly screens out everything that does not fit into the pattern of rationality, maximization and order. One example

---

[1] HEILBRONNER: *An Inquiry into the Human Prospect* (New York, 1975).

is the "energy-war" between the promoters of nuclear energy and the promoters of solar energy. Beneath the surface of this debate is the question, "How much centralized big technology shall we tolerate?" Nuclear energy is generated mainly in large central power plants. Such centralized systems are extremely vulnerable, and, even more important, the operation of nuclear plants demands highly specialized know-how. The enemies of nuclear power are warning us that the nuclear technocrats are establishing an energy-dictatorship, and numbers of people are sympathetic with these attacks on powerful technological systems.

The "post-modern" society is not just the contrary of the "modern", nor is it the same as Daniel Bell's "post-industrial". It implies the freedom and the ability to test new economic and political thought and action in open debate. It is perhaps more a way of thinking than a system. In the present pluralistic world situation, what is required is not a grand synthesis, not a new philosophy which will embrace and harmonize divergent powers and forces, not a universally valid total truth. What is needed above all is the ability to be self-critical of one's preference for liberal democracy and the market system. This sounds easier than it actually is. We are in a tough struggle in which each side is seeking to establish its own position. The more closed and restricted the growth philosophy which is held, the more violent the rejection of a differing view. The relative and provisional nature of new models must be accepted. This demand for self-relativization constitutes a threat to the current intellectual fashion for clear-cut positions and battle-lines. To stand up for relative values and models is to threaten the foundations of the modern faith. Such relativism threatens the clichés of polarization by stressing that reality is much more complex than the usual intellectual stereotypes. If we are to develop structures for genuine communication, we have first to dismantle hegemonistic thought patterns. Only then can there be open debate. It is possible even where fundamental divergences exist, though very often the real divergences are not at all where they are commonly supposed to be. Official differences no longer coincide with real differences. Divisions are less clear-cut than they are in theory proclaimed to be. Everywhere they are being relativized by new facts. Thus in our debate we have to redefine, not only the points of difference but also the points of contact and above all the open questions.

The continuing "limits to growth" debate reveals certain real strategic differences. The *classical growth school of thought* is basically evolutionistic in its conviction that our planet's natural resources still provide a big reserve for growth and development; the main question is how this development is to be organized and directed. Binswanger and Geissberger call it the "*breakthrough-strategy*".[1] Promoters of this breakthrough-strategy

---

[1] *Ways Out of the Welfare Trap*, Frankfurt, 1978.

are convinced that the negative impacts of the growth-economy can be kept under control through an adequate environment technology. In their view, there are no insoluble problems. This is still the conviction of a large majority in the West. Almost all Western economic and political structures and attitudes are based on this technocratic credo. The vision of an emerging technosphere, of a world dominated by artificial systems, is still popular. It is political suicide for a political leader in the West to question the conviction that we are still in a permanently expanding industrial economic system characterized by constant growth. Even though this expansion is a historical novelty — not more than one hundred and fifty years old — there is still a wide belief in a continuous upward progress which must go on.

Among the post-modern trends and strategies working against the modern breakthrough strategy is the proposal for an *equilibrium economy* as the only sound and sustainable form of human society. The scenario for an equilibrium or sustainable society is well known. It does not imply an end to all forms of growth, but a sharp limit upon those forms that damage our life-support base. It does not allow the economic capital to expand at the expense of our ecological capital. To achieve an equilibrium, the stock of economic capital is stabilized, and what it produced is made more durable, reparable and recyclable. Acceptance of this environmental economy and ethics challenges fundamentally present economic assumptions and practices.

Such considerations are not new. European efforts to evaluate progress go back to the beginning of this century. The book of Alfredo Nicoforo, *La misura della vita* (The measure of life), which appeared in 1919, or the pioneering work of Karl W. Kapp in the forties and fifties, in which he tried to publicize the "social cost of private ownership", should be mentioned. But it was not until the late sixties that these ideas began to find a wider response, based on the need for ecological as well as economic accounting, and making use of the new term "social indicators" to measure the quality of life. A leading economist like Gunnar Myrdal could say that "the concept of the GNP, and the whole structure of the theoretical approaches built up with the GNP as a central axis will have to be dethroned".[1]

Participation and Decentralization in a Post-Modern World

One of the most important requisites of the post-modern society is a stop to the process of centralization and a move towards decentralization. As increasing centralization has not produced the expected benefits; there has been in recent years a strong reaction against the whole tendency, a

---

[1] GUNNAR MYRDAL: *Against the Stream, Critical Essays on Economics* (New York, 1972), p. 208.

sudden rediscovery of the virtues of smaller units, a questioning of the modern belief that tended to give more power not only to big corporations but also to national governments which are constantly centralizing their authority. Since the late 1960s, the participation movement has been demanding decentralization of power in both the economic and the political-bureaucratic structures. Active self-help movements are trying to replace bureaucratic management wherever possible. Various containment strategies are working in the same direction: containment of the excessive money economy, containment of waste through partial renaturalization, containment of increasingly centralized welfare bureaucracies. Also related to this trend is the movement for "devolution", the effort to enlarge or revive the authority of regional and local agencies. In many parts of the world, regions or groups of smaller units are trying to increase their power over against that of central authorities. Devolution makes sense in Western Europe, particularly in centralist-bureaucratic France or Italy. It aims at more self-government for regions, countries and towns, and is a major challenge to the present centralized bureaucratic systems.

While this devolution-process is to be promoted, we should have no illusions about the possibility of complete autonomy or separatism in an age of global problems and interdependence. We should seek an economic and social policy which would aim to make devolution possible, recognizing that political and natural resources both set limits to growth. However it is clear that the existing political structures no longer match the underlying economic and social realities and that this is today a source of systemic disintegration. Hence the paradox. On the one hand, the national state bureaucracy is no longer an effective instrument for dealing with the major world economic problems; it is necessary to develop effective international instruments of control and distribution. On the other hand, the demand for decentralization is becoming more and more urgent. Because of the tradition of thinking big, we do not have much sense of appropriate size and scope, of what unit is needed to handle a particular level of problem. What is evident is the increasing weariness of the large bureaucracies that now extend into all areas of life. Today, many people are asking whether all problems can be solved through the state, and this is leading to an authentic people's movement, opposing further concentration of state power. A post-modern scenario would envisage a society beyond the modern expansionist economy and beyond the expansionist state bureaucracy.

There is still today a tendency for technocrats to consider as utopian the active participation by simple citizens in the kind of decision-making now controlled by experts. Yet this same power-élite has not succeeded in overcoming the present chaos of our urban centres. The suggestion that the citizen cannot be burdened with participation can therefore be countered with the assertion that precisely in view of the present complexity of modern technologically organized societies we need more autonomy, a greater variety of groups, and more participation by people in ordering of their everyday life. The demand for participation is not some sort of pre-modern pre-industrial romanticism outmoded by the demands of centralized complex organizations. Rather, appropriate solutions to such everyday problems as organization of work and organization of social services demand participation. In the post-modern society new communication structures and new kinds of service to the community would be more important than the increase of personal income. Small networks of community groups cannot replace the bureaucratic welfare state, but they could take over some of those functions and services which it can no longer perform.

Does the World Power Struggle Prevent a Post-Modern Society?

Such strategies are important on the micro-level but what about the macro-level? Do the military, political and economic realities allow a measure of pluralism? Dahrendorf holds that we are going through a period in which power on a world scale is becoming more diffused, and that as a result the world power structure is gradually changing.[1] We no longer have the bi-polarity of the fifties and sixties but a plurality of power centres. The world structure is not a neat pattern of five great nations which can arrange everything among themselves. We might describe our situation as a process in which there is the gradual replacement of one pattern by another.

The two main conflict areas familiar to us are the East-West struggle which seems to be receding and the North-South conflict which seems to be the battle ground of the future. According to Dahrendorf, each period of history is dominated by specific themes and ways of conflict. The theme of the last three decades — the cold war — was military and political rather than economic. History does not progress by the resolution of conflicts. What happens is that new arenas of conflict emerge which overshadow the old and gradually reduce their importance and relevance. Today while detente between East and West is still being discussed, a new conflict on economic issues is emerging in the North-South arena. It is of the very nature of this conflict that there are no longer clear centres of power.

This period between two dominant patterns of conflict is difficult to describe. Some would like to regard the new conflict in the old terms: as part of the struggle between East and West for domination. Others would like to ignore the old conflict, even though it continues. In Europe, the border-line between the systems remains tense. The East-West conflict

---

[1] RALF DAHRENDORF: "A European Perspective", in *Foreign Affairs*, October 1977, pp. 72 f.

is one of ultimate power. Yet this ultimate power has its limitations. The possession of nuclear weapons did not mean that the war in Vietnam could be won by the USA, and that in the Middle East Egypt could be controlled by Moscow. The extraordinary character of this ultimate power leaves an opening for other types of conflict, for limited wars and for economic struggle. This new economic pattern of international relations has diminished the role of the Soviet Union, because in terms of economic power Moscow is not very relevant. In another sense, the new pattern has also diminished the role of the USA. In military and economic terms it is still the greatest world power, but it is no longer absolutely predominant.

The main result of this process of change is the diffusion and devolution of power. The structures of power are becoming amorphous, although we can already discern the forces which are likely to move into a new pattern. The number of actors is larger, the degree of their cohesion small. But the actors can be grouped and the interests of these groups can be analysed. I follow Dahrendorf in his description of the emerging pattern of power. He sees three main actors:

I. The OECD countries;

II. The threshold countries (many of which are members of the OPEC);

III. The countries of the group of 77.

These groups represent three positions in international economic relations: countries which have achieved a high level of economic-technological development; countries which have begun to develop very rapidly; and the very poor countries which have not themselves the resources to develop. If we are to define the nature of power today, we must identify the major questions posed by these three groups. The main question confronting the last group is, will they find a gradualist way to improve or will they choose revolutionary confrontation? The choices of the OPEC group, probably more than any other development, will determine the course of future economic world order. But perhaps equally important will be the attitude of the OECD countries. Will they find it possible to accept change if this means losing their monopoly of wealth? Or will they become defensive and force the world into a period of costly and sterile confrontation?

The Answer to the Battle of Monolithic Systems

Devolution of power cannot take place without effective international institutions. What is needed is not a political-ideological consensus on a broad range of values, but a dense web of ties with mixed interests and a minimum of common values. Top priority must be given to strengthening the fragile common interests in order to prevent the break-up of the world economy into separate blocs leading to economic warfare. In the formulation of such policies, stress must be laid on what can be agreed upon as minimum standards. This demands from all partners some measure of "ideological erosion". There are no simplifying formulas which can be used. For example, the Kissinger triangle formula (USA/USSR/China) proved to be too narrow. Such balance of power diplomacy failed to take account of the need for solutions to a great variety of global and regional problems. Nor is the trilateral concept of Brzezinski adequate for it has little to say about the Third World. Neither a triangular nor a trilateral policy is enough. We need policies and patterns of action adequate for all three worlds, while recognizing that none of the three is homogeneous. The Third World in particular is undergoing rapid differentiation. Hence we have to be aware of the very relative nature of all existing formulas and world models, and resist all attempts to smuggle monolithic models of thought and action into the analysis of present world structures.

There is a variety of ways of coping with the different situations. But each one is incomplete. The best chance for setting up common structures lies in pluralism, which has two implications. The first is *flexibility*, leading to agreements open to permanent revision. This means no dictate imposed by dominant powers. The second is *the need for fall-back positions*. Every policy, every action-model must recognize the possibility of failure and the need for alternative proposals, and there must be a readiness to accept second-best solutions.

Questions for Discussion

1. How can people in the rich world cooperate in the development of the poor world, while at the same time maintaining an acceptable — but lower — standard of living for themselves? More specifically, what would be the nature of an economic system that would be flexible enough to reduce economic growth in the rich world without producing all the negative side effects that follow when an economy geared for growth does not grow?

2. What conclusions should the rich world draw from the statement, "All the world cannot be as rich as the rich countries because of physical constraints, particularly on energy"?

3. What resources does your community consume which come from other countries and regions, and what do you know about the conditions under which these resources are produced and exported?

4. Would you classify your community as rich or poor? What criteria do you use in measuring this in relation to the situation of communities in other countries?

5. What do you know about the effect of your country's economic and technological policies on the welfare of other countries? And about how these policies look to people in other countries?

6. What are the most urgent issues concerning economic and technological development which people in your church and community would like to have discussed at the world ecumenical meeting in 1979?